W9-CCD-756

FIXING WINDOWS XP ANNOYANCES™

FIXING WINDOWS XP ANNOYANCES™

How to Fix the Most Annoying Things
About the Windows OS

David A. Karp

O'REILLY®

Beijing • Cambridge • Farnham • Köln • Paris • Sebastopol • Taipei • Tokyo

Fixing Windows XP Annoyances™
How to Fix the Most Annoying Things About the Windows OS
by David A. Karp

Copyright © 2006 O'Reilly Media, Inc. All rights reserved.
Printed in the United States of America.
Illustrations © 2006 Hal Myforth

Published by O'Reilly Media, Inc., 1005 Gravenstein Highway North, Sebastopol, CA 95472.

O'Reilly books may be purchased for educational, business, or sales promotional use. Online editions are also available for most titles (*safari.oreilly.com*). For more information, contact our corporate/institutional sales department: 800-998-9938 or *corporate@oreilly.com*.

Print History:

March 2006:   First Edition.

Editor: Robert Luhn

Production Editor: Philip Dangler

Copyeditor: Rachel Wheeler

Indexer: Julie Hawks

Interior Designer: David Futato

Illustrators: Robert Romano, Jessamyn Read, and Lesley Borash

The O'Reilly logo is a registered trademark of O'Reilly Media, Inc. The *Annoyances* series designations and related trade dress are trademarks of O'Reilly Media, Inc.

Many of the designations used by manufacturers and sellers to distinguish their products are claimed as trademarks. Where those designations appear in this book, and O'Reilly Media, Inc. was aware of a trademark claim, the designations have been printed in caps or initial caps.

While every precaution has been taken in the preparation of this book, the publisher and author assume no responsibility for errors or omissions, or for damages resulting from the use of the information contained herein.

0-596-10053-1

[C]

For Cory

Contents

Introduction

Some days I want to pick up my PC and throw it out the window. Other days, I fancy hitting it with a large, blunt object, or perhaps drilling through the CPU with a high-speed auger bit. Yesterday, I dreamt of small gray mice chewing through the power cable. But of course, the wanton destruction of electronic equipment can be rather expensive, not to mention a poor solution to the hundreds of everyday annoyances that evoke such feelings.

Windows XP frequently falls under the "You can't live with it; you can't live without it" category, and with good reason. Windows is an operating system, the underlying software that provides drivers, interface components, and communication services to the applications and games you use on your PC. Ideally, operating system software should be both omnipresent and invisible; like the air we breathe, it allows us to function but should never get in our way. Alas, it doesn't always work out that way.

Windows crashes. It interrupts our work with incomprehensible error messages. It bogs down under the weight of the software we pile on top of it. And it seems to make simple tasks—such as finding files, choosing default applications, and setting up a network—needlessly complicated and hopelessly cumbersome. For these reasons and hundreds more, Windows is annoying.

The good news is that there are solutions to most Windows annoyances. Whether the solution lies in an obscure setting, an add-on program, or just a different way of doing something, most of what bugs us about Windows can be fixed. And that's what this book is about.

How to Use This Book

The information in this book is assembled into "annoyances" and "fixes." If you're having a problem with Windows, look through the Table of Contents for the annoyance that most closely matches your problem, or jump to the Index to find a section based on the solution. Of course, feel free to thumb through these pages, too—you'll likely find fixes to problems you didn't even know could be solved.

Annoyances and their respective fixes are organized into categories, which in turn are divided into these six chapters:

Chapter 1, Windows Interface

> The fixes in this chapter deal with the interface quirks that plague Windows and most of the applications you run on your PC. Among other things, you'll learn how to clean up your Start menu, get to the desktop easily, and switch between applications more quickly.

Chapter 2, Windows Explorer

> Windows Explorer is the heart of file and folder management in Windows XP. The annoyances in this chapter cover Windows Explorer in all of its forms, including tips on how to do things like force it to remember your view settings, save your default application choices, tame File→Open and File→Save As dialog boxes, and get XP's Search tool to behave.

Chapter 3, Multimedia

> Can't hear sound? Having a problem playing a DVD or burning a CD? Want to do more with your digital photo collection? Interested in turning your PC into a DVR and entertainment center? Chapter 4 covers all this and more!

Chapter 4, The Web and Email

> The Internet is a terrific resource, but it's also the source of a lot of major annoyances, such as spyware, spam, and pop-ups. Get a handle on Internet Explorer's role in this mess, and what you can do to improve your online experience.

Chapter 5, Wireless and Networking

> Getting your PC online can be a bit of a headache, not to mention connecting all the PCs in your home or office together to share files and printers. Learn how to make everything work without compromising your security.

Chapter 6, Setup and Hardware

> This opening chapter helps you reinstall Windows, update it safely, get it to start up more quickly and shut down without complaining, and finally, make it work with all your hardware.

Conventions Used in This Book

The following are the typographical and iconographical conventions used in this book:

Italic

> Used for emphasis and to indicate new terms, URLs, filenames, file extensions, directories, program names, and pathnames. For example, a path in the filesystem appears as *c:\Windows\System32*.

`Constant width`

> Used to show code examples, anything that might be typed from the keyboard, the contents of files, and the output from commands.

`Constant width italic`

> Used in examples to show text that should be replaced with your own user-supplied values.

Menus and navigation

> Arrows (→) are used as a shorthand notation to indicate navigation through drop-down menus, which is particularly useful given how frequently settings and features are buried deep in Windows's various menus and dialog windows. If you see an instruction like "select View→ Explorer Bar→Folders," it means that you should open the View menu in the current window, select the Explorer Bar menu item, and then select the Folders menu item. Note that when you need to click other interface elements, such as tabs, checkboxes, and buttons, this will be clearly indicated in the text.

Notes and warnings

> Pay special attention to notes set apart from the text with the following manner.

> **WARNING**
>
> *This is a warning note. When you see one of these, your PC's security or stability—not to mention your own sanity—may be in jeopardy.*

> **NOTE**
>
> *This is a tip, typically containing useful supplementary information, a handy suggestion or shortcut, or a general note relating to the topic at hand. Extra credit if you can spot the pun.*

Got an Annoyance?

Is your mother nagging you about grandchildren? Are your grandchildren nagging you about their mother? Did your cat shred your dog-eared copy of *Lord of the Rings*? Is Sauron giving you a hard time? Can't shake the feeling that your friends don't really like you? If so, I don't want to hear about it. Tell your therapist. Or your plumber.

Something bothering you about Windows? Ahh... now you're talking. If you have an annoyance that needs an immediate solution, pay a visit to the Annoyances.org forums, particularly *http://www.annoyances.org/exec/forum/winxp/* for XP-related issues. Or, if you'd like to submit an annoyance for a future edition of *Fixing Windows XP Annoyances*, send it to *annoyances@oreilly.com*. Tell 'em Dave sent you.

O'Reilly Would Like to Hear from You

We have tested and verified the information in this book to the best of our ability, but you may find that features have changed (or even that we have made mistakes!). You can help us improve future editions by sending us your feedback. Please let us know about any errors, inaccuracies, bugs, misleading or confusing statements, and typos that you find anywhere in this book.

Please also let us know what we can do to make this book more useful to you. We take your comments seriously and will try to incorporate reasonable suggestions into future editions. You can write to us at:

O'Reilly Media, Inc.
1005 Gravenstein Highway North
Sebastopol, CA 95472
(800) 998-9938 (in the U.S. or Canada)
(707) 829-0515 (international/local)
(707) 829-0104 (fax)

Additions and corrections to this book, related miscellany, downloadable software, and the Annoyances forum can all be found at:

http://www.annoyances.org

The O'Reilly catalog page for this and other Annoyances books—where you'll find errata, downloadable software, and other information—is located at:

http://annoyances.oreilly.com

To ask technical questions or to comment on the book, send email to:

bookquestions@oreilly.com

For more information about books, conferences, Resource Centers, and the O'Reilly Network, go to:

http://www.oreilly.com

About the Author

David A. Karp started the Annoyances series of books with the bestseller *Windows Annoyances* all the way back in 1996. Since then, he has written 10 power-user books available in 9 languages, including 5 books on Windows XP. He's also the author of *eBay Hacks: Tips & Tools for Bidding, Buying, and Selling, Second Edition* (see *http://www.ebayhacks.com*) and the editor of *PayPal Hacks* (see *http://www.paypalhacks.com*).

David writes for *PC Magazine* and is a contributing editor for *Ztrack Magazine*. He created and actively maintains Annoyances.org, a popular Windows troubleshooting web site. Noted recognition of his work has come from *PC Computing Magazine*, *Windows Magazine*, *The San Francisco Examiner*, and *The New York Times*.

Educated in mechanical engineering at U.C. Berkeley, David consults on Internet technology while dabbling in user-interface design and software engineering...all of which illustrate his disdain for thermodynamics. Of course, David works hard to conserve energy, even though he knows full well that energy is always conserved.

David is a compulsive tinkerer, an avid skier, and a mediocre Go player. He likes to spend time outside, predominantly on his bicycle or with his camera, but rarely both. David scored 30.96647% on the Geek Test (*http://www.innergeek.us/geek.html*), earning a rating of "Total Geek." He knows the difference between a fireman and a firefighter. He's a master craftsman and a breeder of prize-winning clams. Animals and children trust him. And he knows why you bought this book.

Acknowledgments

Thanks to Robert Luhn, Mark Brokering, and Tim O'Reilly for helping to make this book happen.

My immense gratitude to Torey Bookstein, love of my life, who provides immeasurable support through good times and bad.

Windows Interface

You can rearrange the furniture in your office, put your favorite tchotchkes on the shelves, and prune your plants any way you like. So why can't you customize Windows to your heart's content?

In fact, Windows XP is surprisingly pliable. This is fortunate, because one of the best ways to deal with many Windows annoyances is to tweak, customize, or otherwise hack the operating system to eradicate them.

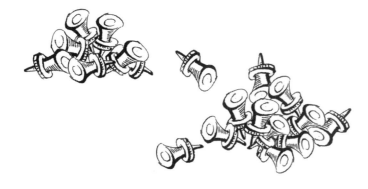

GENERAL INTERFACE

Snappy Scrolling

THE ANNOYANCE: When I scroll a folder in Windows Explorer or a web page in Internet Explorer, it acts "sticky," as though it needs oiling. I presume oiling my monitor is out of the question, but there's got to be a way to make scrolling snappier.

THE FIX: Microsoft calls this behavior "smooth scrolling," and fortunately, you can turn it off. For this, you'll need a Microsoft program called TweakUI (free, *http://www.microsoft.com/windowsxp/downloads/powertoys/xppowertoys.mspx*). Click the Explorer category on the left side of the window (Figure 1-1), and on the right side, uncheck the "Enable smooth scrolling" box. Click Apply when you're done.

To turn off smooth scrolling in web pages, in Internet Explorer select Tools→Internet Options, and click the Advanced tab. Scroll down to the bottom of the Browsing section, uncheck the "Use smooth scrolling" box, and click OK.

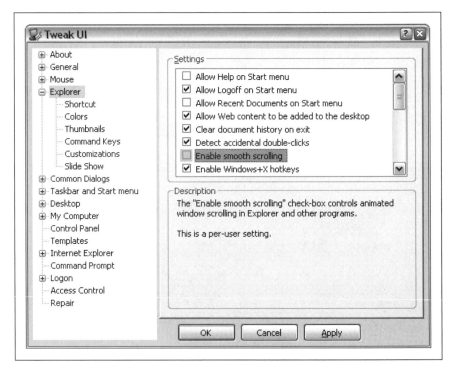

Figure 1-1. Turn off smooth scrolling to make scrolling windows more responsive.

Sharpen Blurry Text

THE ANNOYANCE: The text on my screen is blurry. Do I need glasses?

THE FIX: If the manufacturer's logo on your monitor is also blurry, glasses might be a good idea. Otherwise, there are two things that can cause blurry text in Windows XP.

If everything on your screen is blurry, as opposed to just the text, your display may be set to the wrong resolution. If you have a flat-panel LCD monitor, it has a *native resolution*, which matches the number of the monitor's physical pixels. If your monitor's native resolution is 1024×768, for instance, and Windows is set to 800×600, your screen will have to interpolate that lower resolution, and the display will appear blurry. To fix the problem, right-click an empty area of your desktop, click Properties, and then click the Settings tab. Slide the "Screen resolution" slider until the numbers match your screen's native resolution, and then click OK. (See the next annoyance if this setting makes icons and text too small.)

If text is the *only* thing on the screen that's blurry, you're suffering from the "benefits" of anti-aliasing, illustrated in Figure 1-2. Windows "smoothes" screen fonts to reduce their jagged edges, but this doesn't always look so hot.

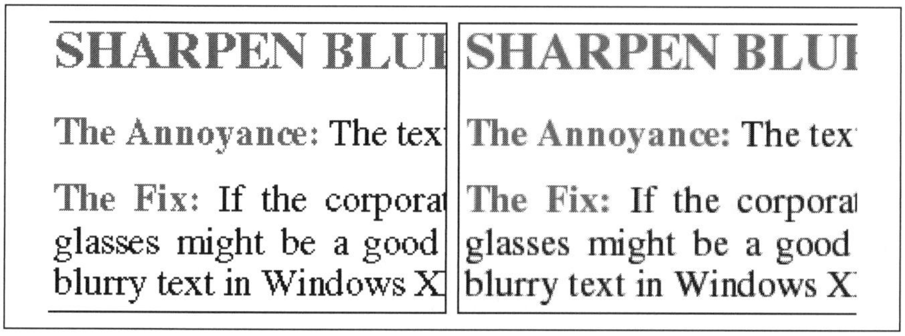

Figure 1-2. Anti-aliasing smoothes jaggy screen fonts, but it can make them look blurry.

To turn off font smoothing, right-click an empty area of the desktop, click Properties, click the Appearance tab, and then click the Effects button. There are two kinds of font smoothing (Standard or ClearType), but odds are you won't be able to tell the difference. Just uncheck the "Use the following method to smooth edges of screen fonts" box and click OK to disable the feature altogether.

> **NOTE**
>
> *If you don't know your screen's native resolution, it's usually—but not always—the rightmost (highest) setting. Since an LCD's native resolution is also the highest it can display, you know you've gone too far if you lose the edges of your desktop and Windows scrolls the display as you move the mouse. When in doubt, see the documentation.*

> **NOTE**
>
> *If you like font smoothing but aren't happy with the way Windows does it, try Microsoft's free ClearType Tuner PowerToy, available at: http://www.microsoft.com/windowsxp/downloads/powertoys/xppowertoys.mspx.*
>
> *Among other things, it walks you through the settings, allowing you to adjust the feature to suit your taste. It even lets you change the contrast to help minimize the drawbacks inherent in anti-aliasing.*

Make Things Big on High-Res Screens

THE ANNOYANCE: I spent a lot of cash for the best, highest-resolution flat-panel LCD display on the market, but everything on the screen is too small. Did I waste my money?

THE FIX: Depends on how much you spent! But the good news is that you can make most things on your screen bigger to compensate for the tiny pixels. To make text bigger, right-click an empty area of your desktop, click Properties, and then click the Appearance tab. From the "Font size" drop-down, you can choose either Large or Extra Large, but for better results, click the Advanced button to enlarge specific elements (title bar, menus, tooltips, etc.) to your taste.

Start by clicking Active Window in the little preview window at the top of the dialog box shown in Figure 1-3 (or selecting Active Title Bar from the Item list), and then choosing a larger number in the Size list in the second row (next to the Font list). Do the same for Inactive Title Bar, Menu, Message Box, Palette Title, and Tooltip.

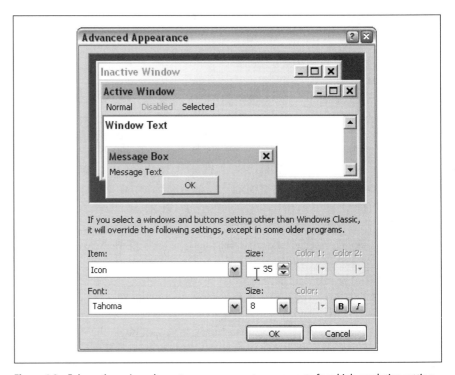

Figure 1-3. Enlarge the various elements on your screen to compensate for a high-resolution setting.

While you're here, you'll probably want to make your desktop icons bigger. By default, they're 32×32 pixels, but if you choose Icon from the Item menu, you can specify any size you like. For best results, restrict your choice to multiples of 16, such as 48 or 64. Finally, adjust the Icon Spacing (Horizontal and Vertical) to accommodate the new, larger icons.

Drag Windows Intact

THE ANNOYANCE: My coworker can see her application windows while she's dragging them around her screen, but on my computer, all I see is outlines. How can I get this much more obvious instant feedback?

THE FIX: Right-click an empty area of your desktop, click Properties, click the Appearance tab, and then click the Effects button. Check the "Show window contents while dragging" box, and then click OK.

Understanding Color Depth

Have you ever noticed that photos appear excessively grainy or contain ugly bands or streaks where a smooth sky or gradient should appear? Do all the colors on your screen become distorted when new images or web pages are displayed? These are symptoms of an *adaptive* palette. When your display is set to 256 colors, there can never be more than 256 individual colors in use at any given time. Because 256 isn't nearly enough to represent all the colors in the spectrum, Windows simply chooses the best 256 colors each time you display an image. The more images are displayed, the more horrendous things can look.

However, since 65,536 colors (16-bit mode, or 2^{16} colors; sometimes called High Color) are sufficient to display photographic images (as are the even better 24- and 32-bit modes), the palette is fixed and does not have to adapt to what is on the screen. This results in a richer, faster display; web pages, games, and photos look better; and you don't have to put up with a constantly changing palette.

To set the color depth, open the Display control panel and choose the Settings tab. Move the Screen resolution slider to the right to increase your display's resolution (more dots equals more screen real estate, but smaller screen elements). To the right is a drop-down list labeled "Color quality" with all of the color depth settings your video card supports. Select the highest color quality setting your video hardware supports (at least Medium 16-bit).

As you adjust your color depth, Windows may automatically adjust other settings depending on your card's capabilities, especially if you're using an older video card. The amount of memory on your video card dictates the maximum color depth and resolution you can use.

The memory required by a particular setting is calculated by multiplying the horizontal size times the vertical size times the bytes per pixel. If you're in 32-bit color mode, each pixel will require 32 bits, or 4 bytes (there are 8 bits to a byte). At a resolution of 1600x1024, that's 1600x1024x4 bytes/pixel, or 6.25 MB. Therefore, a video card with 8 MB of memory will be able to handle the display setting, but a card with only 4 MB will not. The card's refresh rate can also limit the maximum resolution and color depth. Most newer cards easily exceed these restrictions, though, so the case may be moot.

In most cases, choose the highest color depth your system supports at whatever resolution you're currently using. However, since higher color depths may cause your applications to run a little more slowly and eat up more system memory, you may want to downshift to 16-bit color.

—From *Windows XP Annoyances for Geeks, 2nd Edition*

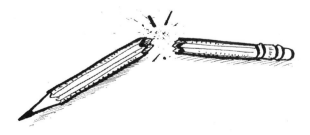

Make Windows Translucent While Dragging

THE ANNOYANCE: When I have a lot of windows open, it's hard to find just the one I want. How can I quickly cut through the clutter?

THE FIX: One of the new features Microsoft is promoting in the successor to Windows XP (Windows Vista) is a so-called 3-D interface that allows you to more easily see what's behind a window while you're dragging it. Windows XP doesn't have anything like this, although most video card makers supply drivers that offer something similar. For example, recent versions of the nVidia drivers (available at *http://www.nvidia.com*; use these *only* if you have a display adapter with an nVidia graphics processor) can create a transparent window effect, as illustrated in Figure 1-4.

> **NOTE**
>
> *Contact the manufacturer of your display adapter (video card) for appropriate drivers for your hardware; see Chapter 6 for more details on installing new drivers and reverting to earlier versions if the new drivers don't work properly.*

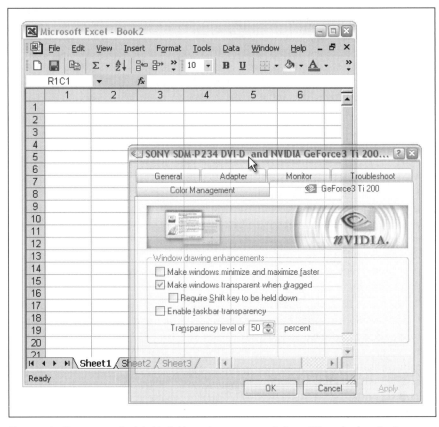

Figure 1-4. You can see what's behind this semi-transparent window while you're dragging it.

If your display adapter driver doesn't offer this feature, you can use a program such as Actual Transparent Window ($19.95, *http://www.actualtools. com/transparentwindow/*).

General Interface

Un-Animate Windows Controls

THE ANNOYANCE: Windows takes forever to open menus and drop-down list-boxes and to scroll lists. How can I give it a kick in the proverbial pants?

THE FIX: To make Windows XP appear fancier and more advanced than the competition (I know, what competition?), Microsoft added animation to several parts of the interface. But waiting (and waiting) while Windows slowly cranks open a menu can be a real drag. To speed things up, open the System control panel, click the Advanced tab, and click the Settings button in the Performance section. Uncheck the boxes for "Fade or slide menus into view," "Slide open combo boxes," and any other animations that annoy you (see Figure 1-5). Click Apply to try out your new settings.

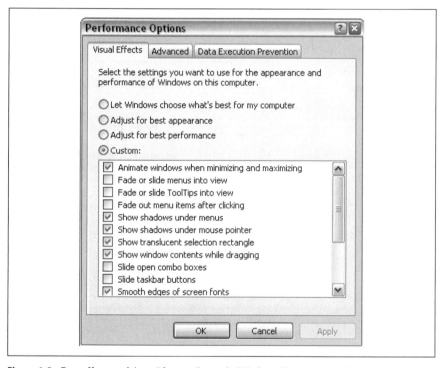

Figure 1-5. Turn off some of these "features" to make Windows XP more responsive.

Using Themes

Themes let you save several individual settings under a single name. There's only one place in Windows to save and retrieve themes, and your theme selection affects settings in several dialogs.

Manage themes by opening the Display control panel and clicking the Themes tab. To load a theme and replace your current settings, select a theme from the drop-down Theme list and click the Apply button.

To save your current settings into a new theme (or replace an existing theme), click the Save As button. Your theme is saved as an individual *.theme* file, by default in the *My Documents* folder. But only themes found in the *\Windows\Resources\Themes* folder are used to populate the Theme list, so place your custom *.theme* files there.

Settings saved with the current theme include your wallpaper, your custom desktop icons (select the Desktop tab, then the Customize Desktop button), your screensaver, your current style, and color selections. Themes essentially cover all of the tabs in the Display Properties dialog, except for the Settings tab.

According to the Windows documentation, themes are supposed to also encapsulate your mouse pointers, sounds, and Windows Media Player skin settings. Unfortunately, this simply doesn't work. When you save a custom theme, these extra settings are ignored. What's worse, when you then load a theme, the mouse pointers, sounds, and WMP skins are all simply reverted to their defaults. You'll need to use schemes (see the "Using Schemes" sidebar) to save your mouse and sound settings and protect them from the themes feature.

—From *Windows XP Annoyances for Geeks, 2nd Edition*

Customize the Windows Look and Feel

THE ANNOYANCE: I'm tired of the "Windows XP" and "Windows Classic" styles, the only two choices in Display Properties. Can't I add my own styles?

THE FIX: Yes, but you'll need a third-party program such as WindowBlinds (free and $19.95 versions are available at *http://www.stardock.com/products/windowblinds/*). With WindowBlinds, not only can you choose from a bunch of interesting, preconfigured "skins" like the one shown in Figure 1-6, but, if you're particularly adventurous, you can design your own.

Once you have WindowBlinds, you can download new skins from any of several online libraries, including *http://skinbase.org*, *http://www.deviantart.com*, and *http://www.deskmod.modblog.com*.

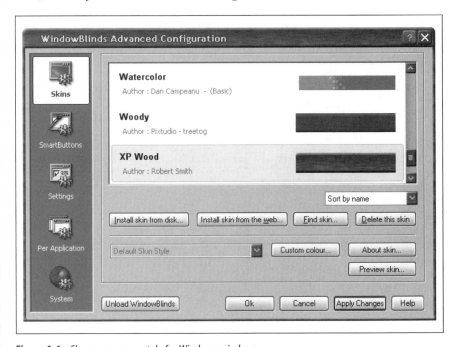

Figure 1-6. Choose your own style for Windows windows.

Simplify the Control Panel

THE ANNOYANCE: I use the Windows Control Panel frequently, but I find the categories confusing and cumbersome. How can I get to Control Panel icons more directly?

THE FIX: You're right; the categories add an extra (and mostly unnecessary) step every time you need to change a setting. To turn off categories in the Control Panel, simply click the "Switch to Classic View" link in the top-left corner. If you don't see this link, click the "Appearance and Themes" category and open Folder Options. On the General tab, select "Show common tasks in folders," and click OK.

For even quicker access, open the Taskbar and Start Menu control panel, click the Start Menu tab, and click the Customize button. If you're using the XP-style Start menu, click the Advanced tab, find Control Panel in the list, select "Display as a menu," and click OK. If you're using the Classic Start menu, check the Expand Control Panel box, and click OK. Now, to open a Control Panel icon, just select Start→Control Panel or Start→Settings→ Control Panel, respectively, and select the desired icon from the list.

DESKTOP

Show the Desktop Without Closing Windows

THE ANNOYANCE: I usually have a lot of application windows open, and it's a pain to have to shove windows out of the way to get to a file on the desktop.

THE FIX: There are a bunch of ways to get to your desktop in a flash. First, hold the Windows logo key (which we'll call *Winkey*, just to be cute) and press D to quickly minimize all open windows. Press Winkey-D again to restore them. Do this many times to give yourself a headache.

But what if your keyboard havey no Winkey? No problemo; just click the Show Desktop button on the Quick Launch toolbar (the little row of tiny buttons on the far left of your Taskbar). Give the button another click to restore the windows.

Want to free up some Taskbar real estate? Eliminate the Quick Launch toolbar buttons you don't use by right-clicking each one and selecting Delete. To really save space, you can banish all the buttons *except* Show Desktop, and place the shrunken Quick Launch toolbar next to the Windows System Tray on the far right, as shown in Figure 1-7.

Figure 1-7. Use this handy button to show the Windows desktop without minimizing all your windows.

> ─── **NOTE** ───
>
> *If you can't move or resize the Quick Launch toolbar, right-click an empty area in the Taskbar and deselect the "Lock the Taskbar" option. When you have things the way you like them, turn "Lock the Taskbar" back on.*

Using Schemes

A scheme is a saved collection of settings in a single dialog box. For example, you can save your current mouse pointer selections under a scheme name by going to the Control Panel, opening Mouse Properties applet, clicking the Pointers tab, and selecting a different pointer. This not only makes it easier to quickly switch between multiple sets of mouse pointers (such as one for when you're wearing your glasses and one for when you're not), but also allows you to quickly undo changes made by Windows and other applications.

Other dialogs that use schemes include the Power Options control panel (the Power Schemes tab) and the Sounds and Audio Devices control panel (the Sounds tab). In previous versions of Windows you could also save your Display Settings into a scheme, but in Windows XP this functionality has been replaced with themes.

—From *Windows XP Annoyances for Geeks, 2nd Edition*

> ─── **NOTE** ───
>
> *If you don't see the Quick Launch toolbar, right-click an empty area on your Taskbar, and go to Toolbars→Quick Launch. And if the Quick Launch toolbar is missing its Show Desktop button? See the "Make a Show Desktop Button" sidebar for instructions on how to add one.*

Make a Show Desktop Button

By default, the Quick Launch tool-bar comes with a Show Desktop button, which allows you to quickly minimize all open windows and access stuff on your desktop. But · what if this button accidentally gets deleted?

Unlike most other toolbar buttons, the Show Desktop button isn't a Windows shortcut. Rather, it's a Shell Command File (SCF), which is really just a plain text file containing a special command that Windows understands. To create a new SCF file, open your favorite plain-text editor (or Notepad), and type the following five lines:

```
[Shell]
Command=2
IconFile=explorer.exe,3
[Taskbar]
Command=ToggleDesktop
```

Save the file as *Show Desktop.scf* (or any other name, provided that you include the .scf filename extension) anywhere you like, including on the desktop. To have the icon appear on your Quick Launch toolbar, place the file in the *Documents and Settings\Administrator\Application Data\Microsoft\Internet Explorer\ Quick Launch* folder.

Want to appease the rabid minimalist within? Do away with the Quick Launch toolbar altogether, and instead install the *Show Desktop.scf* file as a new icon in the Windows System Tray using the free Tray utility available at *http://www. annoyances.org/exec/show/ software/*.

If these tricks don't do it for you, right-click an empty area of the Taskbar, and select "Show the Desktop." It'll look like all your windows have been minimized, but they're just hidden; to bring them back, repeat the procedure but select Show Open Windows instead.

Alternatively, to access any files or icons on your desktop (without disturbing your open applications), you can simply open Windows Explorer and highlight the *Desktop* folder at the top of the folder tree.

From Keyboard to Desktop

THE ANNOYANCE: I'm using a computer without a mouse, and I need to open a file on the desktop. How do I get to it via the keyboard?

THE FIX: If you're already at the desktop, press the Windows logo key (or press Ctrl-Esc if you don't have one), and then press Esc to close the Start menu. Then, press Tab and watch the dotted rectangle move from the Quick Launch toolbar to, eventually, the System Tray. Press Tab one more time, and an icon on the desktop (such as My Computer) will be selected. (You may not see the selection but it's there; use the arrow keys to get to your file.) When it's highlighted, press Enter and it'll open.

If you're not at the desktop, first press Ctrl-Esc, then press Esc and tab to the Quick Launch toolbar. Use the arrow keys to highlight the Show Desktop button, and press the spacebar. When the desktop appears, follow the steps above.

If you don't want to go to all this trouble, just open Windows Explorer, press Tab to move to the folder tree, and then press the Home key to jump to the top of the folder tree, which happens to be the desktop. Tab over to the right window, and use the arrow keys to scoot down to the file you want. When it's highlighted, press Enter to open the file.

Save Your Desktop Layout

THE ANNOYANCE: All I have to do is sneeze, and Windows rearranges my desktop icons. How do I lock them in place?

THE FIX: This reshuffling can happen for a variety of reasons, such as changing screen resolution (typically for a game) or updating Windows settings (e.g., display settings, screensaver, mouse cursors). To save your desktop layout, you'll need a program like the free WinTidy (*http://www.pcmag. com/article2/0,4149,17748,00.asp*) or Desktop Icon Save and Restore (*http:// www.midiox.com/html/desktop.htm*; XP users, download the Windows 2000 version).

If Windows isn't spontaneously rearranging your desktop icons but refuses to let you put them where you want them, there's a fix for that, too. This problem is caused by one of two mechanisms designed to help keep your desktop icons tidy, and you'll have to turn off at least one of them if you want to more freely place your desktop icons. Right-click an empty area of the desktop, select Arrange Icons By, and turn off the Auto Arrange option. If you leave the "Align to Grid" option on, your icons will always appear lined up in rows and columns; turn it off to have complete flexibility when dragging your desktop icons.

Make Icon Labels See-Through

THE ANNOYANCE: The captions under my desktop icons have ugly blocks of solid color behind them, obscuring my pretty, pretty wallpaper.

THE FIX: I know what you mean; you've just got to see as much as possible of that kitten playing with the ball of yarn. The color Windows uses for the blocks behind icon captions is the default desktop color—what you'd see if you had no wallpaper. You can change this color by right-clicking an empty area of the desktop and selecting Properties. Choose the Appearance tab, then click the Advanced button. Choose Desktop from the Item menu, and open the color picker under "Color 1" to change it. Pick a color that closely matches the background in your desktop wallpaper, and click OK and Apply to see the results.

An even better option is to open the System control panel, click the Advanced tab, and in the Performance section, click the Settings button. Scroll down and check the "Use drop shadows for icon labels on the desktop" box, and click OK. The caption backgrounds will vanish, and the text will have shadows so you can distinguish the captions from your desktop wallpaper, as shown in Figure 1-8.

Figure 1-8. You can choose how you want to outline desktop icon captions.

Control the Space Between Desktop Icons

THE ANNOYANCE: There's an awful lot of wasted space between the rows of icons on my desktop; there's got to be a more efficient way to line them up.

THE FIX: As any greengrocer will tell you, the most efficient way to stack oranges is the face-centered cubic arrangement, wherein each piece of fruit is placed in the cavity formed by three adjacent oranges in the lower plane. (For more information, Google "Kepler Conjecture.")

Sadly, Windows XP doesn't have this option, but you can fine-tune the row and column spacing on the desktop. Right-click an empty area of the desktop, choose Properties, click the Appearance tab, and then click the Advanced button. From the Item drop-down menu, choose Icon Spacing (Horizontal), and adjust the spacing—the number of pixels between the edges of adjacent icons—by changing the Size value. A good value is approximately 1.3 to 1.5 times the width of an icon (typically 32 pixels); specify 40 to pack them pretty closely, or 50 to spread them apart. You can likewise change the Icon Spacing (Vertical) value; use the same number for both the horizontal and vertical measurements, and the result will look balanced.

START MENU

Pick a New Username

THE ANNOYANCE: How do I change the name and icon at the top of the Start menu? I don't like being called "AJAX70761."

> **WARNING**
>
> *The name you choose is your username, which is particularly important if you share files with others on your network (Chapter 5) or if you type your username to log into your computer. See the "Welcome Screen" section later in this chapter for more login tips.*

THE FIX: Don't take it personally; Windows doesn't really care what you're called. You can choose a new name pretty easily by opening the User Accounts control panel. Choose your account from the list in the lower part of this window, and then click "Change my name."

While you're here, click "Change my picture" to choose a new icon to appear at the top of your Start menu (unless you're using the "Classic" Start menu) and on the Welcome screen. Note that your choices aren't limited to the generic icons Windows shows you; click "Browse for more pictures" to choose any *.bmp*, *.jpg*, or *.png* file on your system.

Clean Up the Start Menu

THE ANNOYANCE: There's too much junk in the Start menu. How can I strip out the clutter so I can more easily find the programs I need?

THE FIX: There are three "zones" in the Windows XP–style Start menu (Figure 1-9), and following typical Microsoft logic, each one works in a completely different way.

Figure 1-9. Items in each of the Start menu zones get removed and customized in different ways.

The two items at the top of the left column (above the line) are fixed entries devoted to opening your web browser and email program. To change or hide these entries, right-click the Start button, select Properties, click the Start Menu tab, and click Customize. On the General tab, change the settings in the Show on Start Menu section.

The "zone" immediately below is the somewhat-dynamic list of recently used applications. Back on the General tab, in the Programs section, you can choose how many icons can appear here at once; choose zero to hide the list completely. (You can delete any particular item directly in the Start menu by right-clicking it and selecting "Remove from This List.")

NOTE

If you're running Windows XP Professional, you can use the Group Policy Editor to remove any unwanted items from your Start menu. Go to Start→Run, type gpedit.msc, and click OK. Then expand the branches on the left to User Configuration\ Administrative Templates\Start Menu and Taskbar. Double-click any item on the right and click the Disabled radio button in the Setting tab; then click Apply, then OK. Here, you can remove the All Programs menu, Network Connections, Favorites, Search, Help, Run, and all of the "My" folders (Pictures, Music, etc.). When you're done, you may have to log out and then log back in for the changes to take effect.

Next, click the Advanced tab to customize some of the entries in the top-right column of the Start menu, such as Control Panel, Favorites, My Computer, My Music, My Network Places, Network Connections, Printers and Faxes, Run, and Search. (To find out how to hide the My Recent Documents menu, see "Hide the My Recent Documents Menu.") Click OK when you're done.

Finally, you can add programs to the top-left zone. One way to do this is to drag any program or shortcut over the Start button and hold it for at least a second. The Start menu will open, and you can then drop the item in the top-left zone. The easier way is to right-click a shortcut or program executable (.*exe* file) and select "Pin to Start menu." To delete any "pinned" item from this list, right-click the entry and select "Unpin from Start menu."

Block Recent Programs from Appearing in Your Start Menu

THE ANNOYANCE: I don't want every program I've run lately to be listed in my Start menu. Is there a way to keep this list tidy?

THE FIX: Yes, but you'll have to manually exclude each program you don't want to automatically appear in the Start menu's recently used programs list. In some cases, this may require messing with the Registry.

First, open TweakUI (free, *http://www.microsoft.com/windowsxp/downloads/powertoys/xppowertoys.mspx*). Expand the Taskbar & Start Menu branch on the left, and select the Start Menu category. In the list on the right, uncheck the box next to any program you don't want to ever appear in your Start menu, and click OK when you're done.

If the program you want to exclude isn't in the list, you must edit an entry in the Registry. Open the Registry Editor (go to Start→Run and type regedit), and expand the branches to HKEY_CLASSES_ROOT\Applications. Under the Applications branch, you'll see a bunch of subkeys, each representing a program installed on your PC, named for the applications' executables (such as WINWORD.EXE for Microsoft Word). To add a new subkey, right-click the *Applications* key, select New→Key, type the executable filename of the program you want to exclude, and click OK.

Right-click the newly created key, and select New→String Value. On the right, type NoStartPage for the name of the new value. Repeat this for each program you want to add (and thus exclude), and then close the Registry Editor when you're done.

> **NOTE**
>
> *If you don't know the executable filename, find the application's shortcut in your Start menu, right-click it, click Properties, and choose the Shortcut tab. The filename should be in the Target field at the end of a path statement, such as c:\Program Files\Adobe\Adobe Photoshop CS\Photoshop.exe.*

Hide the My Recent Documents Menu

THE ANNOYANCE: The Documents list on my Start menu shows some of my recently opened documents. Since other people sometimes use this computer, I'd rather not have the names of my private documents appear in such a public place. I looked for a setting in the Taskbar and Start Menu Properties window to turn it off, but I can't find one. How do I hide this list?

THE FIX: There are several ways to hide this list (and/or its contents). If you're using the XP-style Start menu, right-click the Start button, select Properties, click the Customize button, and go to the Advanced tab. In the scrolling list, under My Documents, select "Don't display this item," and click OK to confirm your choice. While you're at it, on the Advanced tab, click the "Clear list" button and uncheck the "List my most recently opened documents" box.

If you're using the "Classic"-style menu, you'll need to use TweakUI (free, *http://www.microsoft.com/windowsxp/downloads/powertoys/xppowertoys.mspx*) to hide this list, as shown in Figure 1-10. Open TweakUI, expand the Explorer category on the left, and uncheck the "Show My Documents on classic Start Menu" box. Click Apply, then OK. (You can also hide the list for the XP-style Start menu with TweakUI—just uncheck the "Allow Recent Documents on Start Menu" box.)

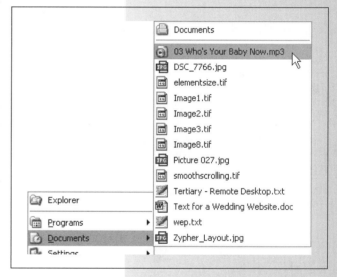

Figure 1-10. You can use TweakUI to hide the Documents menu.

> **NOTE**
>
> *Unfortunately, when you add new programs to your PC, they're appended to the bottom of the list, rather than being inserted into their alphabetic places. You may want to re-sort the list each time you install a new program, as described next.*

Sort Your Start Menu Alphabetically

THE ANNOYANCE: At first, I didn't notice that everything in my All Programs menu was out of order; I thought I was going crazy because I couldn't find anything. Is there any way to make Start menu programs appear in alphabetical order?

THE FIX: You can organize the items in your All Programs menu (or Programs if you're using the Classic Start menu) and its submenus by dragging and dropping. To sort entries alphabetically, right-click any menu item and select "Sort by Name."

Solve the Mystery of Disappearing Start Menu Items

THE ANNOYANCE: To simplify the Start menu I decided to use the "Classic" version, but when I opened it I found that most of the icons in the Programs list were missing. After a few fits of frustration, I eventually stumbled upon the tiny arrow at the bottom of the menu (Figure 1-11) that, when clicked, shows the rest of my programs. Why won't the Classic Start menu show all my programs at once?

THE FIX: Believe it or not, this is a feature, not a bug. The theory is that you're supposed to be interested only in programs you've used recently. Applications you haven't opened in a while are thus hidden from view until you click that little arrow or wait awhile for the complete list to unfurl. Fortunately, this feature is easy to turn off: right-click the Start button, select Properties, click the Start Menu tab and then the Customize button, and uncheck the Use Personalized Menus checkbox.

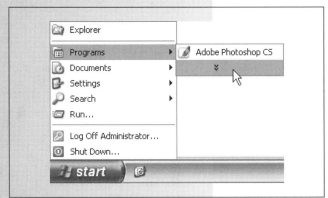

Figure 1-11. If you see this arrow at the bottom of your Programs list, you're using a feature called "Personalized Menus."

Stop Windows from Highlighting New Programs

THE ANNOYANCE: Why are some items in my All Programs list grayed out? It looks like they're disabled, but they open when I click them.

THE FIX: By default, Windows XP highlights newly installed programs to make them easier to find, presumably because you are not yet accustomed to seeing them. The problem is that they don't look so much "highlighted" as grayed out (Figure 1-12). To turn off this feature, right-click the Start button, go to Properties, click the Start Menu tab, and then click the Customize button. On the Advanced tab, uncheck the "Highlight newly installed programs" box.

Show Start Menu Programs in Multiple Columns

THE ANNOYANCE: I have so many icons in my All Programs menu that they run off the screen. I have to wait while Windows slowly scrolls the list to the one I want.

THE FIX: You have a few options here: you can either reduce the size of the menu by deleting unwanted items or organizing them into subfolders, or you can display the icons in multiple columns, as shown in Figure 1-13. For this trick, right-click the Start button, go to Properties, click the Start Menu tab, and then click the Customize button. On the Advanced tab, scroll down the "Start menu items" area and uncheck the Scroll Programs checkbox.

Figure 1-12. Newly installed programs are highlighted in the All Programs list.

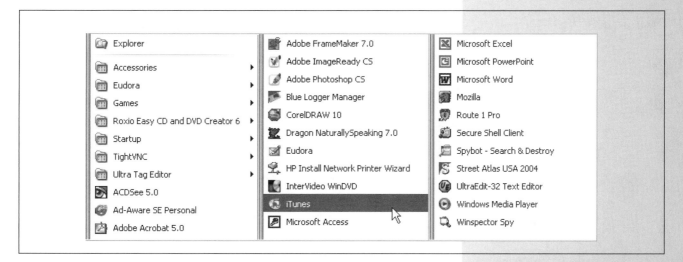

Figure 1-13. If you don't like the way Windows displays long menus, you can configure your menus to look like this.

TASKBAR

Customize the Alt-Tab Window

THE ANNOYANCE: When I switch between programs using Alt-Tab, it's hard to tell which window is which. The icons alone don't provide enough information, and the Alt-Tab window is too small to show the entire title of each window.

THE FIX: There are two ways to customize the Alt-Tab window. The first requires Creative Element Power Tools, available at *http://www. creativelement.com/powertools/.* Open the Creative Element Power Tools Control Panel, click the button next to "Change the size of the Alt-TAB window," and stretch the box to customize the size (Figure 1-14).

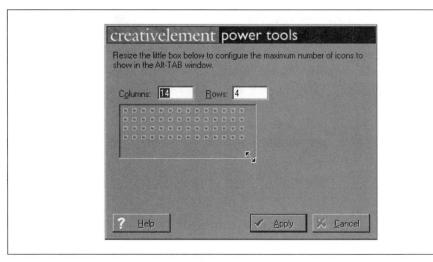

Figure 1-14. You can change the size of the Alt-Tab window to make room for more icons and longer window captions.

If you want more than a larger Alt-Tab window, try Microsoft's free Alt-Tab Replacement PowerToy, available at *http://www.microsoft.com/windowsxp/ downloads/powertoys/xppowertoys.mspx.* Once installed, it shows a preview of each window (Figure 1-15), rather than just the icon.

> **NOTE**
>
> *You can switch between multiple documents in the same application in a similar fashion, by pressing Ctrl-Tab or Ctrl-F6. Some applications (such as Word) show documents in separate windows, so they appear individually in the Alt-Tab sequence. Of course, this can be changed, too; in Word, for instance, select Tools→Options, and, on the View tab, uncheck the "Windows in Taskbar" box.*

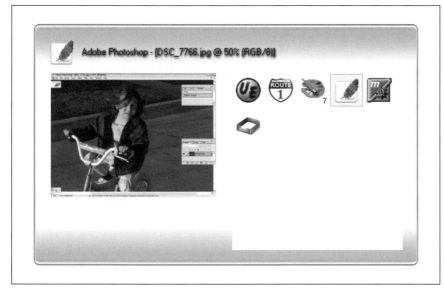

Figure 1-15. Replace the Alt-Tab window with this free PowerToy to see previews of open windows.

Ungroup Taskbar Buttons

THE ANNOYANCE: At some point during the day, Windows starts adding little arrows to my Taskbar buttons and "grouping" my programs. Instead of being able to activate a window by clicking once, I now have to click two or three times to get the window I want (Figure 1-16). Make it stop!

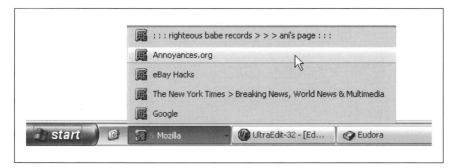

Figure 1-16. Windows consolidates task buttons to prevent the Taskbar from becoming crowded, but these groupings can be cumbersome to use.

THE FIX: By default, Windows XP "groups" similar Taskbar buttons when the Taskbar gets full (when it's not full, the Taskbar behaves normally). To have the Taskbar work the same way all the time, right-click an empty area of the Taskbar and choose Properties. In the Taskbar tab, uncheck the "Group similar taskbar buttons" box.

NOTE

To find out what a particular Tray icon is for, hover the mouse pointer over the icon for a few seconds until a little yellow "tooltip" appears. (Not all icons have these.)

Clean Out the Tray

THE ANNOYANCE: There's a bunch of junk in that little box to the right of my Taskbar, near the clock. I don't know what half the icons are for, and I think they're causing Windows to start more slowly.

THE FIX: That little box is called the Tray (or sometimes the System Tray, Systray, or notification area). It's filled with icons representing currently running programs, most of which are probably unnecessary. And you're right: these programs slow down the Windows startup process, as each takes time to load and consumes precious memory.

The problem is that removing a Tray icon varies from program to program. Most of the time, you can right-click an icon to exit the program (Figure 1-17), or even to change the setting that controls the icon so it won't load again. However, in some cases the program will reappear the next time you start Windows. To get rid of it permanently, you may have to hunt for the setting that controls whether or not the program starts with Windows. Look in the *Startup* folder in your Start menu, and if you find the Tray icon

Hide Stubborn Systray Icons

Windows XP lets you hide Tray icons that otherwise can't be removed, decreasing clutter and increasing Taskbar real estate. Here's how to do it:

1. Right-click an empty area of the Taskbar and select Properties.

2. Check the "Hide inactive icons" box, then click the Customize button. The Customize Notifications dialog will appear.

3. Windows keeps a history of every icon that has ever appeared in the Systray, and they're all shown in this window. The first section, Current Items, lists the icons that are currently appearing in your Tray; all others are shown in the Past Items section.

4. The options in this list are, unfortunately, not terribly intuitive. Start by selecting an entry in the drop-down list that appears next to the title. There are three choices:

    Hide when inactive
    This is the default for all icons, and simply means that the icon is only shown when the application in question tells Windows to display it.

    Always hide
    Choose this to, not surprisingly, hide the icon.

    Always show
    This option does absolutely nothing; it's no different from the "Hide when inactive" option. The only way to have an icon always appear is to configure your own with the Tray utility discussed in "Make a Show Desktop Button," earlier in this chapter.

5. When you're done, click OK, and then OK to close the Taskbar and Start Menu Properties window for your changes to take effect. (For some reason, the Apply button doesn't always work here, at least with regard to hidden or unhidden Tray icons.)

If at least one active Tray icon is hidden, it won't simply disappear. Instead, you'll see a little left-arrow button in its place at the edge of the Tray. Click the arrow to temporarily expand the Tray to show the hidden items. The Tray automatically collapses when you move your mouse away, hiding the icons once again. Unfortunately, there's no way to simultaneously hide this button and hide the Tray icons you don't want.

—From *Windows XP Annoyances for Geeks, 2nd Edition*

there, remove it. If you don't see it in the *Startup* folder, open the Registry Editor, navigate to *HKEY_LOCAL_MACHINE\SOFTWARE\Microsoft\Windows\CurrentVersion\Run*, and carefully remove the entry corresponding to the unwanted program. (For more tips on tidying your Tray, check out the sidebar "Hide Stubborn Systray Icons.")

Figure 1-17. You can right-click most notification icons to close or configure them.

Customize the Start Button

THE ANNOYANCE: That big ugly green Start button is annoying. How can I make it look like an ordinary button, like in earlier versions of Windows?

THE FIX: There's not much you can do about the Start button without changing the way the rest of Windows looks. If you prefer the no-frills Start button found in Windows 2000, Me, 98, and 95, open the Display control panel, click the Appearance tab, and choose "Windows Classic style" from the "Windows and buttons" drop-down. Of course, this will revert the rest of Windows to the older, simpler, non-XP style as well; unfortunately, you can't have the fancy new window style without the big ugly green button to go with it.

Move the Taskbar

THE ANNOYANCE: My Taskbar suddenly jumped to the side of my screen. How do I get it back on the bottom?

THE FIX: To move it, just click an empty area of the Taskbar and drag the bar to a new location. The bar won't move with the mouse like windows do, but if you're patient and move the mouse far enough, the Taskbar will follow. (If it doesn't, right-click the Taskbar and turn off the "Lock the Taskbar" option.) To prevent it from moving again, once it's in place, right-click an empty area of the Taskbar and select "Lock the Taskbar."

Fix Taskbar Bugs

THE ANNOYANCE: Certain elements of my Taskbar—things described elsewhere in this chapter, for instance—are either missing or grayed out. How come?

THE FIX: This and related Taskbar glitches are caused by errant Registry entries and nasty bugs. Luckily, you can use the Taskbar Repair Tool Plus! (free, *http://www.kellys-korner-xp.com/taskbarplus!.htm*), shown in Figure 1-18, to fix these nagging problems.

Among other things, the Taskbar Repair Tool Plus! can fix a grayed-out "Lock the Taskbar" command, recover missing minimized programs and a missing Start button, and squash more than a dozen other bugs relating to the System Tray and the Quick Launch toolbar.

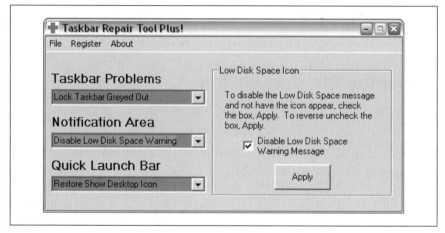

Figure 1-18. Use the Taskbar Repair Tool Plus! to fix a handful of Taskbar, Quick Launch toolbar, and Systray annoyances.

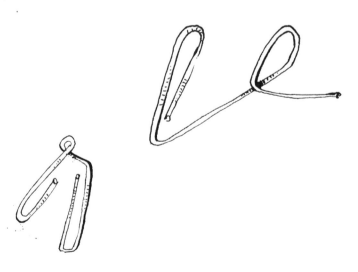

APPLICATION WINDOW

Find Missing Program Windows

THE ANNOYANCE: Certain programs never seem to open successfully. If I double-click a JPG file, for instance, my image viewer never launches—I see its icon in the Taskbar, but that's it. Clicking the icon doesn't do anything; the only thing that has any effect is right-clicking it and selecting Close to make it go away.

THE FIX: Although it may seem that the program has crashed, it's probably opening off-screen. Most programs can remember their last position and size, but few are smart enough to realize that they can't be seen. To find out if an application has opened off-screen, click its Taskbar icon so that it appears pushed in, and then press Alt-Space. If a little menu appears, use the cursor keys to select Move, and then press Enter. At this point, a gray rectangle should appear somewhere on your screen; use your cursor keys to move the rectangle so that it's roughly centered on the desktop, and then press Enter. With any luck, the missing window should magically appear.

If you don't see the menu, minimize all open windows and see if there's a dialog box for the program hiding behind them (in which case, you can click OK or whatever to make it go away). If there's no dialog box, uninstall and then reinstall the program. Still no luck? Contact the manufacturer of the misbehaving application for help.

Evils of DDE

Underneath the purring Windows interface is a well-hidden facility called *DDE* (short for Dynamic Data Exchange) that allows applications to communicate with one another. DDE frequently comes into play when you double-click documents in Windows Explorer, in an open folder window, or on the desktop. If the application associated with a document is not running, Explorer launches the application and the document simultaneously. But if the application is already running, Explorer merely sends a DDE message to the application, instructing it to open the document on its own. This should ensure that only one copy (instance) of a program is open at any given time.

Unfortunately, DDE ends up causing the exact problem it was designed to prevent. In some cases, Explorer opens a document and its application (like it's supposed to), and then sends a DDE message to the application instructing it to open a second copy of the file. The solution? Disable DDE. Although you can't turn off DDE entirely (nor would you want to), you can solve the problem by selectively disabling DDE support for certain file types, as explained in "Seeing Double Windows."

Seeing Double Windows

THE ANNOYANCE: Whenever I double-click a document in Windows Explorer or on the desktop, it opens in two identical windows. Is Windows really that stupid?

THE FIX: Yes, my son, Windows really is that stupid. Luckily, the fix is simple enough, but you must first determine the type of file that causes the problem.

In Windows Explorer, select Tools→Folder Options or open the Folder Options control panel, and choose the File Types tab. Find the appropriate filename extension in the list, and click the Advanced button. (If you see a Restore button here, click it to reveal the elusive Advanced button, and then click Advanced.)

NOTE

You'll need to know the extension (e.g., .doc or .wpd) of the offending file, which Microsoft, in its infinite wisdom, has hidden by default. To make filename extensions visible in Windows Explorer, go to Tools→Folder Options, click the View tab, and select "Show hidden files and folders."

In the subsequent dialog box (shown in Figure 1-19), highlight the bold item in the list—in this case, Open—and click the Edit button. In the "Editing action for type" window, uncheck the Use DDE box (see the "Evils of DDE" sidebar), and then click OK in each successive dialog box to confirm your choice. The duplicate windows should never return (at least until you reinstall the application, and in so doing, reinstall the DDE setting).

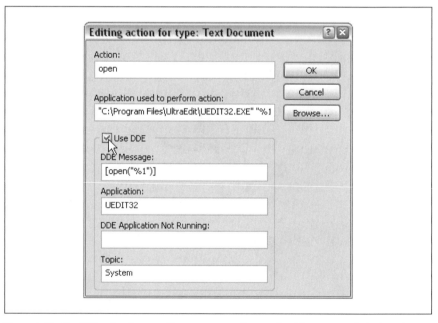

Figure 1-19. The DDE option for some file types causes all sorts of problems, most of which can be solved by simply turning it off.

Make Old Windows New Again

THE ANNOYANCE: I'm using an older program that's really showing its age. How can I make it look like the rest of my applications?

THE FIX: The style you choose in Display Properties affects not only the title bars of your applications, but also the push buttons, menus, toolbars, drop-down lists, and other screen elements in most, if not all, programs that run in Windows. Some older applications, though, may not know to take advantage of these new features.

To force a single application to update all of its push buttons, menus, and so on, type the following into a plain-text editor such as Notepad:

```
<?xml version="1.0" encoding="UTF-8" standalone="yes"?>
<assembly xmlns="urn:schemas-microsoft-com:asm.v1" manifestVersion="
1.0"><assemblyIdentity version="1.0.0.0" processorArchitecture="X86"
name="COMPANYNAME.PRODUCTNAME.PROGRAMNAME" type="win32"/><description>MY
DESCRIPTION</description>
<dependency><dependentAssembly><assemblyIdentity type="win32"
name="Microsoft.Windows.Common-Controls" version="6.0.0.0"
processorArchitecture="X86" publicKeyToken="6595b64144ccf1df"
language="*" /></dependentAssembly></dependency></assembly>
```

NOTE

The capitalized text after "name=" can be customized, but the rest of the text must appear exactly as shown. If you don't feel like typing all this yourself, you can download the text from http://www. annoyances.org/downloads/ manifest.txt.

Save this text into the same folder as the application you're customizing, and give it the same name as the main executable (*.exe*) file, followed by *.manifest*. For example, if you were trying to update an old version of Adobe Photoshop (*photoshp.exe*) installed in the *c:\Program Files\Adobe\Photoshop* folder, you'd save this text file in the same folder, as *Photoshp.exe.manifest*.

The next time you start the application, it should look more up to date. Not all programs can be forced to use styles this way, though, and those that support it may not do so properly.

WELCOME SCREEN

Get Rid of the Welcome Screen

THE ANNOYANCE: I'm sick of the Welcome screen. Why can't I go straight to Windows when I turn on my computer?

THE FIX: You can—if you're the only one using your computer. First, select a password, if you haven't done so already. Open the User Accounts control panel, choose your account from the list, click "Create a password," and then type the password you'd like to use. (Don't worry; you won't have to type it every time.)

Next, go to Start→Run, type control userpasswords2, and click OK. In this different User Accounts window, shown in Figure 1-20, uncheck the "Users must enter a user name and password to use this computer" box. When prompted, type your username and password (twice), and click OK. Thereafter, you won't have to log in manually again, and the Welcome screen will be banished.

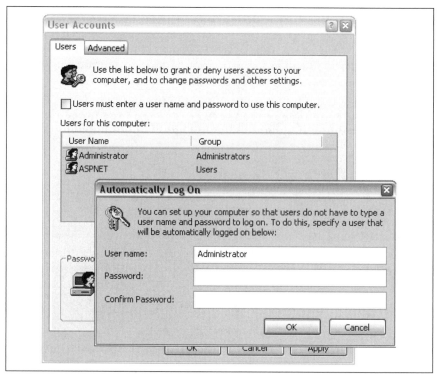

Figure 1-20. Use the Alternate User Accounts window to make it so you don't have to log in every time you turn on your computer.

Fix the Unread Messages Display

THE ANNOYANCE: The Welcome screen is telling me I have unread mail. How does it know? And, besides, it's wrong—nobody ever emails me. How do I get rid of this?

THE FIX: Sorry to hear that. Try joining some discussion groups or something, or if you like, I can add your address to some spam lists!

Regardless, the "unread messages" display only works if you're using Microsoft Outlook or Outlook Express to read your email. If you're not using either of these programs, you'll need to edit the Registry to fix the problem. Go to Start→Run, type regedit, and click OK. In the Registry Editor window, expand the branches on the left side to *HKEY_CURRENT_ USER\Software\Microsoft\Windows\CurrentVersion\UnreadMail*.

Then, on the right side, double-click the *MessageExpiryDays* value; if it's not there, go to Edit→New→DWORD Value, and type `MessageExpiryDays` for the name of the new value. In the Edit DWORD Value box, type 0, and click OK.

Old-Fashioned Logon

THE ANNOYANCE: My computer is used by a lot of people, and I don't think Windows's practice of listing them all is very smart. It's a lot harder for an intruder to guess both a username and a password than only a password. Is there a way to replace the Welcome screen with a good ol' logon box?

THE FIX: In the old days, people used to type in their usernames and passwords to log onto their computers (after, of course, climbing down from the mastodons that delivered them to the office).

You can replace the friendly-but-not-terribly-secure Welcome screen with the old familiar logon box (Figure 1-21) via the User Accounts control panel. Click the "Change the way users log on or off" link, and then uncheck the "Use the Welcome screen" box. Click the Apply Options button when you're done.

Figure 1-21. This old-fashioned logon box is more secure than the Welcome screen.

> ──── **NOTE** ────
>
> *Some other Windows features are affected by this setting. For instance, the Windows XP Shut Down box is also replaced with an older, no-frills version. And without the Welcome screen enabled, pressing Ctrl-Alt-Del opens the Windows Security box instead of the Task Manager.*

Hide the Name of the Last User

THE ANNOYANCE: I've switched to the classic logon screen, but now the username of the last person who used the computer is shown. From a security standpoint, this is not an improvement!

THE FIX: To hide this username, you must dive into the Windows Registry. Go to Start→Run, type `regedit`, and click OK. In the Registry Editor window, expand the branches on the left side to *HKEY_CURRENT_USER\ Software\Microsoft\Windows NT\CurrentVersion\Winlogon*. (Notice that this is in the Windows NT branch, not the Windows branch used elsewhere in this book.) Create a new value in this key: right-click *Winlogon* and select New→String Value, type `DontDisplayLastUserName` for its name, and press Enter. Double-click the new value, type 1 in the "Value data" field, and click OK.

Un-Secure Your Screensaver

THE ANNOYANCE: Every time my screensaver comes on, I have to type my password to make it go away. Is this necessary?

THE FIX: Other than being a sure-fire way to force you to remember your own password, it's not really useful unless you work in a public environment. The idea is that if you walk away from your desk, an intruder can't poke around your system without knowing your password. If you feel that the likelihood of this happening is small, change this setting by right-clicking an empty area of your desktop, selecting Properties, and choosing the Screen Saver tab. Uncheck the "On resume, password protect" box, and click OK.

There's a second option that does pretty much the same thing when your computer hibernates or goes to sleep. If you don't want Windows to send you back to the Welcome screen each time you "wake up" your PC, open the Power Options control panel (or click the Power button in Display Properties), choose the Advanced tab, and uncheck the "Prompt for password when computer resumes from standby" checkbox. Click OK, and you're done.

Windows Explorer

In designing Windows Explorer, Microsoft tried to strike a balance between useful and simple, and the result is a program that is often neither.

Explorer has a tendency to hide useful information, such as file-name extensions and folder sizes, while cluttering windows with pointless links and unnecessary wizards. Sure, you can fix some of these shortcomings by changing settings in dozens of different dialog boxes, but most problems must be resolved with the help of add-on programs or obscure Registry hacks.

Looking at a single folder, and want to know where it is on your system? You'll have to go to View→Folder Options, choose the View tab, and turn on the "Display the full path in the title bar" option. Want the same information in a File→Open dialog box? Sorry, you'll need to purchase an add-on program for that.

Simple features that were present in DOS 20 years ago are still absent from Explorer, such as the ability to rename multiple files at once with wildcards or print out a list of files. You'll need add-on programs for these tasks, too.

The good news is that Windows Explorer is an entirely modular and extremely flexible application and will happily accept your hacks, add-ons, and fixes with aplomb (most of the time). Just think of Explorer as a starting point rather than a finished product, and you'll eventually get the kind of file management you want.

FOLDERS

Show Folder Tree Lines

THE ANNOYANCE: Windows Explorer used to have dotted lines connecting the folders in the folder tree. How can I show these lines in Windows XP?

THE FIX: In Windows Explorer, go to Tools→Folder Options, click the View tab, and uncheck the "Display simple folder view in Explorer's Folders list" box. Click OK, and the folder lines will reappear in Windows Explorer, as shown in Figure 2-1.

NOTE

Windows Explorer is typically seen in its two-pane format, with a folder tree on the left and the contents of the currently selected folder on the right. With the "simple folder view" option enabled, Windows Explorer automatically expands a folder branch when you highlight a folder to show all the folders contained therein. Disable this option, and you'll have to click the little plus signs [+] or double-click the folder names to expand branches.

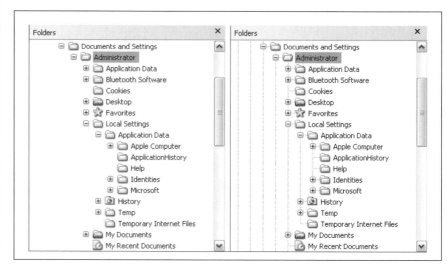

Figure 2-1. Lines in the folder tree help show relationships between folders.

Get the Details View Every Time

THE ANNOYANCE: I like the Details view because it shows all the information about my files at once, but I hate having to go to View→Details every time, only to have Windows Explorer forget my preference when I switch folders.

THE FIX: Windows Explorer won't change the default view settings unless you ask it to. Start by customizing a folder view: select the Details view (or whatever view you like), and choose a sort order by clicking the column headers or by going to View→Arrange Icons by. You can even go to View→Choose Details—or right-click a column heading—to choose which columns appear in the Details view. (See "Sort Photos Chronologically" in Chapter 3 for a nifty way to use one of the extra Details columns here.)

When you're done customizing, go to Tools→Folder Options, choose the View tab, and click the "Apply to All Folders" button. Check the "Remember each folder's view settings" box, and click OK.

Sooner or later, senility will appear to strike and Explorer will start indiscriminately forgetting your view settings in some folders. To fix the problem, find a folder that still matches your preferences, return to the Folder Options window, and click "Apply to All Folders" again. For more on this problem, see the next annoyance.

Remember Settings for More Folders

THE ANNOYANCE: I turned on the "Remember each folder's view settings" checkbox, as described in "Get the Details View Every Time," but it doesn't take long for Explorer to forget the settings I've set for a specific folder.

THE FIX: Explorer stores folder view settings in the Registry and, alas, not in the folders themselves. This awkward design has two rather silly drawbacks. First, if you move or rename a folder, its view settings revert to Explorer's defaults. Second, by default the view settings can be stored for a maximum of only 400 folders on your system. While this may seem like a lot, this limit can quickly be consumed, particularly since an individual folder eats up an additional slot in the Registry each time it's moved or renamed.

To raise the limit, you'll need to mess around in the Registry. Open the Registry Editor (go to Start→Run and type regedit), and then navigate to *HKEY_CURRENT_USER\Software\Microsoft\Windows\Shell*. Create a new value by selecting Edit→New→DWORD Value, and, in the right pane, type BagMRU Size for the name. Double-click the new value, select the Decimal option, type the number of folders you'd like Explorer to remember (e.g., 5000) in the "Value data" field, and click OK. Next, repeat the process for the *HKEY_CURRENT_USER\Software\Microsoft\Windows\ShellNoRoam* key. Close the Registry Editor when you're done.

Jump to a Subfolder

THE ANNOYANCE: I'm trying to get to a folder about seven layers deep, and it's a hassle to have to wait for Windows to update the display as I expand each folder. Isn't there a way to jump to a subfolder without wading through all of its parent folders?

THE FIX: There are a few ways to do this. The easiest is to highlight the top-level folder in the tree and press the asterisk (*) key. This will expand the selected folder, all of its subfolders, all of *their* subfolders, and so on. Then, type the first few letters of the target folder to jump to it.

> **NOTE**
>
> *Best not to use this trick on a folder with a lot of subfolders, such as the root directory or, say, Program Files. Explorer will take its sweet time reading the whole branch, which should give you a pretty good idea of why they're collapsed in the first place. As there's no way to abort the procedure, you'll be waiting quite a while before you can start navigating to any of those subfolders!*

> **NOTE**
>
> *Explorer remembers different preferences for single-folder windows and two-pane folder-tree windows. Once you've used the "Apply to All Folders" button in, say, a two-pane Explorer window, go ahead and double-click a folder icon on your desktop (or right-click a folder in the tree and select Open) and customize the single-folder window that appears as you see fit. Then repeat the above steps to save those settings as the default for that window type.*

Alternatively, if you know the full path of the folder, just type it into Explorer's address bar and press Enter. Windows will even help you by filling in likely candidates as you type (see Figure 2-2); press the down arrow key to pick a folder from the list.

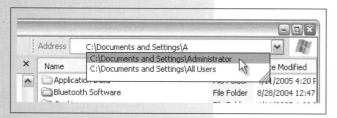

Figure 2-2. Windows Explorer helps you type folder paths to quickly jump to buried subfolders.

Yet another shortcut is to press F3 or Ctrl-F to open the Search pane (see "Search in a New Window" for a way to preserve your current view while searching). Click the "All files and folders" link, type the folder name in the "All or part of the filename" field, and press Enter. Double-click the folder when it appears in the Search Results window to open it.

Shrink the Address Bar

THE ANNOYANCE: I have a small screen, and the address bar and the Standard Buttons toolbar take up too much space. I got rid of the toolbar, but I'd like to keep the address bar. Is there a way to make it smaller?

THE FIX: With screen real estate at a premium (even on large displays), anything you can do to minimize clutter is helpful. The trick is to stuff the address bar into that unused space to the right of Explorer's main menu (File, Edit, View, etc.), as shown in Figure 2-3.

> **NOTE**
>
> *If you don't see the address bar in Windows Explorer, go to View→Toolbars→Address Bar.*

Right-click any part of the menu or the gray part of the address bar, and if there's a checkmark next to "Lock the Toolbars," click it to turn it off. Then grab the word "Address" with your mouse and drag the bar to the right side of the menu. Since some folders (such as Network Connections in the Control Panel) have extra menus, make sure to leave a little space to the right of the Help menu to accommodate them. When you're done, right-click the bar and select "Lock the Toolbars" to turn the lock back on.

Figure 2-3. Stuff the address bar into the menu bar to save space.

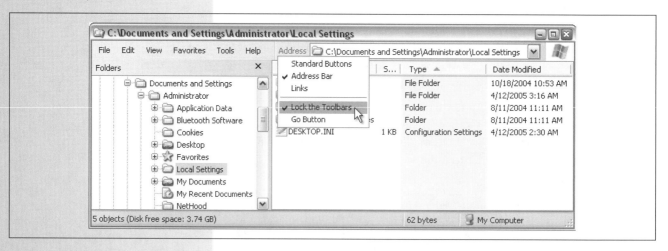

Copy a Folder Path to the Clipboard

THE ANNOYANCE: I want to send someone an email with the location of a file on our network. How do I do this without having to type the path manually?

THE FIX: Go to View→Folder Options, choose the View tab, check the "Display the full path in the address bar" box, and click OK. Navigate to the folder you want to copy, and the full path of the selected folder will appear in the address bar above. Click the text in the address bar once (it should already be highlighted, as shown in Figure 2-4), and press Ctrl-C to copy it. Then press Ctrl-V to paste the text into your email.

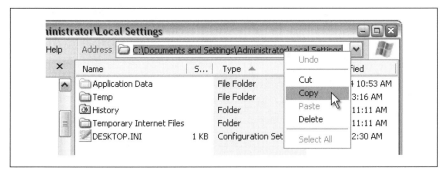

Figure 2-4. Use the address bar to copy the current folder path to the clipboard.

An add-on can help here, too. Among other things, Creative Element Power Tools (*http://www.creativelement.com/powertools/*) lets you right-click any folder (or file, for that matter) and select Copy Filename to place the name and entire path on the clipboard. You can then press Ctrl-V to paste it anywhere you like.

Print a Folder Listing

THE ANNOYANCE: I need a printout of the contents of a folder, but Explorer doesn't have a Print function. Do I have to resort to the Print Screen key on my keyboard?

THE FIX: In the days of DOS, pressing the Print Screen key would send all the text on your screen to your printer. But in Windows, this key simply takes a screenshot of the entire display and puts it on the clipboard as a bitmap. (Hint: press Alt-Print Screen to snap just the active window.)

Fortunately, there's a better way, but it involves a little preparation. Open Notepad, and type the following:

```
dir /o:gn "%1" >c:\filelisting.txt
notepad /p c:\filelisting.txt
```

When you're done, select File→Save and name the file *printfolder.bat*. (The *.bat* filename extension is important.)

Next, in Windows Explorer, go to Tools→Folder Options, and choose the File Types tab. Highlight "(NONE)/Folder" in the list, and click the Advanced button. Then click the New button in the Edit File Type dialog. In the Action field, type Print Listing, and below, in the "Application used to perform action" field, type the full path and filename of the *printfolder.bat* file you just created (e.g., c:\stuff\printfolder.bat). Click OK and then OK again, and click the Close button when you're done.

Thereafter, right-click any folder and select Print Listing to run the batch file and print an alphabetized listing of the folder contents.

If you don't want to fuss with the batch file, use Creative Element Power Tools: just right-click any folder and select Print Folder Contents, or select Copy Folder Contents if you want to paste the listing into another program. (Both tools also calculate the sizes of all subfolders—something you can't do in Explorer without an add-on program.) To get a list of only the selected files, as opposed to all the files in a folder, in Power Tools right-click and select Copy Filename. The Copy Filename tool doesn't calculate your folder sizes, but it works in search results and will even include the full path of each selected file. If you still need to print, just paste the listing into any application and print away.

Print a File from Explorer

THE ANNOYANCE: I need to print a variety of documents on a regular basis, but it's a hassle to open each document in its own application just to print it. There's gotta be a faster way.

THE FIX: Depending on the file type, odds are the feature you want is right at hand. In Explorer, just right-click a document and select Print to send it to the printer.

Now, the printing of documents is the responsibility of individual applications, so if you don't see a Print option for a particular file type, it means there's no application configured for this task. To add a Print option to a file type that doesn't have it, go to View→Folder Options in Explorer, and choose the File Types tab. Select the type in the list, and click the Advanced button. Click New, type Print in the Action field, and then click Browse. Locate the application that opens files of this type (e.g., Notepad for *.txt* files, Microsoft Word for *.doc* files), and then click Open. After the path and filename in the "Application used to perform action" field, add a space and then type /p %1.

Click OK and then OK again, and click the Close button when you're done. Now, right-click a document that matches the file type you just customized and select Print, and you should get a printout of the file shortly!

NOTE

The %1 is a placeholder, which Explorer will replace with the name of the file you've right-clicked. The /p parameter is usually all that is required to instruct the program to print the file, although your application may need a different parameter. Look up "command-line parameters" in your application's documentation for details.

Show the Folder Size

THE ANNOYANCE: Explorer shows the collective size of the files in a folder down in the Status bar, but this statistic never includes the subfolders. Why doesn't Explorer show the size of *all* the contents of a folder?

THE FIX: It does, but not in the Status bar. Right-click a folder and select Properties, and Explorer will calculate the size of the folder and all its contents—including subfolders—reporting both the total number of bytes and the actual disk space consumed. (The latter is always a larger number because files, no matter how small, consume disk space in discrete chunks called *clusters*.) Of course, this gets rather time-consuming if you want to check the sizes of more than a handful of folders.

To display folder sizes right in Windows Explorer (Figure 2-5), install the free Folder Size for Windows extension, available at *http://foldersize. sourceforge.net*. Open Windows Explorer, navigate to any folder on your hard disk, and select View→Details. Right-click any column header (or go to View→Choose Details), and place a checkmark next to Folder Size. This gives you a new Folder Size heading that shows the sizes of both individual

---
NOTE

Due to a limitation in Windows XP's support for "column handlers" like the Folder Size extension, you won't be able to sort Explorer listings reliably by clicking the Folder Size column header. As a partial fix, a second column, Folder Size Sort, is also included in the package. Although it omits the comma separators and "KB" designation, it can properly sort files by size.

Figure 2-5. Use the Folder Size extension to show the size of folders and all their contents in a new column in Windows Explorer.

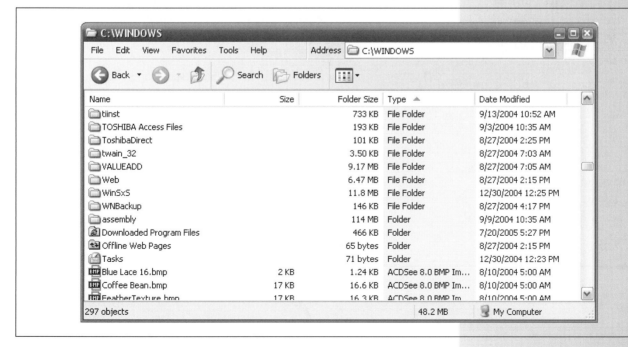

files and the contents of folders (you can turn off the Size column now, since the file size display will be redundant).

At this point, you can rearrange and resize the columns by dragging them with your mouse. If you want to make this new setup the default, so that the Folder Size column shows up for all folders, see "Get the Details View Every Time."

Navigate Folders with the Keyboard

THE ANNOYANCE: I hate using the mouse when I don't have to; is there a way to navigate in Windows Explorer with the keyboard?

THE FIX: The less you touch that rodent, the better; keyboarding is faster, too! Highlight any folder with the arrow keys and then press Enter to open it. To jump to the parent (containing folder) of the current folder, press Backspace.

In the folder tree, move from folder to folder with the up and down arrow keys; use the plus (+) key or the right arrow key to expand a folder branch, or the minus (-) key or the left arrow key to collapse it. (The left arrow key will also jump to the parent if the selected folder is already collapsed.)

Windows Explorer also maintains a "history," like Internet Explorer. Hold down the Alt key and press the left arrow key to jump to any folder you've previously viewed. Once you've gone back in time, so to speak, you can move forward by holding Alt and pressing the right arrow key.

And there's more! Use the Tab key to jump between the folder tree, the file listing, and the address bar (use Ctrl-Tab to go backwards). Press Enter to open the selected item, F2 to rename it, or Alt-Enter to open its Properties sheet (a.k.a. right-click→Properties).

Selecting files and folders with the keyboard is easy, too. To select a range of files, hold down the Shift key while using the up or down arrow keys. To select nonadjacent files, hold down the Ctrl key while pressing the up or down arrow keys, and then hit the spacebar to select or deselect a file.

> **NOTE**
>
> *You can jump to any folder by typing the first few letters of its name, as long as it's visible on the tree (not collapsed). See the sidebar "Helpful Explorer Keystrokes" for more on this and other useful shortcuts.*

Helpful Explorer Keystrokes

Certain keyboard shortcuts can be real timesavers in Explorer, especially when used in conjunction with the mouse. The following tips assume you're using standard double-clicking. If you've chosen to have icons respond to a single click, just replace "double-click" here with "single-click."

- Hold the Alt key while double-clicking a file or folder to view the Properties sheet for that object. Although this is often quicker than right-clicking and selecting Properties, the right-click menu—also known as the context menu—has a bunch of other options, most of which are not accessible with keystrokes.

- Hold the Shift key while double-clicking a folder icon to open an Explorer window at that location (as opposed to a single-folder window). Be careful when using this, because Shift is also used to select multiple files. The best way is to select the folder first.

- Press Backspace in an open folder window or in Explorer to go to the parent folder.

- Hold the Shift key while clicking on the close button [X] to close all open folder windows in the chain that was used to get to that folder. (This, of course, makes sense only in the single-folder view and with the "Open each folder in its own window" option turned on.)

- Select one icon, then hold the Shift key while clicking another icon in the same folder to select it and all the items in between.

- Hold the Ctrl key while clicking to select or deselect multiple files or folders, one by one. Note that you can't select more than one folder in the folder tree pane of Explorer, but you can in the right pane. You can also use Ctrl key to modify your selection. For example, if you've used the Shift key or a rubber band to select the first five objects in a folder, you can hold Ctrl while dragging a second rubber band to highlight additional files without losing your original selection.

- Press Ctrl-A to quickly select all of the contents of a folder: both files and folders.

- In Explorer or any single-folder window (even in the folder tree pane), press a letter key to quickly jump to the first file or folder starting with that letter. Continue typing to jump further. For example, pressing the T key in your \Windows folder will jump to the Tasks folder. Press T again to jump to the next object that starts with T. Or, press T and then quickly press A to skip all the Ts and jump to taskman.exe. If there's enough of a delay between the T and the A keys, Explorer will forget about the T, and you'll jump to the first entry that starts with A.

- Press F6 to jump between the file pane and the address bar (if it's visible). In Internet Explorer (or Netscape or one of the Mozilla browsers, for that matter), use F6 to jump between the address bar and the page you're viewing.

—From *Windows XP Annoyances for Geeks, 2nd Edition*

Hide the Tasks Pane

THE ANNOYANCE: I never use any of those silly links in the "File and Folder Tasks" and "Other Places" boxes on the left side of most single-folder windows (Figure 2-6). Can I get rid of them and get back some screen space?

THE FIX: Absolutely! Go to Tools→Folder Options, select the "Use Windows classic folders" option, and click OK. You won't be missing anything, either; just about every feature in the Tasks pane is accessible in Explorer's menus or by right-clicking.

Figure 2-6. Save space by doing away with the Tasks pane.

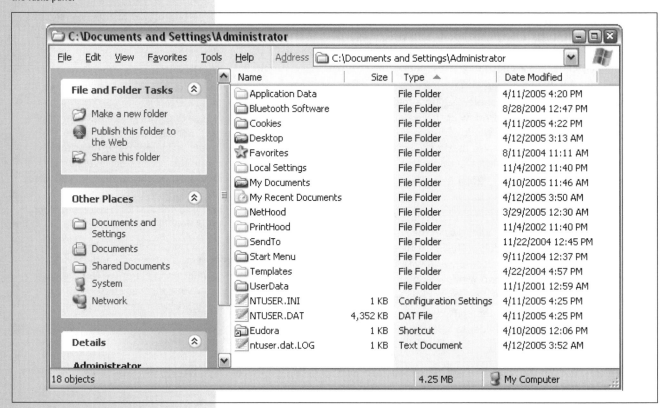

> **NOTE**
>
> *The only one thing you can't do without the Tasks pane is turn on or off the Category view in the Control Panel. With the Tasks pane visible, go to Tools→ Folder Options, select "Show common tasks in folders," open the Control Panel, and click "Switch to Classic View" to show all Control Panel icons together (or click "Switch to Category View" to hide the icons behind the handful of Control Panel categories).*

Get Back the Folder Tree

THE ANNOYANCE: Sometimes when I'm looking at a single-folder window, I want to use the tree so I can jump to other nearby folders. But it's cumbersome to go to View→Explorer Bar→Folders just to show the tree, and the delay each time I open the Explorer Bar menu is intolerable. Is there a faster way?

THE FIX: You've probably noticed that "Folders" is the only entry in the View→ Explorer Bar menu that *lacks* a keyboard shortcut, which is odd, given that it's easily the most useful feature in the bunch. While you can't summon the folder tree with the keyboard, or do anything about that delay, you can click the Folders button on the toolbar to show or hide the folder tree. If your toolbar doesn't have this button, you can add it; if you've turned off the toolbar to reduce clutter, you can turn it back on but slim it down so it contains only the Folders button (as shown in Figure 2-7).

Here's how to customize the toolbar. First, double-click a folder icon on your desktop to open a single-folder window. (Since Windows Explorer saves different toolbars for single-folder windows and folder-tree windows, make sure to do this in a single-folder window, as opposed to one that already has the folder tree.) Display the standard toolbar if it isn't already visible by selecting View→Toolbars→Standard Buttons.

Right-click the toolbar and select Customize. The buttons currently on the toolbar appear on the right side of this window. To add a Folders

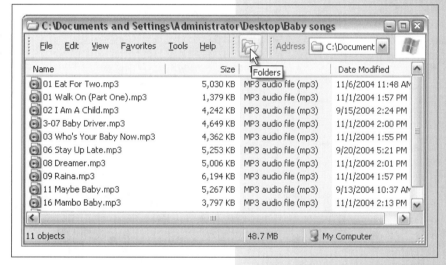

Figure 2-7. Use this button to quickly show or hide the folder tree.

button, select it in the "Available toolbar buttons" list and click the Add button. To create a minimalist one-button (Folders) toolbar, highlight each of the other items in the "Current toolbar buttons" list in turn and click the Remove button to take it off the bar. Keep doing this until there's nothing left except for the yellow Folders button. From the two drop-down menus below, select "No text labels" and "Small icons," respectively, and click the Close button when you're done. Finally, move the lone button so it appears next to the menu; use the steps for moving the address bar discussed in "Shrink the Address Bar," earlier in this chapter.

From now on, you can click the Folders button to show or hide the folder tree in any single-folder window.

Open Explorer in a Custom Folder

THE ANNOYANCE: Every time I open Windows Explorer, it opens the *My Documents* folder and leaves the rest of my hard disk hidden inside the My Computer branch. I'd rather have it go to the drive list in My Computer, or directly to a folder I use more often. How do I do this?

THE FIX: Of course, you can create a shortcut to a folder by selecting the folder in Explorer, then dragging the control menu icon (the little box in the upper-left corner of any window) onto the desktop. But if you double-click this shortcut, all you'll get is a single-folder window. If you want a full-fledged Explorer window complete with the folder tree, try this.

First, create a brand new shortcut by right-clicking an empty area on the desktop and selecting New→Shortcut. For the location, type:

```
explorer.exe/n,/e,,"c:\my folder"
```

Make sure to include the space after .exe, the three commas as shown (without spaces), and quotation marks around your folder path; naturally, replace *c:\my folder* with the folder you'd like to have Explorer display. Or, to open directly to your drive list in My Computer, add the /select parameter between the second and third commas, and specify c:\ as the destination path, like the path shown in Figure 2-8. Click Next, type `Windows Explorer` (or any name that makes sense to you) for the shortcut name, and click Finish.

Figure 2-8. Create a new shortcut to open Windows Explorer in a custom folder.

To open Windows Explorer to the new location, just double-click the shortcut. For more convenient launching, put it in your Start menu, in the Quick Launch toolbar, or on the Windows desktop.

Keep Explorer from Vanishing

THE ANNOYANCE: Windows Explorer keeps crashing; worse, it takes all the other Explorer windows with it—even the desktop! How can this cascade crash be stopped?

THE FIX: By default, the same *instance* of Explorer handles the desktop, the Start menu, and all open Explorer and single-folder windows. That is, only one copy of the *explorer.exe* application is ever in memory. This means that if one Explorer window crashes, they all crash.

To fix this, go to Tools→Folder Options, choose the View tab, check the "Launch folder windows in a separate process" box, and click OK. Thereafter, each Explorer window will represent a separate instance of the program. Although this consumes a little more memory and may slightly increase the time it takes to open Explorer windows, you won't notice the difference at all if you're using a fast computer. (See the "Restore the Desktop" sidebar for another side effect.)

Delete an Undeletable Folder

THE ANNOYANCE: I'm trying to delete a folder, but Windows says it's being used by "another person." Are we talking gremlins here, or has someone broken into my PC to read my manifesto on platypus cloning?

THE FIX: All this means is that there's a running application that either has a file open in that folder or has placed a lock on the folder because the last file it saved was stored there. (The latter can happen even if the folder is empty.) Just close the application in question (or close all open windows if you're not sure which one it is), and try deleting the folder again.

You'll get a similar error if the folder contains a program file (i.e., an *.exe* or *.dll* file) belonging to an application that's currently running. As you'd expect, closing the application should make it possible to delete the file, and thus the folder. The tricky part is when the file is a component of a background process (so there's no visible window to close), part of a stealthy spyware process (see Chapter 4), or part of a program that has crashed. If you suspect the problem is connected to a hidden process, restart Windows and then delete the folder. If you suspect spyware, scour your system with up-to-date antispyware software, such as Spybot - Search & Destroy (free, *http://www.safer-networking.org/en/download/index.html*) or Ad-Aware SE Personal (free, *http://www.lavasoft.com/support/download/?myrehovot.info*).

If you still can't delete the folder, try Safe Mode. Restart your computer, and just after the system beep but before the Windows startup logo appears, press the F8 key to display the Windows Advanced Options Menu. Use the arrow keys to highlight Safe Mode, and then press Enter. Windows will then load in a hobbled state, loading only essential programs and drivers. At

Restore the Desktop

There's a little program that runs invisibly in the background that automatically restarts Explorer if it ever crashes; this ensures that you're never without your desktop or Start menu.

If you turn on the "Launch folder windows in a separate process" option, it sort of breaks this feature. If your desktop ever disappears and *doesn't* come back, press Ctrl-Alt-Del to display the Task Manager. Choose the Processes tab, click the Image Name column heading to sort the list alphabetically, highlight explorer.exe in the list, and click the End Process button; do this for every instance of Explorer you see. When you're done, restart Windows Explorer by going to File→New Task (Run), typing explorer, and clicking OK.

this point you should be able to delete the folder with no problem. Restart your PC when you're done, and Windows will load normally.

If this doesn't work you can use the "Delete in-use files" tool, part of Creative Element Power Tools (http://www.creativelement.com/powertools/). If there's a file you can't get rid of, just right-click it, select Delete In-Use File, and then restart your PC. The next time Windows loads, all files queued for deletion will be removed before any programs that use them load.

Clean Up Context Menus

THE ANNOYANCE: I installed a new program, and it immediately added a new entry to Explorer's right-click menu for folders. How can I get rid of this pest?

THE FIX: If the application's authors followed good programming practices, they should have included an option that lets you remove this right-click entry. (Check the program's documentation for specifics.) But odds are it ain't there.

In Windows Explorer, go to Tools→Folder Options, and choose the File Types tab. Highlight "Folder" in the list, and click the Advanced button. If the entry you want to remove appears here, highlight it and click the Remove button. Otherwise, close the window.

This leaves the Registry as the only means of cleaning up your context menus. Open the Registry Editor (go to Start→Run and type regedit), and navigate to *HKEY_CLASSES_ROOT\Folder\shellex\ContextMenuHandlers*. Expand the branch, and you'll see a handful of subkeys immediately below *ContextMenuHandlers* (see Figure 2-9), each of which corresponds to at least one entry in your folders' context menus.

> **NOTE**
>
> *Before you muck with the Registry, back up the entire ContextMenuHandlers key by highlighting it, selecting File→Export, and saving the key as a .reg file on your desktop. To restore the backup should something go wrong, just double-click the .reg file.*

Figure 2-9. Some stubborn context menu items can only be removed with the Registry Editor.

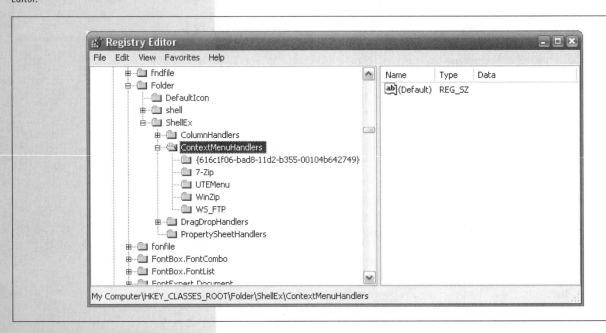

The purpose of some subkeys in *ContextMenuHandlers* will be obvious, while others will appear only as nonsensical strings of numbers and letters. If you see a key that is clearly responsible for the errant context menu item, go ahead and delete it. Otherwise, highlight each key, and look at the values in the pane on the right for clues.

If you encounter a numeric key like *{616c1f06-bad8-11d2-b355-00104b642749}* (see Figure 2-9), it's a *ClassID*, or a pointer to a registered program component referenced elsewhere in your Registry. To find out what it does, highlight the key in question, press F2 to select the name, press Ctrl-C to copy the name, and then press Esc. Next, press Ctrl-F to open the Find dialog, Ctrl-V to paste the string into the "Find what" field, and press Enter to begin a search. As you search through the Registry, you'll find references to the same ClassID in other file types; stop when you get to the first instance you find that isn't located under a *ContextMenuHandlers* key. Most likely, you'll end up in a key that looks like *HKEY_LOCAL_MACHINE\SOFTWARE\Classes\CLSID\{616c1f06-bad8-11d2-b355-00104b642749}*. The name of the program should appear in the right pane (see Figure 2-10); if not, expand the branch and look through the subkeys for clues.

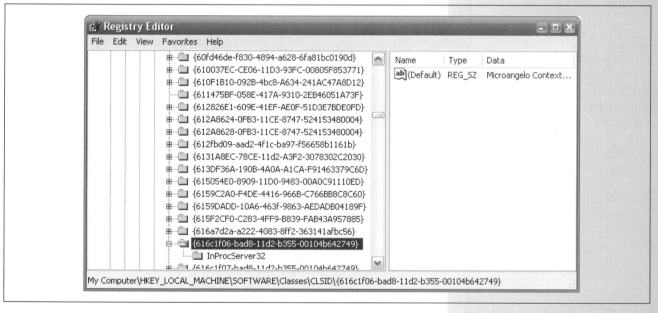

Figure 2-10. Search the Registry for a ClassID to find out what it's for.

NOTE

If you can't find the key responsible, go to HKEY_CLASSES_ROOT\Directory\shellex\ContextMenuHandlers and repeat the above process (or, if you're hunting for an item that appears in files' context menus, conduct your search in HKEY_CLASSES_ROOT*\shellex\ContextMenuHandlers).

If the program to which the ClassID is pointing matches the context menu item you want to delete, return to *HKEY_CLASSES_ROOT\Folder\shellex\ ContextMenuHandlers* and delete the errant subkey there (leaving the one in *HKEY_LOCAL_MACHINE\SOFTWARE\Classes\CLSID* intact).

Customize Folder Icons

THE ANNOYANCE: The standard yellow folder icons make me feel jaundiced. Is there any way to pick a more aesthetically pleasing icon?

THE FIX: Unfortunately, Explorer only lets you customize the icons for individual folders—you can't make a blanket change without the help of a third-party application.

Right-click a folder whose icon you'd like to change, select Properties, and choose the Customize tab, shown in Figure 2-11 (see the "Missing the Customize Tab?" sidebar if it's not there). Click the Change Icon button, and then choose an *.ico*, *.dll*, or *.exe* file containing the icon you'd like to use for this folder. Click OK when you're done.

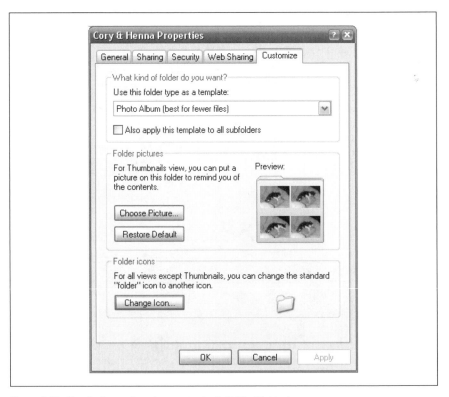

Figure 2-11. Use the Customize tab to customize individual folder icons.

Missing the Customize Tab?

Don't see the Customize tab in the Properties window for a folder? Put it back by opening the Registry Editor (go to Start→Run and type regedit) and navigating to *HKEY_CLASSES_ ROOT\Directory\shel- lex\PropertySheetHandlers*. Create a new key (Edit→ New→Key), and type {ef43ecfe-2ab9-4632-bf21- 58909dd177f0} for its name.

Next, navigate to *HKEY_ CURRENT_USER\Software\ Microsoft\Windows\ CurrentVersion\Policies\ Explorer*. Double-click the *NoCustomizeThisFolder* value in the right pane, type 0 (zero) in the "Value data" field, and click OK. Do the same for the *NoCustomizeWebView* and *ClassicShell* values. (If any of these values are absent, skip 'em.) Finally, navigate to *HKEY_LOCAL_MACHINE\ Software\Microsoft\ Windows\CurrentVersion\ Policies\Explorer* and set the same three keys to 0 (skip this step if this key is missing on your system). Close the Registry Editor when you're done, restart Windows, and try again.

Another approach: back on the Customize tab, click the Choose Picture button to choose a photo to superimpose over the standard folder icon in Explorer's Thumbnail view.

If you want to change the default folder icon for all folders, try the Microangelo On Display utility ($24.95, *http://www.microangelo.us*). Among other things, On Display allows you to customize nearly every icon found in Windows XP, including the default icon used for all folders.

Faster Folder Fix

THE ANNOYANCE: It takes forever to open a particular folder in Windows Explorer. Does the fact that it contains 4,000 files have anything to do with it?

THE FIX: Why, yes—the more files a folder contains, the longer it will take for Explorer to display it. Your first order of business is to run Disk Defragmenter (go to Start→Run and type dfrg.msc) to rearrange the physical data on your hard drive so that it can be read more efficiently. Once that's done, Explorer should load the folder much more quickly.

The other thing you can do is to separate the files into several folders. Organize them alphabetically, for instance, by placing files that start with an A, B, C, or D into a folder called *A-D*. Do the same with *E-H*, *I-L*, and so on. Not only will Explorer display each subfolder in less time, but it might make it easier to find individual files.

FILES

Show Filename Extensions

THE ANNOYANCE: I'm looking at a list of files, and I see several files with the same name. I can't tell my love letters from my hate mail!

THE FIX: By default, Windows Explorer hides file *extensions*, the part of the filename after the last dot. For instance, a Microsoft Word file called *Hi Grandma.doc* will just appear as *Hi Grandma* in Windows Explorer. Naturally, this makes it indistinguishable from *Hi Grandma.jpg* (except, of course, for the tiny file icon). To make it easier to distinguish one file from another, open Windows Explorer, go to Tools→Folder Options, choose the View tab (see Figure 2-12), uncheck the "Hide extensions for known file types" box, and click OK.

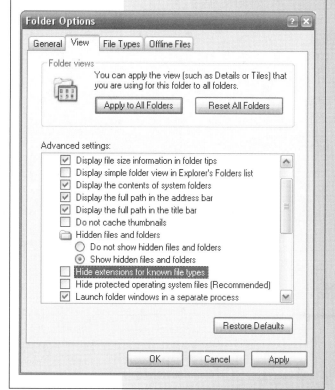

Figure 2-12. Use Folder Options to show filename extensions so you can more easily work with your documents.

NOTE

The Windows Picture and Fax Viewer, the program that appears when you open image files, is a special case and usually won't release its hold on its file types, even when you choose a new default program. See "Down with the Picture and Fax Viewer!" in Chapter 3 for the fix.

Choose Default Programs

THE ANNOYANCE: I like to double-click files to open them, as opposed to opening them from within an application. But sometimes when I double-click a file, the wrong program opens. How do I fix this?

THE FIX: Right-click the file you'd like to open, select Properties, and click the Change button to choose a new default program for that type of file. If you don't see the program you want in the list, click the Browse button to locate the application's executable (*.exe*) file on your hard disk. Click OK in both boxes to confirm your choice.

This doesn't mean you're stuck with a single program to open all files of a certain type, though; you can use the File Types window to assign several programs to each file type, and choose between them on the fly. In Explorer, go to Tools→Folder Options, choose the File Types tab, and then select the file type from the list. You can sort the list by Extension or description (File Type) by clicking the respective column headers. For instance, to customize the associations for JPG image files, click the Extension header, and highlight JPG in the first column. Click the Advanced button (or click Restore and then Advanced) to display the Edit File Type window shown in Figure 2-13.

Figure 2-13. Use the Edit File Type window to associate several programs with a single type of file.

The Actions list shows the applications already associated with the selected file type. To add a new program to the list, click the New button. Type the name of the program in the Action field (e.g., Photoshop or Open with Photoshop), and then click Browse to select the application. Most of your installed applications will be located in the *c:\Program Files* folder, although most Windows components (such as Notepad) are located in *c:\Windows\ System32*. Select the application's main *.exe* file, click the Open button, and then click OK.

When you're done adding new actions, click OK in the Edit File Type dialog box and then the Close button in the Folder Options window. Now, right-click any file of the type you just customized (e.g., any JPG file). Your newly added actions will appear near the top of the context menu, and you'll be able to select "Open with Photoshop," for instance, to open the file with Adobe Photoshop, without having to make Photoshop the default application for JPG files.

Protect Your File Types

THE ANNOYANCE: One of my programs keep selfishly reasserting itself as the default application for opening certain file types. Short of tossing the program, is there any way to prevent this from happening?

THE FIX: Once you've gone to the trouble of customizing your file type associations, as described in "Choose Default Programs," the last thing you want is for some application to indiscriminately replace your settings. Although Windows doesn't provide any easy way to prevent this from happening, there are a few steps you can take if you're sufficiently motivated.

First, open the misbehaving application (let's call it *OmniPave*) and disable any settings that look like "Check to see if OmniPave is the default" or "Check OmniPave file associations at startup." Consult the documentation that came with your software for further help.

No luck? Here's one approach that only works in Windows XP Professional and Media Center Editions, and only if Service Pack 2 is installed. (Sorry, XP Home users.) While it may be overkill, it's effectively fool-proof.

Open the Registry Editor (go to Start→Run and type regedit), open the *HKEY_CLASSES_ROOT* branch, and scroll down the list until you find the filename extension in question, including the leading dot. As an example, we'll look at *HKEY_CLASSES_ROOT\.jpg*.

Right-click the *.jpg* key, select Permissions, and click the Advanced button. Uncheck the "Inherit from parent the permission entries that apply to child objects" box, click the Copy button when prompted, and then click OK. Back in the "Permissions for .jpg" window, shown in Figure 2-14, highlight the first entry in the "Group or user names" list, and uncheck the Full Control box in the Permissions list below. Repeat this for all the entries in the "Group or user names" list, and click OK when you're done. This effectively locks out all changes to this key, until you return to the Permissions window and re-enable the Full Control option.

Figure 2-14. Set restrictive permissions for Registry keys to prevent your file type associations from being overwritten.

Now, with the *.jpg* key still highlighted, look at the *(Default)* value in the right pane. This value contains the name of another key in your Registry, which contains more settings that you'll need to lock down. For instance, if the *(Default)* value is set to jpegfile, you'll have to navigate to *HKEY_CLASSES_ROOT\jpegfile* and set the permissions for this key as described above.

Repeat the process for any other file types you'd like to protect, and close the Registry Editor when you're done. From now on, Windows will not permit any application to modify these keys, thus protecting your file types. Of course, it remains to be seen how your applications react; a program may crash after being denied access to the Registry, but most will likely ignore the error and load normally.

> **NOTE**
>
> *If you have Windows XP Home Edition, you can't set any permissions on your Registry keys. But you can still create manual backups of your favorite file types by selecting them in the Registry Editor, going to File→Export, and saving each key in its own file. If your file types are ever overwritten, just double-click the .reg files you created to restore your backups. If you don't feel comfortable messing with the Registry, the QuickAssociation utility (free, http://www.pcmag.com/article2/0,1895,1654639,00.asp) can back up—and lock down—file types you've spent time customizing.*

Predict Moves and Copies

THE ANNOYANCE: Sometimes when I drag a file, it gets copied. Other times, it gets moved. It doesn't really make sense. How can I predict what will happen, and more importantly, how can I choose?

THE FIX: The problem is that drag and drop works differently in different situations. If you drag a file or folder from one place to another on the *same physical drive* (e.g., from *c:\docs* to *c:\files*), the object is moved. If you drag an object from one physical drive to *another* physical drive (e.g., from *c:\docs* to *d:\files*), the object is copied, resulting in two identical files on your system. (There are other specific exceptions, most too obscure to mention here.)

Fortunately, you can control what happens—regardless of the drives in question—by using a combination of keystrokes. To copy an object in any situation, hold the Ctrl key while dragging. To move an object in any situation, hold the Shift key while dragging.

To help you out when you're dragging files, Explorer provides some visual feedback. If there's a tiny plus sign (+) next to the mouse pointer, the files will be copied; if there's a curved arrow, Explorer will create shortcuts to the files. A standard, unadorned arrow means the files will be moved.

> **NOTE**
>
> *If you press Ctrl or Shift before you click, Windows may assume you're using these keys to select multiple files. If Explorer isn't behaving as you expect, make sure to press these keys only after you've started dragging, but before you let go of the mouse button.*

To choose what happens to dragged files each time *without* pressing any keys, drag your files with the right mouse button. When you release the button at the destination, a special menu will appear (see Figure 2-15). Select the action you want (Copy Here, Move Here, or Create Shortcuts Here), or click Cancel to abort.

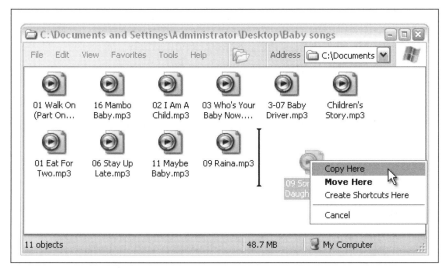

Figure 2-15. Drag files with the right mouse button to choose whether they get moved or copied.

Copy Files to a Hidden Destination

THE ANNOYANCE: Dragging and dropping has become a real drag. Every time I want to move a file, I have to open the destination folder first, and then fuss with the windows until the file and the destination are both visible simultaneously. Is there an easier way to do this?

THE FIX: Actually, there are several! The first requires a little patience. Drag the file over to Explorer's folder tree, and hover the pointer near the top or bottom of the tree; with a steady hand, you can make Windows Explorer scroll the tree. Once the desired folder comes into view, hover the file over the folder until it expands (this usually takes a second or two). Keep doing this to dig down to the appropriate subfolder if necessary, and release the button when the destination is finally visible to drop the file into place.

Another method uses good ol' copy and paste. Right-click the file (or files) you want to copy, and select Copy (or Cut, if you want to move the file). Open the destination folder, right-click an empty area, and select Paste.

If you prefer to use the mouse, use the Copy To, Paste, and Move To buttons on the Explorer toolbar (if it's visible). Better yet, use a program like Creative Element Power Tools (*http://www.creativelement.com/powertools/*), which comes with a Move To/Copy To tool you can use by right-clicking, and even lets you create new folders on the fly.

> **NOTE**
>
> *The keyboard shortcuts for the cut, copy, and paste operations are Ctrl-X, Ctrl-C, and Ctrl-V, respectively.*

FILE DIALOGS

Customize File Dialogs

THE ANNOYANCE: The folders listed in the gray bar along the left side of most File→Open and File→Save As dialog boxes aren't terribly useful. Can I put my own folders in there?

THE FIX: Absolutely, but as you've undoubtedly figured out, you can't do it from within the file dialogs themselves (except in Microsoft Office applications, as discussed later in this fix).

If you have Windows XP Professional or Media Center Edition, open the Group Policy Editor (go to Start→Run and type gpedit.msc). On the left, navigate to *User Configuration\Administrative Templates\Windows Components\ Windows Explorer\Common Open File Dialog*, and then in the right pane, double-click the "Items displayed in Places Bar" entry (see Figure 2-16). Select the Enabled option, and in the five Item fields, type the full path of each folder you'd like to appear in your Places bar. (If you want to save some typing, see "Copy a Folder Path to the Clipboard" for a shortcut.)

Figure 2-16. Use the Group Policy Editor to customize the Places bar in file dialogs.

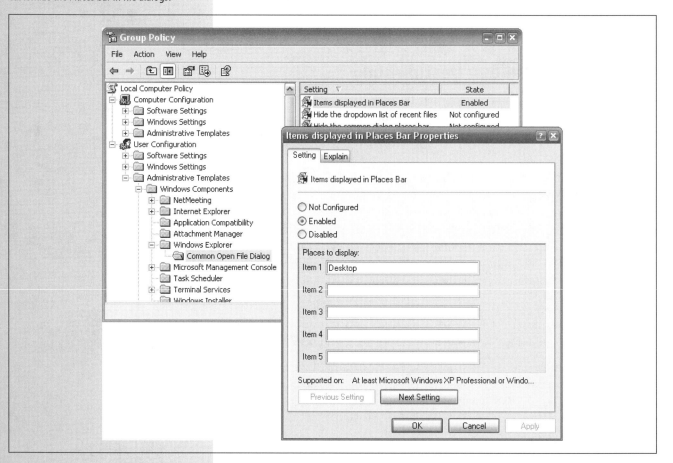

Click OK when you're done. Your custom Places bar will appear in the file dialogs in most of your applications right away, although you'll need to restart any running applications to get them to recognize your changes. The big exception is Microsoft Office applications, which use nonstandard dialogs.

Microsoft saw the need to allow users to customize the Places bar, but only made it easy in Microsoft Office applications (Versions 2002 and later). In the File→Open or File→Save As dialog boxes, highlight any folder in the listing, click the Tools button, and then select "Add to My Places" to add it to the end of the list. To remove a folder from the bar, right-click it and select Remove. (If you want to rearrange the folders and the Move Up and Move Down menu items are grayed out, you must remove and re-add folders until they're in the order you want.)

If you have Windows XP Home Edition, or you just want a friendlier interface than the Group Policy Editor, you can use Creative Element Power Tools (*http://www.creativelement.com/powertools/*) to configure your Places bar in all parts of Windows, including Microsoft Office apps.

> **NOTE**
>
> *Want to keep some of the default folders in the Places bar? Just type in their special code names, such as* Recent *(for My Recent Documents),* Desktop, MyDocuments, MyComputer, *and* MyNetworkPlaces. *You can also display other special folders by entering their code names, such as* CommonDocuments, CommonMusic, CommonPictures, MyFavorites, MyMusic, MyPictures, Printers, *and* ProgramFiles. *(The so-called "common" folders are special shared folders used by multiple users on the same machine.)*

List Recently Used Folders

THE ANNOYANCE: I often find myself working on the same projects every time I turn on my computer, but the File→Open dialogs always take me to *My Documents*, rather than the last folder I used. Is there any way around this?

THE FIX: The default folder is actually decided by the application you're using, so you might find that some programs automatically open the folder you used last, while others send you back to *My Documents*. Regardless, you can enhance your file dialogs with some nifty shortcuts.

> **NOTE**
>
> *You can try clicking the Recent folder (sometimes labeled My Recent Documents) in the Places bar (see "Customize File Dialogs," but this only shows the most recently opened documents, not the folders that contain them.*

There are a handful of different programs designed to augment or enhance file dialogs. Perhaps the fanciest example is Direct Folders ($24.95, *http://www.codesector.com*), which not only lists the folders you've recently accessed with the file dialogs in each of your applications, but decorates the dialog windows with other tools as well (see Figure 2-17). After installing Direct Folders, just click the star icon in the title bar to list your recently visited folders, plus favorites, and even the folder currently displayed in the topmost Explorer window.

If you want a more minimalist approach to file dialog enhancement, Creative Element Power Tools (*http://www.creativelement.com/powertools*) adds quick access to recently-used folders with a much simpler interface.

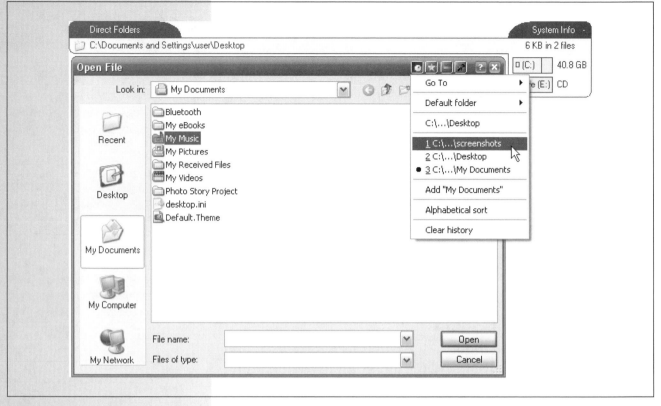

Figure 2-17. Use Direct Folders to augment your file dialogs with a list of recently used folders, plus other useful tools.

It also saves the size and view settings (Details, icon, etc.) of your file dialogs, and can show the full path of the current folder right in the dialog title bar. Another program that works similarly is FileBox eXtender ($20; *http://www.hyberionics.com*). All three companies offer free, fully working demos of their tools.

SEARCHING

Search in a New Window

THE ANNOYANCE: When I'm viewing a folder in Windows Explorer and I press Ctrl-F or F3 to search for something in that folder, the folder tree is replaced with a Search pane (see Figure 2-18). I want my tree back!

THE FIX: There are a bunch of ways to get to the Search tool in Windows, but few are as convenient as starting a search based in the current folder with Ctrl-F. Of course, it's decidedly *inconvenient* when you lose your current view every time you start a search this way. And what's worse is that there's no way to get the folder tree back without a lot of clicking (pressing Ctrl-F again doesn't do it); you have to go to View→Explorer Bar→Folders (or press the Folders button if the toolbar is visible, as discussed in "Get Back the Folder Tree") to show it again.

The workaround is to open Search in a new window by right-clicking a folder in Windows Explorer and selecting Search; it's not as quick as Ctrl-F or F3, but it does the trick.

To force Windows Explorer to open a new window every time you press Ctrl-F or F3, you'll need Creative Element Power Tools, available at *http://www.creativelement.com/ powertools/*. Once you've installed the software, open the Creative Element Power Tools Control Panel and turn on the "Fix the Windows Search tool" option.

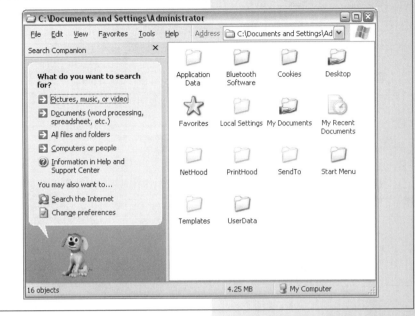

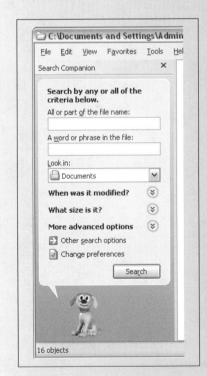

Figure 2-18. Start a search, and the folder tree disappears!

Jump to Advanced Search

THE ANNOYANCE: Every time I open the Search tool, I'm asked "What do you want to search for?" and then I have to pick from a list. Is my Photoshop file a "picture" or is it a "document"? These unnecessary steps drive me crazy. How can I go right to the Search window?

THE FIX: To skip this menu in the future and go straight to the "All files and folders" Search tool (see Figure 2-19), return to the "What do you want to search for?" page and click "Change preferences." Click "Change files and folders search behavior," and select Advanced. Explorer will remember your preference, and you won't have to deal with the menu again unless you want to.

Take the Dog for a Walk

THE ANNOYANCE: The dog was cute at first, but it's always making scratching sounds while I'm trying to work. How do I keep him quiet?

THE FIX: You can't turn off the sounds, but you can turn off the dog. In the main Search window, click Change Preferences, then click "Without an animated character." You can also click "With a different character" to choose between Rover (the puppy), Merlin (a wizard), Earl (a surfboarding banana), or Courtney (anybody's guess).

Figure 2-19. Change your preferences so you don't have to jump through hoops to get to the actual Search tool in Windows XP.

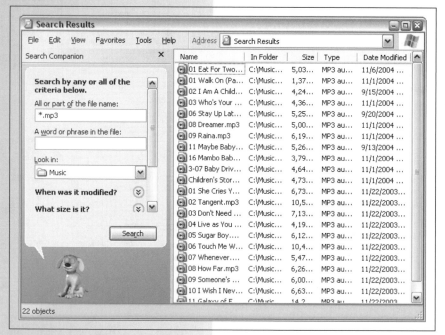

Figure 2-20. You can't see anything in this tiny window.

See the Whole Megillah

THE ANNOYANCE: When I perform a search, I have a hard time making out the full filenames or complete folder names in the search results.

THE FIX: The columns in Explorer's Search Results are too small by default (see Figure 2-20). Start by enlarging the window horizontally. Then, drag the column dividers with your mouse to enlarge the Name and In Folder columns, as shown in Figure 2-21. Alternatively, you can double-click the column dividers—this will automatically resize the columns to accommodate their contents.

Windows Explorer should remember your column preferences for future visits to the Search window, but it doesn't always get it right and sometimes inserts unwanted columns (such as the pointless Relevance column) or reverts to the default layout. Unfortunately, there's no way to definitively save your favorite Search window layout, as you can in the main Explorer window (see "Get the Details View Every Time"), so you may have to reassert your preferences from time to time.

Figure 2-21. Much better!

Searching

Reveal Missing Paths in Search Results

THE ANNOYANCE: I'm looking at a list of search results, and some of the folder names (shown in the "In Folder" column) are missing or incomplete, like in Figure 2-22. How do I find out where these files are located?

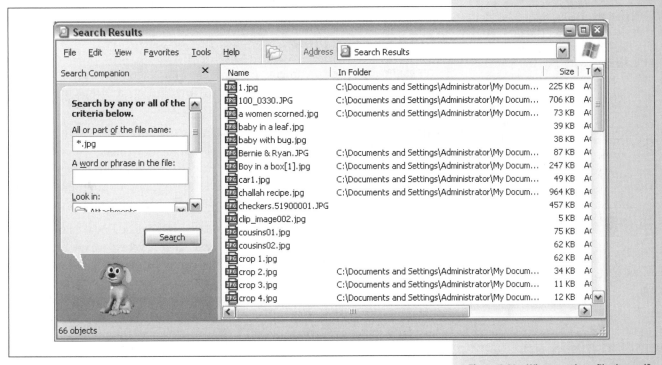

Figure 2-22. Where are these files located?

THE FIX: Those folder names are missing because the files are located inside ZIP files, which Windows XP searches along with ordinary folders. (See the "What Are ZIP Files?" sidebar for details.) Alas, there's a bug in the Search tool—the In Folder column is left blank for any file found inside a ZIP file. The only way to find the location and name of one of these ZIP files is to select File→Open Containing Folder.

If you want to avoid this problem altogether, you must disable Windows XP's built-in support for ZIP files. To do this, go to Start→Run, and type the following at the prompt:

```
regsvr32 /u %windir%\system32\zipfldr.dll
```

Click OK when you're done, and the change will take effect immediately.

Of course, this fix has its consequences. For one, Search will no longer look inside ZIP files, so files contained only within them won't turn up in your search results—it will complete searches more quickly, but its results may leave out certain items. Also, Windows will no longer be able to open or create ZIP files.

What Are ZIP Files?

ZIP files work somewhat like folders in that they "contain" files, so it's not surprising that they're represented as folders in Windows Explorer. But ZIP files aren't folders; they're compressed archives that squeeze down their contents so they take up less space and can be emailed or downloaded from a web site more quickly.

Why ZIP Is Number 1

There are lots of compression schemes out there, although none have achieved the popularity of ZIP. In fact, a few years back, a new archive format was introduced that claimed much better compression than ZIP: archives made with this new scheme ended up being roughly one hundredth the size of corresponding ZIP files. The only problem was that this was a one-way process; files that were compressed and later extracted unfortunately bore no resemblance to the original source files. Might as well stick with ZIP....

—From *Windows XP Annoyances for Geeks, 2nd Edition*

If you can't live without built-in ZIP support, go back to Start→Run, and this time, type the following at the prompt to reinstate the feature:

```
regsvr32 %windir%\system32\zipfldr.dll
```

Better yet, leave Windows's ZIP support disabled and instead download a third-party ZIP utility such as WinZip ($29.95, *http://www.winzip.com*).

Find Recent Files

THE ANNOYANCE: The Documents menu in the Start menu shows only some of the documents I've worked on recently. How do I get a complete listing of recently modified files?

THE FIX: The Recent Documents folder contains shortcuts to files you've double-clicked in Windows Explorer, as well as documents you've opened and saved in certain applications, and the last dozen of these are shown in your Documents menu. But, for whatever reason, not all programs support this feature. Fortunately, you can find all recent files with a quick search.

Go to Start→Search→For files and folders, and select Local Hard Drives from the drop-down "Look in" list. Next, click "When was it modified," choose the appropriate option (say, "Within the last week"), and click the Search button. When the search completes, sort the listing by date by clicking the Date Modified column header. (Don't see the Date Modified column? Select View→Details and then right-click any column header to display a list of available columns.) Double-click any file to open it.

Save Your Searches

THE ANNOYANCE: I need to run the same searches over and over. Is there a way to quickly repeat past searches?

THE FIX: Once you've performed a search, or at least started one, you can save your settings in a file. In the Search Results window, select File→Save Search, choose a location and name for the file (a good place is your desktop), and click the Save button. To repeat the search, just double-click the file and then click Search. (It would be nice if the search started automatically, but no such luck.)

Save Your Search Results

THE ANNOYANCE: Okay, I saved my search, but when I close the Search window and then double-click the file, all my previous search results are gone. What happened?

THE FIX: The Save Search feature doesn't save search results; it only saves the search *parameters*, such as the folder path that's being searched, the text to search for, the date range (if you specified one), and other options.

Although Windows has no way of creating a permanent record of search results, you can do this with the "Copy file and folder names to the Clipboard" tool in Creative Element Power Tools (*http://www.creativelement.com/powertools/*). After completing a search, press Ctrl-A to highlight all the files in the Search Results window, right-click, and select Copy Filename. Open any plain-text editor (such as Notepad), press Ctrl-V to paste in your results, and save the file listing.

Find a File Where Search Doesn't Look

THE ANNOYANCE: I've been searching for a file for weeks. I don't think I deleted it, but I can't find it anywhere. Why can't the Search tool find it?

THE FIX: When you search, you're not necessarily looking in every nook and cranny of your hard disk. For starters, Search only looks in the folder specified in the drop-down "Look in" list, so you'll want to select Local Hard Drives to broaden your search.

Next, click "More advanced options," and place checkmarks next to the first three options shown in Figure 2-23.

It's also possible that Windows isn't configured to show you all of your files. In the Search Results window, go to Tools→Folder Options, choose the View tab, and select the "Show hidden files and folders" and "Display the contents of system folders" options. Now run your search—that lost file just may turn up.

> **NOTE**
>
> *Of course, it's possible your file has found its way into one of the four folders in which Search will never look: the Recycle Bin (c:\Recycler), the Fonts folder (c:\Windows\Fonts), the System Restore archive folder (c:\System Volume Information), or the Nethood folder (c:\Documents and Settings\{user}\ NetHood). To see all the files stored in these special folders, open a Command Prompt window (go to Start→Run and type* cmd.exe*) and use the* CD *and* DIR *commands to enter each folder and view its contents, respectively.*

Figure 2-23. Turn on these options to look in more places.

Search Inside Files

THE ANNOYANCE: I tried searching for files containing some text by typing the text into the "A word or phrase in the file" box, but I didn't get any results. I tried again with text I *knew* was in one of the files, but I still got nothing!

THE FIX: You're not doing anything wrong; sometimes, this feature simply doesn't work. If you want to find files based on their contents, you'll need to use a different program. Check out one of the free third-party desktop search applications described in "Faster Searches," next.

Faster Searches

THE ANNOYANCE: It takes forever for Windows to conduct a simple search. How can I speed things up?

THE FIX: Windows has a little-known feature called the Indexing Service that can marginally speed up searches. To enable indexing, open a Search window, click "Change preferences" then "With Indexing Service," and choose Yes. At this point, Windows begins cataloging your files whenever your PC isn't being used, so that (eventually) Windows can merely consult the catalog instead of physically searching through all your folders and files.

However, Windows's rudimentary indexing service is no match for some third-party desktop search tools, which rely on their own brand of indexing to serve up search results in a jiffy. Probably the first such tool that comes to mind is Google Desktop Search (free, *http://desktop.google.com*), but its awkward web-based interface and scant file type support make it a poor choice. Instead, try Yahoo Desktop Search (free, *http://desktop.yahoo.com*), which offers an interface more similar to Windows Explorer's and includes support for hundreds of file types (see Figure 2-24).

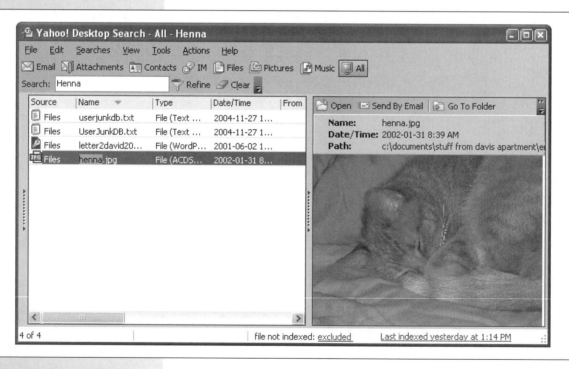

Figure 2-24. Use a third-party desktop search tool to find files faster.

Other free choices include Copernic Desktop Search (*http://www.copernic.com*) and MSN Search Toolbar with Windows Desktop Search (*http://toolbar.msn.com*). If you're serious about searching, check out the reviews at *http://www.searchenginewatch.com*.

Multimedia

In the old days, video problems meant using a butter knife to pry a tape out of your VCR. But in our modern Windows XP era, video hassles result from the complex interplay among player software, hardware (and its drivers), a baffling assortment of codecs, and Microsoft's DirectX extensions. And of course, there's also sound to consider, plus television piped through your PC (via the Media Center Edition of Windows XP), as well as managing digital photos and burning CDs and DVDs. I'll tackle these and other media annoyances in this chapter.

VIDEO

Play Stubborn Videos

THE ANNOYANCE: When I try to open a video clip in Windows Media Player, it says it can't play the file. Not surprisingly, the More Information button doesn't provide any useful information.

THE FIX: Chances are you don't have the required codec installed on your system. A *codec* (which stands for *c*ompressor/*dec*ompressor) is software responsible for storing data in a video file and subsequently extracting it; in order to play any given video, you must use the same codec that was used to create the video in the first place, regardless of the player application you're using.

To figure out what codec was used, you'll need a program such as GSpot (free, *http://www.headbands.com/gspot/*) or AVIcodec (free, *http://avicodec. duby.info*). Just drag and drop the video file onto GSpot or AVIcodec, and the program will display the file's codec. (If it doesn't, the file is probably corrupted, or was encoded with a nonstandard scheme.) Armed with the name or four-digit *4CC* code of the codec (shown in Figure 3-1), surf over to *http://www.fourcc.org/fcccodec.htm* and download your codec from the list. If the 4CC code isn't there, a quick Google search should turn up some useful leads.

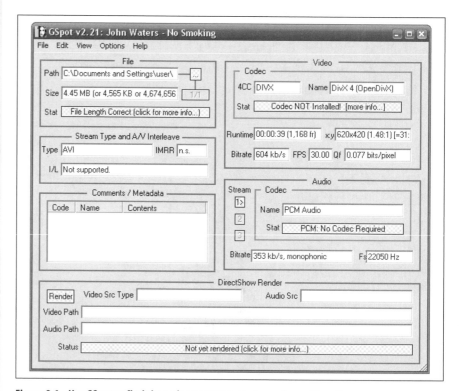

Figure 3-1. Use GSpot to find the codec necessary to play a given video clip.

Of course, Windows Media Player might have trouble playing a video because there's something wrong with the video file. First, make sure your video file is complete; if you downloaded it from the Web, download it again. (If it's an incomplete download, see the next annoyance for a workaround.) If you can't get a better version of the file (and it's an MPEG video), you may be able to fix it with the MPEG Header Corrector (free, *http://www.vcdhelp.us/html/tutmpegheadercorrector.html*).

Play Incomplete Downloads

THE ANNOYANCE: I'm in the middle of downloading a video and I want to start playing it before the download is complete, but Windows Media Player just gives me an error. This whole "waiting" thing is so passé.

THE FIX: For starters, Windows Media Player (WMP) won't play most kinds of videos while they're *in use*; in this case, while they're currently being saved by another program. (The

exception is streaming video—files with the *.asf* or *.wmv* extension.) To get around this limitation, make a copy of the file being downloaded and open it; open the folder containing the file and, using the right mouse button, drag the file to another part of the same folder. Release the mouse button and select Copy Here from the pop-up menu. You should be able to open this duplicate file with no problems.

With some video formats (particularly *.avi* files), there's a catch: the *index*, essential information about the sequence of frames in the video, is located at the end of the file. An incomplete file thus won't have an index, and can't be played. The solution is to use a reindexing utility to rebuild this data and make the file playable. DivFix (free, *http://www.divx-digest.com/software/divfix.html*) does this quite nicely, but it only works on true *.avi* files (see Figure 3-2). If DivFix doesn't work on your file, the Windows Media Encoder (free, *http://www.microsoft.com/windows/windowsmedia/9series/encoder/*) can index some other types of video files, although you may find some aspects of the interface a bit daunting.

Cryptic Media Player Error Codes

Windows Media Player can play just about any file you throw at it, but sometimes it spits out an arcane error code instead. If you get an error, check this list to see what's going on:

- **80040200** means that Windows can't find the right codec for the video clip, either due to an unfamiliar file format or to security settings preventing a codec download. You'll also get this error if you didn't restart your computer after installing the required codec.

- **C00D000F** means that the web server where the video lives is busy; try again later.

- **C00D10B3** means that Windows Media Player is offline. To fix this problem, select Tools→Options, choose the Player tab, check the "Connect to the Internet" box, and click OK.

- **C00D11B3** means that Windows Media Player is having trouble connecting to the Internet. See the solutions for C00D000F, C00D10B3, and C00D11D4.

- **C00D11BA** means that there's a problem with your sound card; see the "Sound and Music" section later in this chapter.

- **C00D11D4** means that there's a problem with your Internet proxy settings. In WMP, select Tools→Options, choose the Network tab, and then click the Configure button. These options should match the proxy setup for your network; if you don't know what settings to use, select "Do not use a proxy server." Duplicate the settings for all the protocols in the "Streaming proxy settings" area on the Network tab.

- **C00D277F** means there's a problem with the licensing for the file you're trying to play; see "Iron Out License Issues" for the fix.

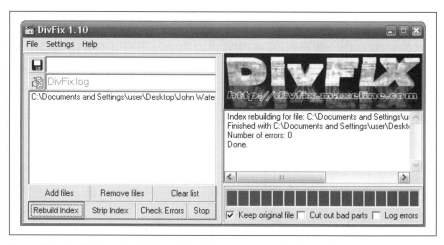

Figure 3-2. Use DivFix to reindex incomplete videos so you can play them as-is.

Fix the Aspect Ratio

THE ANNOYANCE: The video clip I'm trying to play appears squashed (too narrow) or stretched out (too wide). How do I fix this?

THE FIX: Of course, the easy fix is to just look at your computer monitor from an angle so the video *appears* correct. But if you want a more permanent solution (and not a crick in your neck), update the codec as described in "Play Stubborn Videos"), as a later version may fix the problem.

It's also possible that the *aspect ratio* of the actual video clip is botched. To correct this, you'll have to open the file in a video-editing program that can resize video frames. Although the Windows Media Encoder can *crop* frames, it can't stretch or shrink a video. To change the aspect ratio of a video clip, use River Past Video Perspective ($29.95, *http://www.riverpast. com/en/prod/videoperspective/index.php*) or Open Video Converter ($25.00, *http://www.008soft.com/products/open_video_converter.htm*), or, for more control, try a more advanced video application such as Adobe Premiere Elements ($99.99, *http://www.abobe.com*).

Shed Light on Blank Videos

THE ANNOYANCE: When I play a video clip in Windows Media Player, I hear something, but I see nothing. I feel like Sergeant Shultz from *Hogan's Heroes*!

THE FIX: First, make sure you have the latest codec (see "Play Stubborn Videos"). If the codec is in order, you likely have a video overlay problem.

See if you can temporarily fix the problem by maximizing or resizing the Windows Media Player window, or covering it with another window and then bringing it to the front. If you notice a difference, your video card driver may be to blame. Visit the video card manufacturer's web site and download the latest driver. If this doesn't help, you'll have to downgrade Windows's support for video overlays until you can play videos successfully.

In WMP, select Tools→Options, choose the Performance tab, and click the Advanced button to display the Video Acceleration Settings tab (Figure 3-3). Uncheck the "Use overlays" box, click OK, and try playing the clip again. If the problem persists, return to this tab and uncheck the "Use video mixing renderer" box.

NOTE

Typically, Windows Media Player paints a special rectangle on your screen, and your video driver is responsible for super-imposing the moving video over it. This "overlay scheme" allows your PC to play video smoothly, but in some cases it can cause performance problems or compatibility problems (such as blank video).

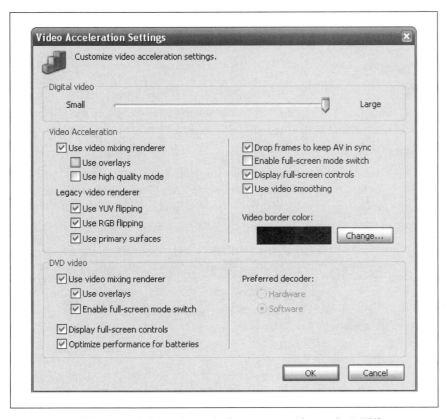

Figure 3-3. Disable some or all of the video overlay features to get videos to play in WMP.

NOTE

To disable video overlays in RealOne Player, go to Tools→Preferences→Hardware→Video card compatibility. Move the slider to the left until "Enable optimized video and disable overlays" appears beneath.

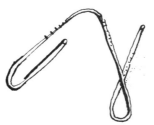

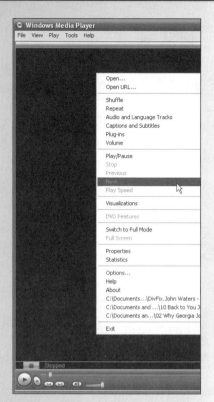

Figure 3-4. You may be able to right-click a video and select Next to skip the ads or intro.

Skip Intro Ads

THE ANNOYANCE: When I play video clips on some web sites, I have to sit through an ad or intro clip. Is there any way to skip directly to the video I want?

THE FIX: Right-click the center of Windows Media Player's video playback area and select Next, as shown in Figure 3-4. This works if the ad(s) and main video are stored as separate files on the server, as it simply instructs the player to jump to the next video in its queue. If Next is grayed out, either the ad and video are part of the same clip, or the publisher has disabled this shortcut.

Save Videos from the Web

THE ANNOYANCE: Why can't I save a video clip I'm watching on the Web? There's gotta be a way to do this!

THE FIX: This is a tricky one; videos on web sites are often jury-rigged to make downloading very difficult. It's possible in most cases, but it takes a few steps.

The first thing you need to do is get the full URL of the video clip. If the video is playing in a standalone Windows Media Player (or RealPlayer) window, it's easy enough: select File→Properties (in RealPlayer, select File→Clip Properties→View Clip Info), and look at the Location field (Figure 3-5).

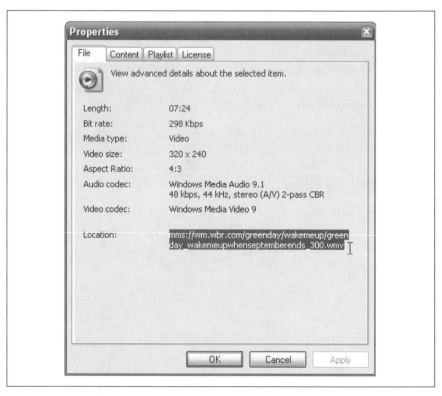

Figure 3-5. Get the URL of an online video clip.

If the video is embedded in a web page (including in a pop-up window), right-click the video itself. If it's a RealPlayer video, you'll be able to select "Play in RealPlayer" to open the clip in a standalone window and nab the URL as described previously. If it's a Windows Media video, you should be able to select Properties to display the Properties window (Figure 3-5), which will show you the URL.

Still can't find the video's URL? If you're using Mozilla or Firefox, right-click an empty area of the web page and select View Page Info. Click the Media tab, and then scroll down the list until you see the URL of the video, which will probably be the only entry that isn't an image file (*.jpg*, *.gif*, etc.). If you find it in the list, click Save As to save a copy of the file on your hard disk.

If you're using Internet Explorer, right-click an empty area of the web page and select View Source (this works in Mozilla/Firefox, too); some familiarity with the HTML language will make it easier to find the information you need. Press Ctrl-F and search the code for text that would likely appear in a video clip URL, such as .asf, .wmv, .ram, or rstp:. Somewhere in the code, you should see a full (or partial) URL for the source video clip, like the one in Figure 3-6.

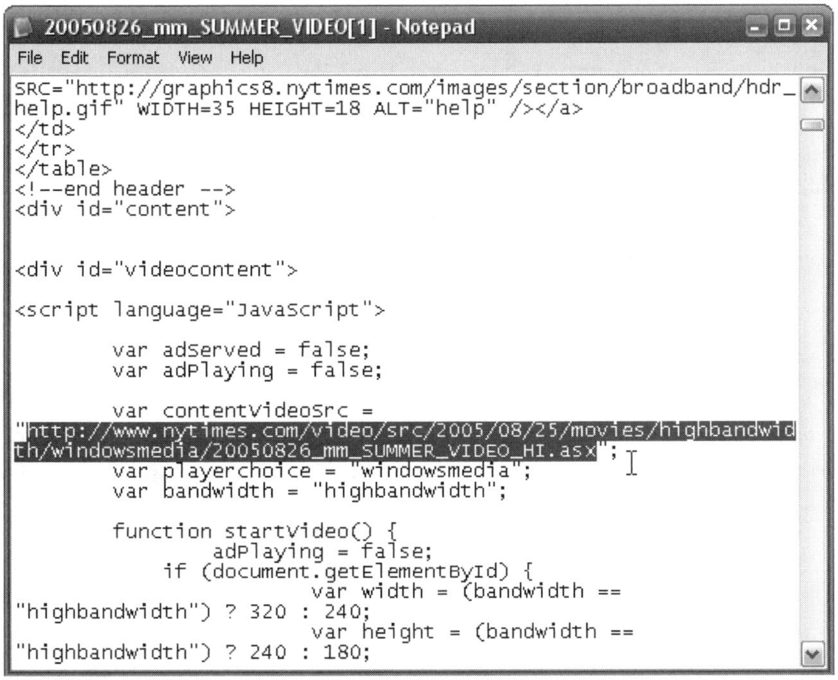

NOTE

Most publishers of online videos specifically disable the "Save As" feature that normally appears in Windows Media Player, but if it's there, go ahead and use it. Only if the Save feature is disabled do you have to use this procedure.

Figure 3-6. Examine the HTML source code of a web page to find the URL of an embedded video clip.

At this point, you should have a URL that looks something like rstp://www. some.server/videos/penguin.asf. Copy the URL (highlight it and press Ctrl-C) and paste it (Ctrl-V) into a program designed to download a video stream, such as WMRecorder ($29.95, *http://www.wmrecorder.com*) or CoCSoft Stream Down ($39.00, *http://stream-down.cocsoft.com*; see Figure 3-7). If all goes well, you should have a file on your hard disk in about the same amount of time it would take to watch the video from start to finish; just double-click the file icon to play the clip.

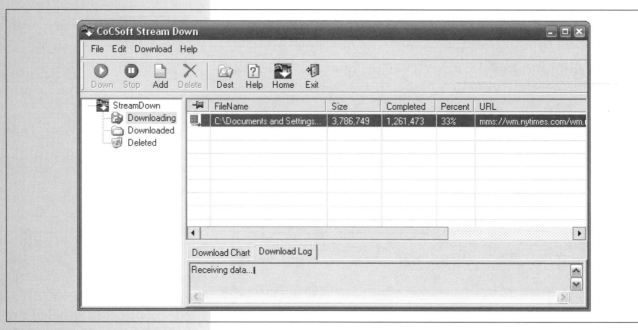

Figure 3-7. Use a program like CoCSoft Stream Down to download streaming video clips to your hard disk.

Only streaming videos have URLs that begin with *rstp://*—if your URL starts with *http://*, you'll probably be able to download the file without any special software. To do this, open Notepad, and type the following code:

```
<a ref="http://www.some.server/videos/penguin.mov">link</a>
```

Save the file to your desktop, and give it the .html filename extension. Double-click the new file to open it in your default browser, right-click the link, and then select Save Link Target As.

Rewind or Fast-Forward Streaming Video

THE ANNOYANCE: I'm watching a video on the Web and I'd like to be able to skip around in it, but I can't rewind or fast-forward the video.

THE FIX: Unfortunately, this is a limitation of the video file, and not simply an option that can be turned on or off. A lot of streaming video clips (particularly *.wmv* videos) have this problem; since the creators expected you to watch the videos as they download, they didn't anticipate the need to rewind or fast-forward.

To rewind or fast-forward a video, it must be indexed, and you can only add an index if the video file is stored on your hard disk. (See "Save Videos from the Web" for a way to download an online video.)

To index a *.wmv* file, download the free Windows Media Encoder from *http://www.microsoft.com/windows/windowsmedia/9series/encoder/*, and open the Windows Media File Editor. Drag and drop the video onto the Editor window, and select File→Save and Index. You'll now be able to rewind and fast-forward the clip to your heart's content.

Reduce Video Buffering

THE ANNOYANCE: I'm trying to watch a video on a web site, but all it says is "buffering." It's not asking me to wax my car, right?

THE FIX: Most online video clips are designed to *stream*, allowing you to start watching before your PC has finished downloading. To keep the video playing smoothly, video players often download a few seconds of video ahead of the playback (a technique called "buffering" or "caching"), and sometimes this means you have to wait. The good news is that you can choose *when* to wait: now, or later.

In Windows Media Player, select Tools→Options, click the Performance tab, and select "Buffer [5] seconds of content" in the "Network buffering" section. To shorten the lead-time so that videos will start playing sooner, enter a small number, such as 3. Depending on the speed of your Internet connection and number of visitors the web server is currently juggling, those 3 seconds of content could take anywhere from 2 seconds to 20 minutes to download.

Unfortunately, entering a small number means that WMP has to stop playback more often to buffer more content. If WMP frequently stops playing to buffer more data, raise the buffer number to 10 or 20 seconds. You'll get smoother playback, but you'll have to wait longer before your online videos play.

NOTE

The buffering settings have no effect on video clips stored on your hard disk. To eliminate buffering messages altogether, see "Save Videos from the Web."

Make Your Own Director's Cut

NOTE

Before using Windows Movie Maker, run Windows Update to ensure you have the latest version of this tool. Since the original release of Windows XP, Windows Movie Maker has undergone significant changes.

THE ANNOYANCE: I downloaded this really long movie, but all I want is a small portion of it. Is there a way to chop it up into little pieces?

THE FIX: You can use Windows Movie Maker, which comes with Windows XP, to extract segments of video from a long video clip. (You'll find it in your Start menu, under Accessories.)

From Movie Maker, select File→New Project. Drag and drop your video file onto the Windows Movie Maker window, and it will appear as a new "Collection."

Across the bottom of the window, you'll see something called a *storyboard*; click the Show Timeline button to switch to the more useful Timeline view. Now, drag your video from the Collection pane to the uppermost Video line (not the Audio/Music line), so that it appears as a horizontal band, as shown in Figure 3-8.

Figure 3-8. Use Windows Movie Maker to crop or glue together video clips.

Using your mouse, carefully drag the left and right edges to "crop" the video, removing the material you don't want. As you shrink the rectangle representing your clip, the corresponding video segment gets shorter; when you're done, you're left with only a small segment of the original movie. Test the results by using the player controls in the upper-right corner.

Now, say you want to glue together two or more separate clips from your video. Although Windows Movie Maker doesn't let you "cut" a video segment into separtate usable pieces on the timeline (you'll need a more advanced video-editing application, such as Adobe Premiere, for that), you can drag the original clip from the Collection pane again, creating a second copy in your timeline. Then, shrink down the second clip to a different scene. You can even drag the clips around in the timeline to rearrange them.

When you're happy with your selection, select Save Movie File from the File menu.

> **— NOTE —**
> *Use the magnifying glass tools to zoom in or out—which effectively expands or shrinks the timescale—so it's easier to see what you're doing.*

Make a Montage

THE ANNOYANCE: I have a bunch of short video clips I'd like to play in succession, but the playlists in Windows Media Player are too cumbersome. Is there a way to more permanently glue multiple clips together into one large movie?

THE FIX: Windows Movie Maker can do this (see "Make Your Own Director's Cut"); just drag multiple clips into the window, then onto the timeline, and arrange them as you like. Unfortunately, this is somewhat time-consuming, and some quality is lost when the movie is recompressed as it is being saved.

Apple's QuickTime Pro Player ($29.99 upgrade from the free player, *http://quicktime.apple.com*) makes this process a lot easier. Start by opening one of your clips in QuickTime Player, and use the timeline slider to navigate to a point in the clip—the beginning, the end, or anywhere in between—into which you'd like to insert another clip. Then, drag and drop the second clip into the middle of the QuickTime Player window. This new clip will show up as a gray stripe on the timeline, as shown in Figure 3-9. (You can continue to add as many movies as you like, provided that QuickTime Player supports the clip formats.)

Figure 3-9. Use Apple's free QuickTime Player to easily concatenate multiple video clips.

> **— NOTE —**
> *Be careful when installing Apple's iTunes software, which can overwrite your purchased Quicktime Pro software with the latest free QuickTime player software without asking.*

When you're done, select File→Save As and supply a filename for your new composition. Choose "Save normally" to save only a skeleton file that references the separate source video clips, or choose "Make movie self-contained" to create a new self-contained movie that doesn't depend on the original source files.

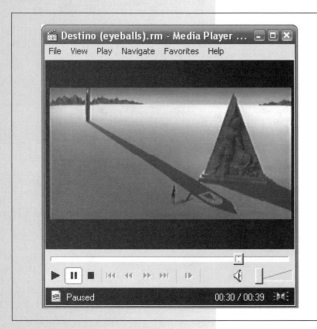

Figure 3-10. The Real Alternative Media Player Classic allows you to play RealMedia content without the messy RealPlayer.

Get an Alternative to Real Player

THE ANNOYANCE: I want to play RealMedia-format video and audio, but I really don't like the cumbersome RealPlayer software. Do I have any alternatives?

THE FIX: Yes, as a matter of fact, you do! Rather than putting up with the ads, messages, spyware, and other nonsense that comes along with RealPlayer, you can use the ultra-simple Real Alternative player (free, *http://home. hccnet.nl/h.edskes/finalbuilds.htm#realalt*), shown in Figure 3-10.

Along the same lines, you can use the QuickTime Alternative player (free, *http://home.hccnet.nl/h.edskes/finalbuilds.htm#quicktimealt*) instead of Apple's QuickTime Player.

Simplify Windows Media Player

THE ANNOYANCE: Windows Media Player 10 is large, cluttered, and difficult to use. How can I trim the fat off this beast?

THE FIX: Open the View menu, and select Skin Chooser. In the left pane, click Corporate, and above it, click the Apply Skin button. From now on, you can switch between the full-blown Windows Media Player extravaganza and the bare-bones player by pressing Ctrl-1 and Ctrl-2, respectively.

Use Alt-Tab with Windows Media Player

THE ANNOYANCE: When Windows Media Player is running, I can't switch to another program using Alt-Tab. Why won't Media Player let me go?

THE FIX: Most of the time, you can press Alt-Tab once to switch from the current window to the window immediately underneath it. But in Windows Media Player, there's a bug that prevents this from working. The problem is caused by a second, hidden window behind Media Player. To work around this, hold Alt and press Tab twice to switch to the other application.

Synchronize Audio and Video

THE ANNOYANCE: The sound and video on my PC aren't synchronized; whenever I play a clip, it looks like a badly dubbed Kung-Fu movie.

THE FIX: This is usually a problem with your hardware drivers. Install the latest drivers for your video card and sound card, and then run Windows Update to make sure you have the latest video-related updates and DirectX drivers (also available at *http://www.microsoft.com/directx/*).

If new drivers don't fix the problem, open the Sounds and Audio Devices Properties window (it's in the "Sounds, Speech, and Audio Devices" category of the Windows Control Panel). Choose the Audio tab, and in the Sound Playback area, click the Advanced button. Choose the Performance tab and move the Hardware acceleration slider a notch closer to None. Click OK, and then click OK again when you're done. Repeat the process until video clips play correctly.

NOTE

If you have syncing problems while playing a DVD movie, press Stop, and then resume playback. Sometimes that's all it takes to get a movie back on track.

Fix Bad Color in Videos

THE ANNOYANCE: The color seems messed up when I play videos in Windows Media Player; sometimes I see colored lines running through the video.

THE FIX: Like many other video problems, this one is typically caused by bad drivers and video codecs, all discussed earlier in this chapter. But if your drivers and codecs are up to date, a little tweaking may be all that's necessary to correct the color in your videos.

Open Windows Media Player, and select Tools→Options. Click the Performance tab, and in the "Video acceleration" area, drag the slider to None. If it's already there, move it to the right to see if that fixes the problem.

If the problem persists, select View→Enhancements→Video Settings. In the pane that appears at the bottom of the screen, click the Reset link.

If the video plays fine at first but then develops color problems, disable the video overlay, as described in "Shed Light on Blank Videos."

SOUND AND MUSIC

Choose an Input Source

THE ANNOYANCE: I installed some dictation software and connected a microphone, but I'm not capturing any sound. I know my family is sick of my incessant griping, but I thought my computer liked me!

THE FIX: Open the Windows Volume Control (double-click the speaker icon in the Windows System Tray or go to Start→Run and type sndvol32), and select Options→Properties. If more than one device is listed in the "Mixer device" drop-down list, either select the one that corresponds to the one your microphone is connected to, or connect your microphone to the device selected here. Next, select the Recording option, and place checkmarks next to all of the items in the "Show the following volume controls" list immediately below. Click OK when you're done.

When you return to the main window, now titled Recording Control, place a checkmark in the Select box in the Microphone column (Figure 3-11), and then move the Volume slider so that it's somewhere in the middle.

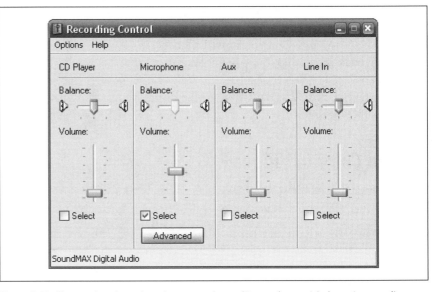

Figure 3-11. If your microphone doesn't appear to be working, make sure it's the active recording input.

If your dictation software lets you choose the recording source, make sure you select the same device you picked in the Windows Volume Control. Still no sound? Run the calibration utility that came with your dictation software to ensure that the recording volume is set correctly. If all else fails, replace the microphone.

Let There Be Sound

THE ANNOYANCE: I can't hear any sound coming from my speakers. All I can hear now are the voices in my head.

THE FIX: Some might consider this a blessing; the incessant sounds that come from computers can drive anyone completely crazy...

But if you absolutely must have sound, check the most obvious (and most overlooked) factor first—cabling. Make sure the cable that connects your speakers to your sound card is properly connected. Likewise, make sure your speakers are plugged into the AC and turned on, with the volume up. If this doesn't solve your problem, try the following tips.

NOTE

For best results with voice-dictation software, use a USB microphone/headset instead of the conventional setup that plugs directly into your sound card. Not only will the quality and clarity improve, but you'll bypass troublesome sound card drivers.

Open the Sounds and Audio Devices control panel. In the "Device volume" section, make sure the Mute box is not checked, and drag the Device volume slider so that it's somewhere in the middle. Next, click the Advanced button to open the Windows Volume Control. Select Options→Properties. If more than one mixer device is listed, select the one that corresponds to the device your speakers are connected to. Next, select the Playback option, place checkmarks next to all of the items in the list below, and click OK.

Back in the Play Control window (see Figure 3-12), make sure that none of the controls are muted and all of the volume control sliders are turned up. If you still don't hear sound at this point, click the Advanced button, center both the Bass and Treble controls, and make sure the Digital Output Only box is not checked.

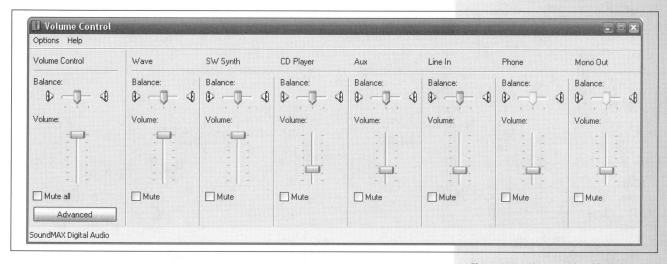

Figure 3-12. Most sound problems are caused by incorrect settings in the Windows Volume Control.

Back in the Sounds and Audio Devices Properties window, click the Audio tab, and in the drop-down menu in the "Sound playback" section, choose your sound card; there may be more than one device listed here, but only one is likely connected to your speakers. Click Apply and try again. If you don't hear anything, click the Advanced button (still in the "Sound playback" section), choose the Performance tab, and drag the Hardware acceleration slider to the left to increase compatibility. Click OK and then Apply when you're done.

Still no decibels? Check your sound card driver; visit the card manufacturer's web site and download and the latest driver. (If you're not sure what sound hardware you have, choose the Hardware tab in the Sounds and Audio Devices Properties window for a list.) Also, run Windows Update to make sure you have the latest sound-related updates and DirectX drivers (also available at *http://www.microsoft.com/directx/*).

Fix Silent CDs

THE ANNOYANCE: I can hear sounds in games and web pages, but I hear nothing when playing music CDs.

THE FIX: First, check the Windows Volume Control to make sure that your CD drive isn't muted and that the volume is cranked up high enough (see "Let There Be Sound" for details).

If audio CDs remain silent, check your audio cables. Unlike sounds generated by your PC, the audio from music CDs is routed from your CD drive directly to your sound card by a special cable, like the one shown in Figure 3-13. (You'll find the cable only in desktop PCs; don't go looking for one in your laptop.) Make sure the cable is securely connected to both your CD-ROM drive and your sound card or motherboard; try replacing the cable if all else fails.

Figure 3-13. If you can't hear audio CDs, this cable may be missing or improperly connected.

Play Music at the Correct Speed

THE ANNOYANCE: No matter what sound I play, it sounds like Alvin and the Chipmunks. Only audio CDs play normally, including, ironically, my *Alvin and the Chipmunks Greatest Hits: Still Squeaky After All These Years* CD.

THE FIX: This behavior is probably caused by a timing problem (big surprise) with your sound card's clock. This can usually be fixed by adjusting your sound card's hardware acceleration.

Open the Sounds and Audio Devices Properties window in the Control Panel, and on the Volume tab, click the Advanced button in the "Speaker settings" section. Click the Performance tab, and drag the Hardware acceleration slider to the left one notch (see Figure 3-14). Click OK, and then click Apply. Play the sound again, and if it's still too fast, lower the Hardware acceleration setting further.

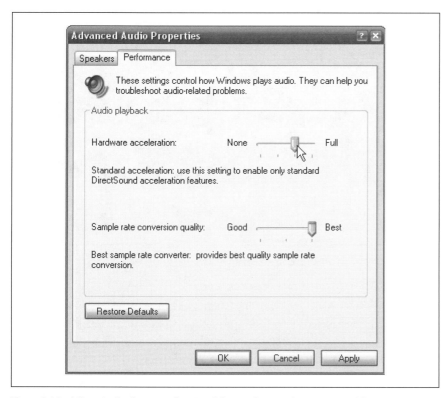

Figure 3-14. Adjust the Hardware acceleration slider to solve sound corruption problems.

Other sound corruption problems can be fixed by turning off the equalizer settings in your music player. In Windows Media Player, for example, go to View→Enhancements→Graphic Equalizer. In the pane at the bottom of the screen, click the Turn Off link. (If the link says Turn On, the equalizer is already turned off.)

Whether or not these adjustments fix the problem, this is not the behavior of a properly functioning sound card. Make sure you have the latest drivers, and consider replacing the card (or sending in your PC for repair) if nothing else works.

Get Crossfades Working

THE ANNOYANCE: I use Windows Media Player, and I can't seem to get my music to crossfade. I can't tolerate dead air.

THE FIX: Crossfading eliminates the silent gaps between two songs by fading in the next song while the current song is ending. To enable crossfading in WMP, go to View→Enhancements→Crossfading and Auto Volume Leveling. In the Enhancements pane that now appears at the bottom of the window, click the "Turn on Crossfading" link (Figure 3-15).

Figure 3-15. Crossfading, which overlaps songs to reduce dead air, only works in certain circumstances.

Crossfading works only on data files (such as MP3 or WMA files), and then only with songs encoded with the same sampling rate (e.g., 192 kbps or 256 kbps). Crossfades won't work if you are playing a standard audio CD, or a data CD that was originally burned with Windows Media Player.

For more competent crossfading, try a different music player, such as WinAmp (free, *http://www.winamp.com*) or even Apple's iTunes (free, *http://www.itunes.com*).

> **NOTE**
>
> *It's also possible that crossfading is actually working, but you can't tell because your music files have more than a few seconds of silence at the beginning or end. To see if this is what's happening, play a few songs that don't begin or end in a fade. You can also help compensate for this by moving the crossfade slider to the right to increase the amount of overlap.*

Extract Sound from a Video

THE ANNOYANCE: I downloaded a music video that plays fine in Windows Media Player, but my portable MP3 player won't touch it; it only plays strict music files.

THE FIX: Use the Windows Media Stream Editor, a component of the Windows Media Encoder (free, *http://www.microsoft.com/windows/windowsmedia/ 9series/encoder/*), to extract the audio from a *.wmv* video file and save it into a standalone Windows Media Audio (*.wma*) file.

First, open the Windows Media Stream Editor, shown in Figure 3-16, and click Add Source. Open the *.wmv* file, and expand the branches by highlighting the file in the list and pressing the asterisk (*) key. Check the box next to the Audio entry and click the Add button. Then, click Create File, supply an output filename, and click Save. When you're ready, click Start to begin the extraction.

When the process is complete, you'll have a standard *.wma* file; see the next annoyance for ways to convert it to MP3 or any other format, if necessary.

Figure 3-16. Use the Windows Media Stream Editor to extract audio tracks from video clips.

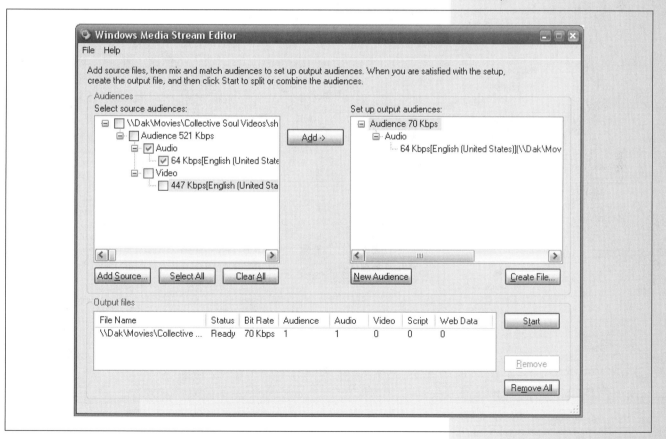

Convert Audio Files

THE ANNOYANCE: I have a bunch of music in one audio format, but my music player won't play them.

THE FIX: Unless there's a specific patch or upgrade for the player that adds support for your file type, you'll probably have to convert your files to a format your player recognizes. For instance, the iTunes Music Store only distributes music in the copy-protected AAC (*.m4p*) format, which only works on Apple's iPod music player. And the iPod itself can't play files in Microsoft's *.wma* format.

To convert an audio file from one format to another, you could open the file in a full-blown sound-editing application such as Sound Forge ($319.96, *http://www.sonymediasoftware.com/download/step2.asp?DID=559*), but there's a cheaper and easier solution if all you're doing is format conversions. You can download Apple's iTunes software (*http://www.apple.com/itunes/*) for free, even if you don't have an iPod or plan to buy music from the iTunes Music Store, and it can convert songs easily and quickly (Figure 3-17). iTunes supports MP3 (all bitrates), AAC (*.m4p*, *.m4a*, and *.m4b*), AIFF, Apple Lossless, and WAV formats.

> **NOTE**
>
> *Converting from one format to another involves recompressing the audio, which reduces sound quality. So, when you first rip your music from CD or purchase it online, choose a format you won't have to convert later. Many people choose the MP3 format because almost every music player supports it, even though some other formats offer slightly better quality and/or smaller file sizes.*

Figure 3-17. Use Apple's free iTunes software to quickly convert audio files from one format to another.

To convert your files, first start iTunes, and select Library on the left. Then drag and drop your music files onto the iTunes window. (If you move the files into your iTunes music folder before dragging them into the iTunes application, iTunes will, by default, organize them into folders based on their embedded tag information.)

Next, select Edit→Preferences, choose the Advanced tab, and then choose the Importing sub-tab. Select a file format from the Format Using listbox (such as MP3 Encoder to convert to the MP3 format), and then select a compression level from the Setting listbox. If you don't know which settings to use, MP3 at 192 kbps is a good compromise between quality, flexibility, and file size. Click OK to confirm your choices. Finally, highlight one or more songs in your Library (as shown in Figure 3-17), right-click, and select "Convert Selection to MP3" (or AAC, or whatever). iTunes will place the newly converted files alongside the originals, both in the Library and in same folder on your hard disk, while leaving the original files intact.

Fix MP3 Tags

THE ANNOYANCE: I've gone to a lot of trouble to name my song files, but Windows Media Player ignores the song titles and artist names when I play my music. What gives?

THE FIX: Windows Media Player and other music players usually don't pay any attention to filenames, but rather look for information in *ID3 tags* that are embedded in the music files. The vast majority of music players support ID3 tags, which store information about the artist, track, album, year, genre, and about a hundred other things. In fact, most ripping programs will identify the CD you're ripping by its serial number, go online and fetch the relevant ID3 information, and embed that information in the MP3 files the program generates.

To get your music player to display and organize your music properly, you'll have to properly tag your music files. Most music players allow you edit ID3 tags, and even Windows Explorer lets you edit a file's tag information by right-clicking, selecting Properties, choosing the Summary tab, and clicking Advanced. Windows Media Player (via the Advanced Tag Editor feature) and iTunes let you modify the tags of several files at once, but with a big stack of files you'll need more power. At this point, you should turn to Ultra Tag Editor ($19.95, *http://www.atelio.com*), which can scoop up the information in your filenames and plug it into the files' ID3 tags; it can also clean up existing tag information and even use the tags to create new names for your music files.

To fix your tags, open Ultra Tag Editor, use the tree to navigate to the folder containing your files, and place checkmarks next to the specific files you want to fix. Choose the Ultra Tagger tab below, and then select "Generate Tag from Filename" from the Action listbox (Figure 3-18).

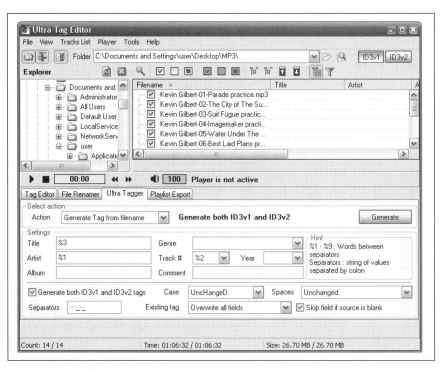

Figure 3-18. Use Ultra Tag Editor to generate MP3 tags from filenames.

— N O T E —

Although programs such as Ultra Tag Editor are flexible, they assume that your filenames all follow the same naming convention (e.g., Artist–Album–Title.mp3). If you use a mish-mash of different file-naming conventions, you can use a program such as Power Rename (part of Creative Element Power Tools, available at http://www.creativelement.com/powertools/) to homogenize your filenames rather than hand-renaming hundreds of individual files.

Now, Ultra Tag Editor needs you to tell it where in your songs' filenames to find the artist name, track title, track number, album name, and so on, so you'll need to examine the filename of a typical music file on your hard disk, which might look something like *Artist-Album-Title.mp3*.

First, determine the delimiter used to separate the information in your filenames—a hyphen (-), in this case—and type it into the Delimiters field. Next, type %1 into the field containing the first piece of information (e.g., Artist), %2 into the field containing the second (e.g., Album), %3 into the third (e.g., Title), and so on. (Imagine that your filenames look like %1-%2-%3-%4....mp3.)

When you're done, click the Generate button to preview the new tags, and click Write Tags to commit.

Connect to Your MP3 Player

THE ANNOYANCE: Windows Media Player won't recognize my portable MP3 player.

THE FIX: Your music player should've come with its own drivers and software, which you can use to add or sync music and otherwise configure the player. The iPod, for instance, uses the iTunes software (available at *http://www.apple.com/itunes/*), while the Phatbox uses the Phatnoise Media Manager (available at *http://www.phatnoise.com/downloads/*). Visit the web site of the manufacturer of your music player for the latest version of the required software.

Now, if you're not terribly fond of the software you have, or if you don't want to abandon your meticulously organized Windows Media Player library, you can visit *http://www.playsforsure.com* to see if Windows Media Player supports syncing directly with your device, either as-is or with a firmware upgrade. If your player isn't on the list (many aren't), you're stuck with the software you've got.

Your last hope: the manufacturer may have included drivers that make your player act like a removable hard disk, allowing you to add music simply by dragging files in Windows Explorer.

Iron Out License Issues

THE ANNOYANCE: I'm trying to play some music, but Windows Media Player keeps complaining about licenses. I'm tired and I just want to hear the Bee Gees!

THE FIX: Music that you purchase online is usually copy-protected, which means you can only play the tunes on the computer where you originally bought them. If you change computers, or even upgrade certain hardware components (like your hard drive), Windows may think you're trying to get around the copy protection and will refuse to play the music.

If you're prompted to "migrate" a license, you'll be able to play the file on another computer. Beware, though, that you can only migrate a license for a given file 10 times; thereafter, the file can't be played. For this reason, you should frequently back up your licenses by selecting Tools→Manage Licenses (License Management in WMP 9.0) and clicking the Back Up Now button, as shown in Figure 3-19. Later, you can click the Restore Now button—should the need arise—to transfer licenses without using the migration feature, and thus move your music from PC to PC without limits.

> **NOTE**
>
> *If you get a licensing error for songs you ripped yourself with WMP, you likely ripped them with the "Copy protect music" option enabled. Although there's no officially sanctioned way to remove copy protection from your songs, you can prevent newly ripped songs from being protected. Select Tools→ Options, choose the Rip Music tab (Copy Music in WMP 9.0), and uncheck the "Copy protect music" box.*

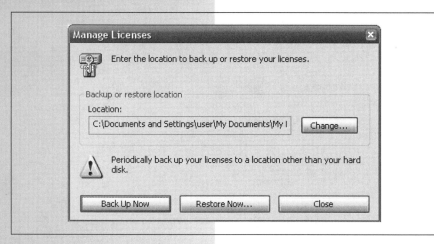

Figure 3-19. Back up your Digital Rights Management licenses to prevent licensing problems later on.

If you purchased the music online, Windows Media Player can attempt to acquire a new license for you. Select Tools→Options, choose the Privacy tab, and check the "Acquire licenses automatically for protected content" box. Most online music stores will also let you download the song(s) again (thus generating new licenses), provided your account is still active.

If you get an error stating that your licenses are corrupted, you may be able to fix the problem by deleting your license database. First, back up your licenses. Then open Windows Explorer, navigate to *\Documents and Settings\All Users\DRM*, and rename the *DRM* folder to *DRM.backup.* (Note that this is a hidden folder; see Chapter 2 for instructions on displaying hidden files and folders.) Return to Windows Media Player and use the Restore Now button to restore your licenses, which recreates the database.

PHOTOS

Down with the Picture and Fax Viewer!

THE ANNOYANCE: When I double-click image files, they open in the Windows Picture and Fax Viewer. I'd rather have them open in Photoshop or another, more capable image program, but changing the settings in Windows Explorer's File Types window doesn't seem to have any effect.

THE FIX: Annoying, isn't it? Microsoft included this rudimentary image viewer in Windows XP, and took steps to ensure that it couldn't easily be disabled.

To turn off the Windows Picture and Fax Viewer for good, open the Registry Editor (go to Start→Run and type regedit), and expand the branches to *HKEY_CLASSES_ROOT\SystemFileAssociations\image\ShellEx\ContextMenuHandlers*. Delete the *ShellImagePreview* key, and close the Registry Editor when you're done; the change will take effect immediately.

NOTE

If you want to use another image viewer without mucking around in your Registry, there are ways to open images other than double-clicking. For instance, you can drag and drop an image file onto the window of any viewer to open it, or right-click an image file and select Open to use an alternate viewer. (Select Open With, and, if need be, Choose Program if your favorite program doesn't appear in the right-click list.)

Get Accurate Color Output

THE ANNOYANCE: Whenever I print photos on any color printer, they don't match what I see onscreen.

THE FIX: This is a common problem, and one, unfortunately, without a clearcut, foolproof solution. The problem is that your monitor, printer, scanner, and digital camera all handle color a little differently. It's up to you to calibrate Windows so that all of these devices can communicate without botching your color photos too badly.

First, you'll need to gamma-correct your monitor, which ensures that its brightness and color balance settings are optimized for your setup. Many high-end monitors have gamma adjustment features, but barring that, you can use the free QuickGamma utility (Figure 3-20), available at *http:// quickgamma.de/indexen.html*. (A similar utility also comes with Adobe Photoshop, although the author of QuickGamma claims better accuracy.) The process essentially involves adjusting controls until two different grayish regions appear indistinguishable when you squint. If you're a perfectionist, you should elect to adjust red, green, and blue values independently.

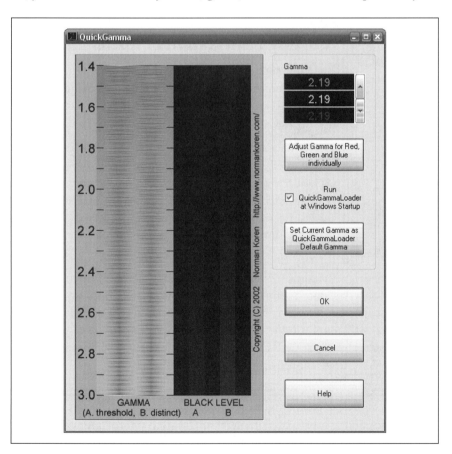

Figure 3-20. Use QuickGamma to adjust your monitor so colors are displayed more accurately.

NOTE

For better control over the color profiles used with your various devices, install the Microsoft Color Control Panel Applet (free; http://www.microsoft. com/downloads/).

Figure 3-21. Use the free Image Resizer utility to shrink a bunch of photos in one step.

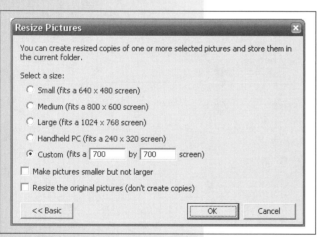

NOTE

Use Power Rename, discussed in the next annoyance, to rename all the newly shrunk files in one step. See "Make a Digital Slideshow," later in this chapter, for another way to share your digital photos.

Next, obtain an ICC profile for your color printer, scanner, camera, and any other imaging devices. You should be able to get ICC profiles from the respective hardware vendors or, barring that, from a site such as *http://desktoppub. about.com/od/iccprofiles/*. Likewise, you can find many scanner profiles at *http://www.littlecms.com/iphoto/profiles.htm*. Another good place to get (and share) ICC profiles is *http://www.chromix.com*. Coming up empty? Search Google for your specific product and model (e.g., "Epson 1520 ICC").

Once you have the correct color profile, install it by opening Start→ Settings→Printers and Faxes. Right-click your color printer's icon, and select Properties. Choose the Color Management tab, click the Add button, select the *.icc* or *.icm* file you wish to install, and click Add. Next, select the Manual option, highlight the new profile, and click OK when you're done.

Now, playing with gamma correction and color profiles will only take you so far. Variations in ink or toner, as well as paper, can all affect color reproduction, so you'll have to employ a little trial and error to get the desired results. Professionals use more sophisticated tools, such as colorimeters, to get better color matching, not to mention higher-quality monitors, printers, and scanners. So don't be surprised if you don't get perfect color every time.

Quickly Shrink Many Photos

THE ANNOYANCE: I have a few hundred digital photos I'd like to share on the Web, but my 8-megapixel camera makes huge files. How can I shrink 'em down en masse?

THE FIX: The easiest way to shrink a lot of files is to use Microsoft's free Image Resizer, available at *http:// www.microsoft.com/windowsxp/downloads/powertoys/ xppowertoys.mspx*. Once it's installed, simply highlight your photo files (JPG, GIF, or BMP), right-click, and select Resize Pictures. Click Advanced and select the Custom option, as shown in Figure 3-21.

In the Custom boxes, type the maximum width and height (in pixels) for each photo. Most of the time, you'll want to specify the same number in both Custom fields to accommodate both landscape and portrait orientations; don't worry, the aspect ratios of your photos will remain intact. For instance, if you type 700 in each field (a good size for web photos), each photo will be shrunk so that the larger dimension is no more than 700 pixels.

Click OK when you're done. Depending on the number of files and the speed of your PC, the resizing process can take anywhere from a split second to a minute or more. By default, your original photos aren't changed; instead, new, smaller versions should appear in the same folder, renamed automatically to prevent conflicts.

Sort Photos Chronologically

THE ANNOYANCE: We just had this big party (a commitment ceremony), and we've gotten hundreds of photos from a dozen different people. I'd like to put them in chronological order by the time of day each was shot, but the dates and times of the files are all out of sync. What makes matters worse, each camera used a different filename format, so I can't even sort them alphabetically. I don't want to sort a thousand pictures by hand—there's got to be an automatic way!

THE FIX: The Date Modified column in Windows Explorer (go to View→Details if you don't see it) probably won't reliably sort your photos. If the photographer did any post-processing (e.g., color correction, cropping, retouching) in a program such as Photoshop, the file's date will reflect the last time the file was saved, not when the photo was originally shot. Also, file dates and times are typically set when a digital camera saves photos to its memory card, not necessarily when the photos are taken. (The discrepancy occurs because many high-end cameras hold the shots in memory before saving them.)

Luckily, embedded in each digital photo is a goldmine of information stored by the camera as part of the EXIF (EXchangeable Image File) format used in *.jpg* files, *.tiff* files, and raw formats such as Nikon's *.nef* files. EXIF data includes the date and time the photo was taken, the camera settings used (f-stop, exposure, metering mode), the photographer's name (sometimes), the dimensions of the image, and more. If the camera supports it, GPS data indicating the exact geographical location of the camera when the photo was shot can even be included.

To view EXIF data for a single photo, right-click the image file, select Properties, choose the Summary tab, and then click the Advanced button. Alternatively, highlight the photo in Windows Explorer, and a brief EXIF summary will appear in the Status bar (go to View→Status Bar if you don't see it).

Better yet, view selective EXIF data for a bunch of photos at once: in Windows Explorer, go to View→Details, then View→Choose Details (or right-click any column header and select More). Place a checkmark next to any new details you'd like to display; EXIF data appears lower down in the list. For instance, place a checkmark next to Date Picture Taken, and click OK. Now, sort the photos chronologically by clicking the Date Picture Taken column header. Voilà!

But what if you want to make this sorting more permanent? Use the free Stamp utility (available at *http://www.snapfiles.com/get/stamp.html*) to rename your files with their EXIF dates. After you do this, your photos will appear in chronological order even when sorted alphabetically.

> **NOTE**
>
> *Of course, you won't find EXIF data in scans of film, nor in digital photos that were modified by software that doesn't support the format. (For the record, Adobe Photoshop and ACDSee both retain all EXIF data in most circumstances, but lower-end programs such as MS Paint and many image converters do not.)*

NOTE

If you're uploading your photos to an online photo sharing/printing service, do your research before you spend too much time sorting your photos. Some sites (such as Kodak Gallery) don't allow you to sort your photos alphabetically, while others (such as Shutterfly) allow you to automatically sort your albums by filename, file dates, or even EXIF dates. Of course, your web site's sorting mechanism won't do much good if you don't clean up your EXIF dates before you upload your photos.

What Stamp doesn't do, unfortunately, is allow you to compensate for the differences among the various cameras' internal clocks. The discrepancies might be as small as three or four minutes among your local guests, or several hours for visitors from different time zones. As a result, your photos may not sort properly even *after* you use Stamp—a problem requiring the following fix.

First, download the free trial of Creative Element Power Tools (available at *http://www.creativelement.com/powertools/*), and use the Change Date tool to change the file dates so they match when the photos were taken. Highlight all the photos you want to fix, right-click, and select Change Date. Select "Date/Time from file metadata," choose "Date & time photo taken by digital camera" from the list, and click Apply.

Next, you'll need to determine the discrepancies between the internal clocks of the various cameras. Pick one photographer to use as the baseline, and then figure out how far off each other photographer is from that baseline. To do this, you'll need to find common points of reference: one or two representative photos of the same instant by each photographer. After a minute or so of studying, you might find that, say, Kathryn's camera was about 3 hours faster than the baseline, while Henry's camera was 6 minutes and 11 seconds slower.

To fix the times, highlight all of Kathryn's photos, right-click, and select Change Date. This time, select "Relative Date/Time," and then make your adjustments with the controls below (see Figure 3-22). Then do the same for everyone else's photos.

When you're done, the photos should be in perfect order when sorted by date. The last step is to change the filenames to incorporate these new times. Alas, Stamp won't read the file dates/times if the photos have EXIF data, but Power Rename (also part of Creative Element Power Tools) can do the job easily. Highlight all the photos, right-click, and select Power Rename.

NOTE

If you've already renamed the photos with Stamp, place a checkmark next to Power Rename's Crop option, select "from beginning," and type a number representing the amount of text to remove from the beginning of the filename.

In Power Rename, place a checkmark next to "Add stamp," select "file date & time," and then click the Format button. From the "Choose a format" list, select "Custom format," and then use the date/time placeholders from the list to assemble a date format conducive to

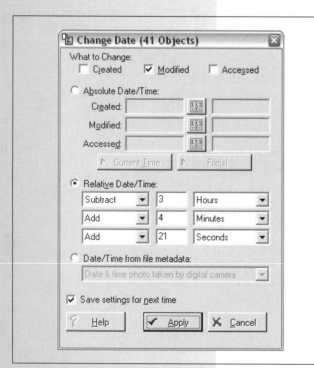

Figure 3-22. Use the Change Date tool to fix discrepancies between the times of different photographers' digital photos.

sorting. Your best bet is to start with the year (yy or yyyy), followed by the month, day, hour, minute, and finally, the second, like this:

```
yyyy-mm-dd_hh-mm-ss
```

For example, Power Rename would take a file with the date July 26, 2005 at 4:53:06pm and add this to the beginning of the filename:

```
2005-07-26_16-53-06
```

Click OK and then the Apply button to rename the files. With all your photos date-and-time-corrected and renamed accordingly, they'll appear in chronological order even when sorted alphabetically!

Control Thumbnails in Explorer

THE ANNOYANCE: I have a folder full of digital photos, and Windows Explorer insists on showing them as thumbnails. I can switch to the Details view, but if I open another folder and then come back, Widows reverts to the Thumbnail view!

THE FIX: Getting Windows Explorer to save your settings can be a real hassle, as discussed in the previous chapter—and in some cases, you'll just have to live with Windows XP's forgetfulness.

To make Windows Explorer remember your view preferences for the folder, select Tools→Folder Options and choose the View tab. Scroll down, place a checkmark next to "Remember each folder's view settings," and click OK. Thereafter, when you make a change, leave, and come back, Explorer should remember your settings (for a time, anyway).

One exception is the way Explorer deals with special folders. For instance, the contents of the *My Pictures* folder are always shown as thumbnails. To work around this, you can either move your photos to a different folder (and not a subfolder of *My Pictures*), or use Microsoft's free TweakUI utility (*http://www.microsoft.com/windowsxp/downloads/powertoys/xppowertoys. mspx*) to change the location of the *My Pictures* folder so your existing photos can be left in peace.

Next, change Explorer's assumptions about a given folder by right-clicking the folder icon and selecting Properties. On the Customize tab, select "Documents (for any file type)" from the drop-down menu, and click OK when you're done. You'll probably have to close the folder and reopen it for the change to take effect.

Another approach is to change the way Windows Explorer displays thumbnails so that they look like ordinary icons; it's not the same as the Details view, but it's a step in the right direction. Open TweakUI, expand the Explorer category, and select Thumbnails. On the right, change the Size to 32, and click OK when you're done.

> **NOTE**
>
> *If a folder contains the hidden file thumbs.db, Windows Explorer will usually show the folder in Thumbnail view. Delete this file to restore normal behavior. (To reveal hidden files, go to Tools→Folder Options, choose the View tab, and select the "Show hidden files and folders" option.)*

Choose Thumbnail Folders

THE ANNOYANCE: I'd like Windows to show thumbnails of all the photos in a particular folder, as well as the contents of all subfolders. Is there a way to set this as the default view?

THE FIX: Not really. Windows Explorer has two ways of remembering your settings: you can set defaults for all folders, and you can save the specific settings you choose for any individual folder. While there's no way to set the view settings for, say, a single folder branch on your hard disk, there are a few workarounds.

First, Windows Explorer should always show the contents of your *My Pictures* folder (and all its subfolders) as thumbnails, so you can get the desired result by storing all your digital photos in *My Pictures*.

Alternatively, you can use a dedicated image viewer, such as ACDSee (*http://www.acdsystems.com*), to view your photo folders. It'll display the contents of all your folders as thumbnails, as shown in Figure 3-23, meaning that you no longer have to worry about how and when Windows Explorer turns photos into thumbnails.

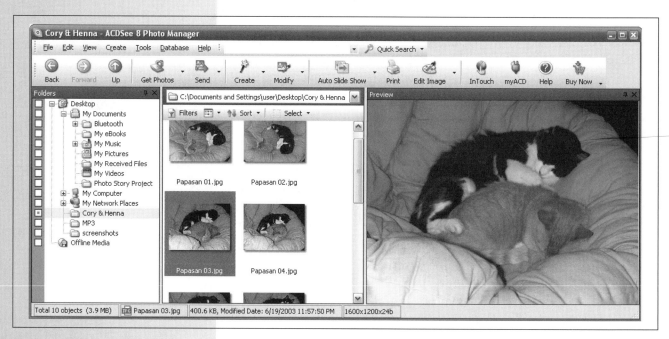

Figure 3-23. For more flexibility than Explorer affords, use a program such as ACDSee to view thumbnails of your photos.

Make Thumbnail Icons

THE ANNOYANCE: I don't much care for Windows Explorer's Thumbnail view. Is there another way to display thumbnails in Explorer?

THE FIX: Yes, and it's a pretty nifty little hack!

In Explorer, when you view a folder containing cursors (*.cur* files), animated cursors (*.ani* files), or icons (*.ico* files), their file icons are previews of their contents, rather than simply generic icons. To expand this feature to apply to *.bmp* files as well, open the Registry Editor (go to Start→Run and type regedit) and expand the branches to *HKEY_CLASSES_ROOT\Paint. Picture\DefaultIcon*. Double-click the (*Default*) value, type %1 in the "Value data" field, and click OK.

At this point, you can increase the size of the thumbnails by increasing the generic icon size. Open the Display control panel, choose the Appearance tab, and click the Advanced button. Select Icon from the Item menu, and type a larger value in the size box to the right, such as 48 or 64.

Unfortunately, this won't work for *.jpg* or *.gif* files (or any other formats). If you have Adobe Photoshop, Explorer will display icon previews for Photoshop files (such as *.psd* files), but that's about it.

> **NOTE**
>
> *If this doesn't work, it means the .bmp file type is no longer associated with MS Paint, and you'll have to modify a different Registry location. Navigate to HKEY_CLASSES_ROOT\. bmp. Here, the (Default) value will contain the name of the key (also in HKEY_CLASSES_ ROOT) that you need to change; just substitute this key name for Paint.Picture in the Registry path above, and make the change.*

Make a Digital Slideshow

THE ANNOYANCE: I'd love to show my vacation pictures nice and big, like an old-fashioned slideshow, but my PC's screen is pitifully small. How can I make a satisfying slideshow with digital photos?

THE FIX: One easy way is to burn your pictures onto an ordinary DVD-ROM or CD-ROM, pop them into your DVD player (provided it supports JPG-laden discs), and watch them on your TV. If you're using Windows XP Media Center Edition, you can burn your photos to a DVD using a process similar to the one described later in this chapter, in "Burn Recorded Programs to DVD." Otherwise, you can use Windows Explorer (or your favorite disc-burning software, for that matter) to burn your JPG photos to an ordinary data disc, as described in "Burn CDs for Free."

> **NOTE**
>
> *If your DVD player doesn't support picture DVDs, it may support picture CDs; or, if you want to create a more polished presentation, you can use third-party disc-burning software to author full-blown, menu-driven DVD slideshows, complete with transition effects and sound. See "Write Video to DVD" for details.*

Another alternative: most digital cameras have a video-out port, allowing you to plug them directly into a television set (using a simple RCA or S-Video cable) and display your photos right on the TV screen. This isn't limited to photos you shot with your camera, either; you can always add JPGs to your camera's memory card via Windows Explorer.

Your TV or DVD player may even have a memory card reader, which would let you display your photos on your TV by simply inserting the card and pressing some buttons on the remote control.

By far, though, the most impressive solution is to connect a DLP projector to your PC's monitor port, and display your photos in high resolution on the wall. Although the cost is much higher, the quality and experience easily trumps any standard television set.

WINDOWS MEDIA CENTER EDITION

Watch TV... On Your TV

THE ANNOYANCE: I'd like to hook up my Windows Media Center Edition (MCE) machine to a TV so I can watch broadcasts, recordings, and even DVDs on the big screen. But when I try this, all I see is black. Does my PC have something against Bruce Campbell movies?

THE FIX: It's nothing personal, and it's probably easy to fix.

When you connect a TV to your computer, you should see your entire desktop, Start menu and all. If you see nothing at all, your PC's TV-out port may be disabled. If you're using a laptop, you may have to press a special keystroke combination to "activate" the TV-out and external VGA ports. On some Dell laptops, for instance, hold the Fn key while pressing F8 to switch between the internal display, the external display, and both; consult your computer's documentation for details. Press these keys repeatedly until you see a picture.

If you see a picture for everything *except* the video, you have a video overlay problem. See "Shed Light on Blank Videos," earlier in this chapter, for a number of workarounds.

Naturally, make sure you're using the right cable. Your PC's TV-out port might use a standard S-Video plug, or it might require a proprietary connector (at extra cost, of course). If your computer lacks a TV-out port, you'll need to get an adapter cable that can connect the PC's external VGA port to your TV. If your TV has a VGA port, you can make the link with a standard VGA cable. If not, you can get a VGA-to-RCA or VGA-to-S-Video adapter cheaply from eBay or conveniently from your local electronics store.

Mimic Media Center

THE ANNOYANCE: Windows MCE is really pretty, but I only have the plain (non-MCE) version of Windows XP. How can I copy MCE's spiffy look and feel?

THE FIX: Get the Royale Windows XP theme from *http://www.microsoft.com/nz/windowsxp/downloads/bliss/newbliss.mspx*. As a special treat for you Windows users in New Zealand, you can get special Kiwi versions of the Bliss background wallpaper from *http://www.microsoft.com/nz/windowsxp/downloads/nzbliss.aspx*!

Fix Broken TV Listings

THE ANNOYANCE: My television listings are wrong. How do I get the right ones for the channels I receive?

THE FIX: First, make sure your PC's clock is set correctly: open Date and Time Properties in the Control Panel and set the time and date. Click Apply, and then choose the Internet Time tab and make sure the "Automatically synchronize with an Internet Time Server" box is checked, so that your clock is always correct.

Next, your Zip Code in MCE might be wrong, which could cause you to get program data for a different region. Or you may be using an antenna, yet downloading programming data intended for cable or satellite broadcasts. From the main Media Center menu, choose Settings→General→Media Center Setup→Set Up TV Signal, and follow the prompts. When asked whether you'd like to configure your TV signal automatically, choose "I will manually configure my TV signal." On the following page, choose whether your signal comes from cable, satellite, or antenna (terrestrial broadcast), after which you'll be prompted to set up your TV Program Guide. When prompted, type your Zip Code, and then click Next to confirm your choices and download the programming data for your area.

Of course, it's possible that all your settings are correct. If only a single program or a single channel is off, it could be a temporary glitch or last-minute programming change. Try manually downloading the latest programming data to iron out any such discrepancies. From the main Media Center menu, choose Settings→TV→Guide→Get Latest Guide Listings.

If all your program data is off, you'll have to be a bit sneaky about it. The simplest solution is to spoof a different location by entering a Zip Code adjacent to your own; you may have to try a few different codes to find the one that delivers the data you need.

Send a Digital Signal to Your HDTV

THE ANNOYANCE: I just spent all this money on a high-definition (HD) television, but the video I feed it from my Windows MCE PC looks terrible. What can I do?

THE FIX: The ports on your PC and the available connectors on the back of your TV limit your options. Ideally you want an all-digital connection, so avoid any analog plugs, such as your PC's TV-out/S-Video port or 15-pin VGA connector. Instead, use a Digital Video Interface (DVI) cable to connect the DVI port on your PC with the matching plug on your TV.

If your PC doesn't have a DVI port, you'll need to replace your video card with one that has DVI support; if you're using a laptop, you'll need to add a PCMCIA DVI card. (Tired of acronyms yet?)

If your HDTV doesn't have a DVI port, it probably has a newer High-Definition Multimedia Interface (HDMI) plug, which is essentially the same thing (albeit with audio); you can get HDMI-to-DVI adapters readily on eBay, and still achieve an all-digital connection. If your TV has no digital video inputs—or they're already being used—your next-best option is to use a DVI-to-composite adapter (also available on eBay); although your TV's composite inputs are analog (not digital), they do support progressive-scan video, which will still look a lot better than S-Video or (gasp) RCA connectors.

Once you've got the cabling in order, the next step is to set the resolution on your PC to optimize the picture quality, as described in "Sharpen Blurry Text" in Chapter 1. Set it too low, and it'll look pixelated; set it too high, and you might have overscanning problems (where the video runs off the screen). Try a few standard resolutions until you find one that looks good (1024×768 usually works pretty well). If you still have trouble, use PowerStrip (a free trial is available at *http://entechtaiwan.net/util/ps.shtm*) to find the optimal resolution and timing settings for your TV.

Of course, no matter what you do, the standard-definition TV tuner in your PC will never provide the same quality, clarity, and color as a true HDTV tuner card. See the next annoyance for more information.

> **NOTE**
>
> *Many HDTVs have only a single digital (HDMI or DVI) input, which may already be occupied (if you're lucky) by a DVD player with a digital output. If you don't want to settle for an analog connection between your PC and TV, you'll need an HDMI or DVI switch, the best examples of which can be found in some high-end digital home theater receivers.*

Capture HDTV Programming

THE ANNOYANCE: I'd like to watch HDTV broadcasts on my computer, but I only seem to be able to get standard-definition (SD) programming. What gives?

THE FIX: You can only receive high-definition programming with a true HDTV tuner. In North America, you'll need an ATSC tuner card for your PC; in Europe and other parts of the world, you'll need a DVB tuner. HD tuners will receive terrestrial broadcasts, but not necessarily cable or satellite broadcasts. For that, you'll likely need an HD tuner with a cable card slot; contact your cable/satellite provider for details.

While the tuner is the most important component, there are other pieces of the HD puzzle. For instance, HD broadcasts use a lot more data, which means you'll need a PC with at least a 2.4-GHz processor for simultaneous capture and playback (required for basic timeshifting of HD programming). You'll need a larger hard disk, too; while an hour of SD programming typically consumes 1 GB of disk space, an hour of HD programming will eat up about 10 times as much space. Thus, even a shiny new 300-GB hard disk will only net you about 25–30 hours of HD storage.

Finally, you'll need HD programming data. If only SD data is available for your area, you may have to use different software (see "Alternatives to Media Center") that gets its data elsewhere.

Fix HDTV Timeshifting Problems

THE ANNOYANCE: MCE can timeshift record all standard-definition television broadcasts, but only some HDTV programming. With some HD broadcasts, MCE simply stops recording.

THE FIX: This is probably due to the *broadcast flag*, a copy-protection scheme instigated in North America in 2005. All HD tuners that pay attention to the broadcast flag will refuse to record any protected HD programming. The only way around this is to use an older HD tuner sold before the broadcast flag took effect (sometimes available on eBay); these tuners will ignore the broadcast flag and record all HD programming without restriction.

Tidy Up Your Remote Control Receiver

THE ANNOYANCE: To use an infrared remote control, I have to plug this silly external receiver box into my PC. It's ugly, and my cat keeps knocking it over.

THE FIX: Despite the growing popularity of home-theater PCs, fewer computers today have built-in infrared ports than those sold 10 years ago.

If your PC has at least one USB port on the front, you can replace your infrared receiver box with an ultra-small USB infrared dongle, which is scarcely larger than the tip of your thumb. Although it'll stick out about an inch, it's an easy and inexpensive way to do away with the messy cables. To find an infrared dongle compatible with Windows XP, search Google and eBay for "USB IRDA."

A tidier, albeit more radical (and expensive) solution is to replace your PC's case with one that has a built-in infrared receiver, such as a VFD-enabled SilverStone enclosure (*http://silverstonetek.com*). Just connect the internal cable to the USB plug on your motherboard, and you're good to go.

As for your cat, perhaps a nice ball of yarn will entertain him (and you) for a little while.

Use Any Remote Control

THE ANNOYANCE: I got this el-cheapo remote control with my TV tuner card. It works, but it's big and poorly laid out. How can I get a spiffy TV remote to work with Windows MCE?

THE FIX: You have a few options. For one, you can get a learning remote from any consumer electronics store, and program it to mimic the remote control that came with your hardware. You can also replace your remote (and accompanying receiver) with another MCE-compatible remote control. To find a compatible remote, search Google and eBay for "MCE remote."

Using special software such as OmniRemote Pro ($24.95, *http://www.pacificneotek.com*), you can also program your PalmOS handheld computer to act as a remote. Although tapping a screen is rarely as comfortable or intuitive as pressing physical buttons, there is an undeniable cachet to controlling one computer with another.

To use your ordinary TV remote control with your PC, you'll need a programmable infrared receiver. Provided the receiver and accompanying driver are compatible with MCE, you'll be able to map any button on your existing remote to an MCE command.

Alternatives to Media Center

THE ANNOYANCE: I'm fed up with the Windows Media Center software; it's clumsy, hopelessly tied to corporate cross-marketing interests, and totally inflexible. Is there any other software package that can do timeshifting, recording, and scheduling with the hardware I already have?

THE FIX: There are a bunch of alternatives to the Media Center software, and most will work with a wider variety of hardware than MCE supports.

Free PVR software alternatives include GB-PVR (*http://www.gbpvr.com*) and MediaPortal (*http://mediaportal.sourceforge.net*). Commercial products, while not necessarily better than their free counterparts, include Meedio Pro (from $44.95, *http://www.meedio.com*), SnapStream BeyondTV ($69.99, *http://www.snapstream.com*), and SageTV Media Center ($79.95, *http://www.sage.tv/sagetv.html*).

Each product has its advantages and disadvantages. When choosing a PVR software package, the most important consideration is an onscreen interface that you like. Aside from that, it should support HD programming and DVD burning, work with a wide variety of remote controls, and accept plug-ins or extensions that add functionality (such as news readers and weather forecasters).

Of course, you don't have to stick with Windows if you want good PVR software. Both MythTV (*http://mythtv.org*) and Freevo (*http://freevo.sourceforge. net*) are free and run on the likewise free Linux operating system.

Burn Recorded Programs to DVD

THE ANNOYANCE: I recorded some shows with MCE that I'd like to keep; is there any way to burn them to DVD so that I can free up the hard disk space for more recordings?

THE FIX: As long as you have a DVD writer, archiving your recorded programs to DVD is a snap with MCE.

Insert a blank DVD into your burner. If your burner supports it, use DVD+R or DVD+RW media instead of DVD-R or DVD-RW discs.

Next, press the START button on your remote, select More Programs, and then select Create CD/DVD. Choose the second option, Video DVD, and then enter a name for the disc.

Select one or more programs to include on the DVD. When you're done, select View DVD to see the list of programs queued to go on the disc; at this point, you can rearrange them before you burn. Select Create DVD to burn the disc.

> **NOTE**
>
> *Test the DVD right away in a real DVD player (not in your PC), before you delete the recording from your PC. If it doesn't play properly, see "Fix DVD Playback Problems," later in this chapter.*

Build Your Own HTPC

THE ANNOYANCE: I'd like to use Windows MCE on a home-theater PC I built myself, but I can't seem to buy a standalone copy of MCE anywhere!

THE FIX: In typical corporate fashion, Microsoft has only made Windows Media Center Edition available preinstalled on specially outfitted PCs. You could buy a PC with MCE and turn it into a full-blown home-theater PC (HTPC), but most of the time it makes more sense to build your HTPC from scratch and then install one of the available alternatives to MCE. (See "Alternatives to Media Center.") You could also wait for Windows Vista, and use the MCE-like software incorporated into all editions of the new OS.

CDS AND DVDS

Burn CDs for Free

NOTE

Your CD or DVD burner may have packet-writing software installed, such as Roxio's DirectCD or Nero's InCD, which lets you write files to CD-R and DVD-R/+R discs a little bit at a time instead of all at once. Unfortunately, discs made in this way aren't easily readable in other CD/DVD players.. The steps in this fix assume that you've disabled any packet-writing software and are using nothing more than the software that's built into Windows XP. Note: if you want to write data to erasable media—such as CD-RW or DVD+RW/-RW discs—you'll need third-party CD-burning software (which likely came with your drive), since XP lacks this talent.

THE ANNOYANCE: I've heard that Windows XP comes with built-in support for CD burning, but I can't make heads or tails of it. How do I make CDs without purchasing expensive add-on software?

THE FIX: Windows XP does indeed include rudimentary support for CD and DVD burners. To get started, in Windows Explorer, right-click your burner's drive icon, select Properties, choose the Recording tab, check the "Enable CD recording on this drive" box, and click OK. Insert a blank disc in your burner, and a dialog box should pop up and ask you what you want to do with the disc. Choose one of the options here, or click Cancel to banish XP's cumbersome wizard.

To make a data disc, open Windows Explorer and drag the files onto your burner's drive icon. You can create folders, rearrange or rename the files, and even delete things from the disc; nothing is permanent until you burn the disc. When you're done adding data, right-click the drive icon (or the "Files Ready to be Written to the CD" note above the file listing, if it's there), and select "Write these files to CD" (Figure 3-24).

Likewise, you can create audio CDs (as well as data CDs containing music files, such as MP3s) using the latest Windows Media Player. Open WMP

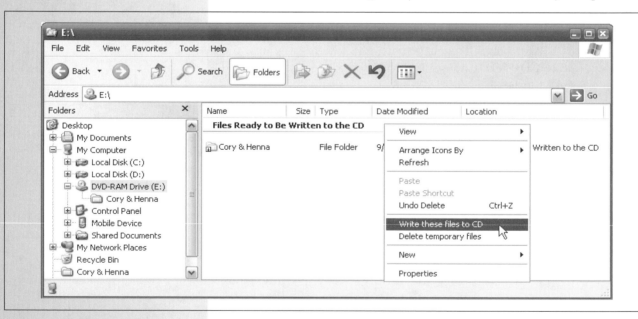

Figure 3-24. Use Windows Explorer to create basic data discs.

and click the Library tab. In the tree on the left, right-click the *My Playlists* folder, and select New. Drag and drop any music files (or tracks from the *All Music* folder in your library) into this window, and rearrange them in the desired order. When you're done, click the Start Burn button at the bottom right (and confirm that you want to save the new playlist, if you haven't done so already).

If you want more flexibility, or just a more streamlined interface, spend the bucks for a third-party application such as Roxio Easy Media Creator ($99.95, *http://www.roxio.com*) or Nero Ultra Edition ($79.99, *http://www. nero.com*). In addition to their snazzier and easier-to-use interfaces, both programs can burn many more disc formats, support disc images, and come with advanced tools to help make better audio CDs and video DVDs.

NOTE

To burn movies to DVD using Windows XP Media Center Edition, see "Burn Recorded Programs to DVD," earlier in this chapter.

Write Video to DVD

THE ANNOYANCE: I have a video I shot and stored on my PC in a *.wmv* file. I burned the file to a DVD, but it won't play in my DVD player.

THE FIX: That's because you created a data disc (a DVD-ROM). To create a DVD that will play in a set-top DVD player, you need to author a DVD-Video disc—a process that typically requires third-party software. (If you have Windows XP Media Center Edition, see "Burn Recorded Programs to DVD" for a built-in solution.)

Both Roxio Easy Media Creator ($99.95, *http://www.roxio.com*) and Nero Ultra Edition ($79.99, *http://www.nero.com*) can create movie DVDs, and many other programs (such as Ulead's VideoStudio; $99.99, *http://www. ulead.com/vs/runme.htm*) offer more advanced authoring tools. However, if your video file isn't compatible with the software package you're using, you'll have to convert your video to a different format; consult the documentation for your product for the specific requirements.

Fix DVD Playback Problems

THE ANNOYANCE: I've burned a DVD movie with dedicated authoring software, but it still won't play in my DVD player.

THE FIX: First, try a different brand of disc. Avoid the el-cheapo blank DVDs in the bargain bin at your local computer store, and instead spend the extra nickel on some brand-name discs (I've found Verbatim discs consistently reliable).

Next, make sure your standalone DVD player supports your disc format. Some older players can't read movies burned to DVD+R/RW or DVD-R/RW discs, so you may need to buy a new player, or settle for playing movies through your PC. (The format that seems to be the most widely supported is DVD+R, although your mileage may vary.)

Finally, visit your DVD burner manufacturer's web site and see if there's a firmware update. Sometimes, a firmware bug will prevent otherwise good discs, written with a good burner, from playing on a perfectly good DVD player—and that's not good.

Make Better-Sounding Music CDs

THE ANNOYANCE: The music CDs I burn sound awful. I thought this was a digital process, impervious to quality issues, but my discs sound worse than the eight-track tapes sitting on the floor of my Dodge Charger.

THE FIX: First, check your music files to make sure they sound okay, and re-rip any songs that have pops, squeaks, or any other quality problems.

CD burning is indeed a digital process, but low-quality discs commonly cause playback problems in standalone CD players (especially car stereos). As discussed in "Fix DVD Playback Problems," try a different disc brand, and make sure your CD burner's firmware is up to date.

Another cause of poor sound quality is a mismatch between the rated speed of your discs and the actual speed at which you burned your music. If, for example, you're using 4X-rated CDs in a 24X burner (or vice versa), you could have problems. Again, higher-quality media are less likely to suffer from this problem, but if all else fails, get faster CDs or a faster burner.

Fix Inconsistent Volume in Your Music

THE ANNOYANCE: When I listen to a music CD I burned, the volume of each song seems to be different.

THE FIX: This is a fact of life when you mix audio files from different sources: some songs will naturally be louder than others. Although you can edit individual audio files to change their volume levels with a program such as Sound Forge ($319.96, *http://www.sonymediasoftware.com/download/ step2.asp?DID=559*), you should avoid any process that involves resaving (and thus recompressing) your files, which lowers the quality. Your best bet is to use a CD-burning program with a "sound-leveling" feature that normalizes the volume of all the tracks as the CD is being written. As luck would have it, Windows Media Player can do this.

To use this feature, open Windows Media Player, select Tools→Options, and choose the Devices tab. Select your disc burner, click the Properties button, and choose the Quality tab. In the "Volume leveling" section, check the "Apply volume leveling to music when it is burned" box, and then click OK.

Watch DVD Movies on Your Hard Disk

THE ANNOYANCE: I ripped a DVD movie onto my laptop's hard disk so I could watch it on the airplane without having to lug around my external DVD drive. Unfortunately, Windows Media Player won't play it. Is there any way to play a movie without the original disc?

THE FIX: Windows Media Player can't play raw DVD files, but most third-party DVD player applications can. For instance, in CyberLink's PowerDVD ($39.95, *http://www.cyberlink.com*), click the little drive button and select "Open DVD File on hard disk drive." Navigate to the folder containing the ripped files, select the VIDEO_TS.VOB file, and click Open.

Back Up to CD or DVD

THE ANNOYANCE: I'd like to back up my files to CD or DVD, but MS Backup doesn't support these drives. What's the deal?

THE FIX: Microsoft Backup supports backing up to a hard disk, floppy, or tape drive, but it can't back up to CD or DVD, despite Windows XP's built-in support for CD writers. There are two workarounds.

First, select File from the "Backup destination" drop-down list, and Backup will store your data in a file on your hard disk. Then use your CD- or DVD-writing software to burn the single file to disc (see "Burn CDs for Free").

Alternatively, install packet-writing software, such as Roxio's DirectCD, which lets you write to a CD or DVD as if it were just another hard drive. Just remember that discs written in this way aren't readable on all players (whereas discs written with ordinary disc-burning software can be read just about anywhere).

View All the Files on a CD-R

THE ANNOYANCE: I burned a bunch of files onto a CD-R last week, and then burned some more files on it this morning. But when I put the disc in another computer, all I can see are the files I put on it today! Did I erase the first bunch of files?

THE FIX: Not exactly—although that's what it looks like. Every time you burn files to a disc, you're creating another "session," or track, on that disc. When you burned your last session, you may've deleted the old files when you added the latest batch of files. The good news is that—unless you erased a rewritable disc—the "deleted" files are still there, only hidden. To retrieve them, you'll need an application that can create a disc image from a single track, such as Roxio's Easy Media Creator ($99.95, *http://www.roxio.com*). Once you've created the disc image, you can either write it to another disc (by itself) or open it with IsoBuster ($25.95, free working demo, *http://www.isobuster.com*) and extract the files by dragging and dropping.

The other possibility is that you've popped the disc into an old CD-ROM drive that can't read multi-session CDs. (All CD-RW and DVD-RW/+RW drives can read multi-session discs.) In this case, there's little you can do to make the earlier sessions readable, short of borrowing another drive or replacing yours. Luckily, brand-new CD/DVD readers are cheap.

Read Stubborn Discs

THE ANNOYANCE: My CD drive works fine with some discs, but not others. Is this a problem with the discs or the drive?

THE FIX: It could be either. If it's an old drive, it may not support all the disc formats you're throwing at it. Check the drive manufacturer's web site for a firmware update that might fix the problem.

A far more most common problem is dust. Gently wipe the troublesome disc with a clean, soft, dry cloth, or barring that, your shirt. Wipe in a straight line, from the center of the disc out to the edge; don't rub in a circular motion.

If all else fails, it might be time to replace that aging drive with, say, a shiny new DVD writer.

Express CD Duplicating

THE ANNOYANCE: I installed two CD drives in my system specifically so that I could quickly copy CDs. But my CD-burning software insists on copying the files to the hard disk first, which slows down the whole process. Isn't it possible to make CD-to-CD copies directly?

THE FIX: It is, but to successfully burn a CD or DVD, your computer must supply data to your burner at a steady rate. When it can't, you get something called a *buffer underrun*—an error that indicates that your burner isn't getting data fast enough. To avoid this problem, your CD-burning software tests the speed of your CD reader; if it's not fast enough to keep up with the writing process, it will cache your CD data to your hard disk each time you copy a disc.

There are a few ways to attack this problem. First, most CD-burning software performs a speed test only once, and then saves the results of the test for future sessions. To force your software to retest your CD drive, just delete these test results. The storage location varies with the software you're using, but the data is usually in the Windows Registry. Roxio's Easy Media Creator, for example, stores this test data in the *HKEY_LOCAL_MACHINE\ SOFTWARE\Roxio\Roxio Shared\CDEngine\CDReader* branch; deleting the *CDReader* key will force the program to retest your drives.

Another approach is to lower the bar. If your CD reader can't keep up with your writer, select a slower writing speed in your burning software. Paradoxically, slowing the burn speed may speed up the overall process.

Play Stubborn Audio CDs

THE ANNOYANCE: I have a CD that supposedly has audio on it, but it won't play in my stereo CD player or on my computer.

THE FIX: The method you use to play a disc depends on how the CD was burned.

If it's a pure data disc (e.g., containing MP3 files), open Windows Explorer, navigate to your CD drive, and try opening one of the files stored on the disc. If you get an error when you double-click the file, point your browser to *http://www.filext.com*, type the filename extension (e.g., *.mp3*) into the search box, and click Go to display information about the file type.

It's also possible that you have an "enhanced CD" on your hands (sometimes called CD Plus). This is a type of disc that contains both audio tracks and computer data. In most cases, Windows Explorer will only be able to see one type of data: either the audio tracks or the computer data will show up, but never both. If only the data appears, though, you should still be able to play the audio tracks by manually opening Windows Media Player, selecting Play→DVD, VCD, or CD Audio, and then selecting the drive containing the disc. The only surefire way to access all the data on your disc is to use third-party CD burning software to create an ISO image from the disc, and then use ISO Buster (see "View All the Files on a CD-R") to extract the files from the image.

Fix Smudged DVD Subtitles

THE ANNOYANCE: I'm watching a foreign-language DVD on my laptop. The picture and sound are fine, but the subtitles are illegible.

THE FIX: This is usually caused by a video resolution that is set too low. If your display is set to 640×480 or 800×600, raise the display resolution by right-clicking an empty area of your desktop and selecting Properties. Choose the Settings tab, and move the Screen Resolution slider to at least 1024×768. Click OK and try again.

If this doesn't help, try using a different DVD player application.

Windows Media Player Quits Before Burning the CD

THE ANNOYANCE: When I try to burn music tracks to an audio CD, Windows Media Player starts putting a few tracks on the CD and then just ejects the disc, saying that there's not enough space.

THE FIX: I'll assume that your arithmetic skills are up to par and that the total length of all the tracks doesn't exceed the capacity of the CD. In this case, it's possible that other drives on your system are interfering with the CD-burning process. If more than one CD or DVD drive is connected to the same IDE controller, they can fight for system resources, with this kind problem being the result. To fix the problem, make sure that your burner is the only CD or DVD writer on the chain; if one drive is connected to the primary IDE controller, make sure that the other one is plugged into the *secondary* controller and that neither is in conflict with another device (such as the hard disk, which is typically configured as the master device).

Next, see if any other CD/DVD-burning software is installed. If there is, uninstall it and try WMP again; also, see if any updates are available for your software. Of course, you can also try burning the disc in a different program; it may be a problem solely with Windows Media Player.

Write CD Text Data to Music CDs

THE ANNOYANCE: When I play an audio CD I created with Windows Media Player, the track names don't show up on my CD player's display.

THE FIX: When burning the disc, you need to include CD Text data. Unfortunately, Windows Media Player can't do this, so you'll need a full-featured CD-burning program to use this feature; see "Write Video to DVD" for some suggestions.

The Web and Email

The Web makes our world simultaneously bigger and smaller. It's hard to imagine computing without a connection to the Internet, but it's also hard to forget all the annoyances that come along for the ride, such as pop-ups, spam, and droves of incomprehensible error messages.

Having access to the Internet opens your PC to a host of technological dangers; sometimes it's the dangers themselves that cause problems, while other times it's the programs designed to protect your PC (such as firewall software) that end up doing more harm than good. The fixes in this chapter will help you streamline your Internet experience without needlessly compromising your security.

For networking and wireless annoyances related to connecting to the Internet, see Chapter 5. For help with web-based audio and video, see Chapter 3.

THE WEB

Lock Down Internet Explorer

THE ANNOYANCE: I've heard that Internet Explorer is riddled with security holes. Has Microsoft fixed these problems? If not, why not?

THE FIX: Over the years, Microsoft has fixed dozens of security holes in Internet Explorer, and if you've been using XP's Windows Update feature regularly, you already have these patches installed. But the larger issue is IE's underlying design—and its cozy connection with the underlying operating system—which permits any web site to install software on your PC. At first, web site designers used this capability sparingly, mostly to install widgets and small helper programs to add trivial features to their pages. But it didn't take long for unscrupulous hackers and greedy corporate executives to learn how to exploit Internet Explorer's open nature, which is why we now have spyware, adware, browser hijackers, pop-ups, and other nasty surprises. Despite these problems, Microsoft has too much corporate strategy tied up in this design to change it now, which leaves you with two choices: hobble Internet Explorer by turning off the most dangerous features, or use a safer alternative such as Mozilla Firefox (more on that later).

If you want to stick with Internet Explorer for now, you can take steps to make it safer. Open the Windows Control Panel and open Internet Options (or, in IE, go to Tools→Internet Options). Choose the Security tab, select the Internet icon at the top, and then click the Custom Level button to display the Security Settings dialog box, shown in Figure 4-1.

Next, go down the list and set each of the options as shown in Table 4-1. Depending on which edition of Windows XP you have and whether or not the latest service pack is installed, some of these options may be different or missing.

Figure 4-1. Use the Security Settings window to turn off some of the more dangerous Internet Explorer features.

Table 4-1. Maximize IE security with these settings

Option	Set to
Run components not signed with Authenticode	Disable
Run components signed with Authenticode	Disable
Automatic prompting for ActiveX controls	Disable
Binary and script behaviors	Disable
Download signed ActiveX controls	Disable
Download unsigned ActiveX controls	Disable
Initialize and script ActiveX controls not marked as safe	Disable

Option	Set to
Run ActiveX controls and plug-ins	Disable
Script ActiveX controls marked safe for scripting	Disable
Automatic prompting for file downloads	Disable
File download	Enable
Font download	Prompt
Java permissions	High safety
Access data sources across domains	Disable
Allow META REFRESH	Enable
Allow scripting of Internet Explorer Webbrowser control	Disable
Allow script-initiated windows without size or position constraints	Disable
Allow web pages to use restricted protocols for active content	Disable
Display mixed content	Prompt
Don't prompt for client certificate selection when no certificates or only one certificate exists	Disable
Drag and drop or copy and paste files to/from Explorer	Disable
Installation of desktop items	Disable
Launching programs and files in an IFRAME	Disable
Navigate sub-frames across different domains	Prompt
Open files based on content, not file extension	Enable
Software channel permissions	High safety
Submit nonencrypted form data	Enable
Use Pop-up Blocker	Enable
Userdata persistence	Enable
Web sites in less privileged web content zone can navigate into this zone	Enable
Active Scripting	Disable
Allow paste operations via script	Disable
Scripting of Java applets	Enable
Logon	Prompt for username and password

Click OK when you're done changing the security settings. Next, click the "Trusted sites" icon, click the Sites button, and remove the checkmark next to the "Require server verification (https:) for all sites in this zone" option. Then type the following URLs into the "Add this Web site to the zone" field, clicking the Add button after each one:

```
http://*.update.microsoft.com
https://*.update.microsoft.com
http://*.windowsupdate.com
http://*.windowsupdate.microsoft.com
```

These four URLs permit the Windows Update feature to continue working unencumbered by your new security settings. The asterisks are wildcards, allowing these rules to apply to variants (such as *http://download.windowsupdate.com*). Feel free to add the domains for other web sites you trust, and then click OK when you're done.

Now that you see what's required to make Internet Explorer safer (albeit not bulletproof), you might be tempted to dump IE entirely in favor of a better design. If so, you're in for a treat! Mozilla Firefox, available for free from *http://www.mozilla.org*, is an open source, standards-compliant web browser that is faster, much safer, and more feature-rich than Internet Explorer. It does a better job of blocking pop-ups, has a more customizable interface, and can be enhanced with powerful extensions (see "Improve Any Web Site" for an example). We'll look at Firefox and another Mozilla offering, Mozilla Suite, in several of the annoyances in this chapter.

Turn Off Internet Explorer

THE ANNOYANCE: I've stopped using Internet Explorer completely, but the fact that it's still on my PC makes me nervous. Is there any way to uninstall it?

THE FIX: Yes and no. Since Microsoft has so much at stake with Internet Explorer, the designers of Windows have gone to great lengths to make IE appear indistinguishable and inseparable from the rest of the operating system. However, several court cases (which Microsoft lost) have forced the company to include a way to hide Internet Explorer, effectively making it appear as though it has been uninstalled without hobbling IE-dependant features such as the help system and Windows Update.

If you're using Windows XP with Service Pack 1 or later, open the Add or Remove Programs control panel, and click the "Set Program Access and Defaults" button on the left. In the "Set Program Access and Defaults" window (see Figure 4-2), you can choose a default web browser, email program, media player, and other Internet-related applications, as well as preventing unwanted programs from being used.

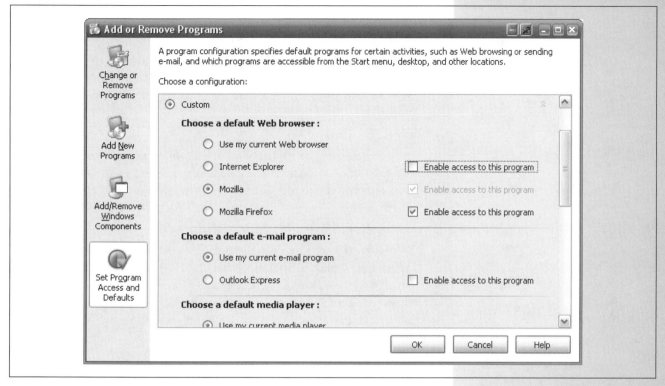

Figure 4-2. Use the "Set Program Access and Defaults" window to completely block access to Internet Explorer.

Choose the Custom option, and then click the double arrow to the right. In the "Choose a default Web browser" section, make sure your favorite web browser is selected, and then clear the "Enable access to this program" checkbox next to Internet Explorer. Click OK when you're done.

Choose a Default Browser

THE ANNOYANCE: I've dropped Internet Explorer and switched to Firefox, but IE windows still appear when I click links in email messages. How do I make those links open in Firefox automatically?

THE FIX: Make Firefox (or whatever browser is your favorite) the *default browser*, associating it with the *.htm* and *.html* file types and the HTTP and HTTPS protocols (among others).

When you install any web browser, including Firefox and even new versions of Internet Explorer, you should be given the opportunity to make the newly installed program the default. But if, for example, you didn't make Firefox the default at that time, or another program made itself the default without asking, you must change the appropriate settings.

The easiest and least-destructive method is to use the browser's own self-default settings. For example:

Mozilla Firefox
> In Mozilla Firefox, go to Tools→Options, and choose the General category. Place a checkmark next to the "Firefox should check to see if it is the default browser when starting" option, and click the Check Now button.

Mozilla Suite
> In Mozilla Suite, go to Tools→Options, open the Advanced category, and then choose System. Place checkmarks next to the file types and protocols you'd like to associate with the browser, and click OK when you're done.

Internet Explorer
> To make Internet Explorer the default browser, go to Tools→Internet Options (or Control Panel→Internet Options), and choose the Programs tab. Place a checkmark next to the "Internet Explorer should check to see whether it is the default browser" option, and click OK. Exit Internet Explorer, and then reopen it and answer Yes when asked if you want Internet Explorer to be the default.

If these steps don't work, reinstall the browser or use the "Set Program Access and Defaults" option in the Add or Remove Programs control panel, as described in "Turn Off Internet Explorer."

Fix Internet Shortcuts

THE ANNOYANCE: My newly installed browser works great, but after I installed it, the Internet Shortcuts on my desktop stopped working.

THE FIX: An Internet Shortcut is a small text file (*.url*) containing the address of a web site and some other information. (You can create an Internet Shortcut by, for example, dragging the little icon to the left of the URL in the browser's address field to the Windows desktop.) Internet Shortcut files aren't associated with any particular browser, but rather with Windows's internal protocol handler (see the "How Internet Shortcuts Work" sidebar for details).

To fix the problem, open the Control Panel, go to Folder Options, and choose the File Types tab. Select URL/Internet Shortcut from the list (ignore "(NONE)/Internet Shortcut" if you see it), and click the Advanced button. (If it's not there, click New, type url, and then click OK.)

Double-click the Open item in the Actions list (or, if Open is not there, click New and then type Open in the Action field), and type the following command into the "Application used to perform action" field:

```
rundll32.exe shdocvw.dll,OpenURL %1
```

How Internet Shortcuts Work

When you double-click an Internet Shortcut pointing to, say, *http://www.annoyances.org*, Windows Explorer sends the file to *shdocvw.dll*, which reads the file and sends the URL within to the browser associated with the HTTP protocol (i.e., your default browser).

This two-step approach means that *two* associations are needed to get Internet Shortcuts to work properly: Internet Shortcuts should point to *shdocvw.dll*, and HTTP links should point to your default browser. The reason that a simple reinstallation of your browser may not fix the broken shortcut problem is that most browsers only set themselves as the default and assume all the other pieces are in order.

The Web

Next, check the Use DDE box. Leave the DDE Message field blank, type shdocvw in the Application field, leave the DDE Application Not Running field blank, and type System in the Topic field, as shown in Figure 4-3. Click OK in all three dialog boxes to confirm your choices.

If Internet Shortcuts still don't work after this change, or if they open in the wrong browser, see "Choose a Default Browser."

Change Internet Shortcut Icons

THE ANNOYANCE: I chose Firefox as my default browser, but Internet Shortcut icons on my desktop still have the Internet Explorer logo. I'm so mad at IE for facilitating a spyware infestation on my system that I don't ever want to see that big blue "e" again!

THE FIX: Not surprisingly, Microsoft likes its IE logo, and they don't want you to change it. Good thing we don't care what Microsoft likes.

Figure 4-3. If Internet Shortcuts stop working, associate them with the shdocvw library.

You've undoubtedly discovered that changing the icon through the File Types window doesn't work—you'll have to get your hands a little dirty to customize this icon. Open the Registry Editor (go to Start→Run and type regedit), and navigate to *HKEY_CLASSES_ROOT\InternetShortcut\shellex\IconHandler*. Rename the *IconHandler* key (highlight it and press F2) to IconHandlerBackup, and then close the Registry Editor. Open the Control Panel, and go to Folder Options. Choose the File Types tab, select the "URL/Internet Shortcut" entry from the list (ignore "(NONE)/Internet Shortcut" if you see it), and click the Advanced button. Click the Change Icon button, and then click Browse to locate an *.ico*, *.dll*, or *.exe* file with the icon you want to use.

Remember Web Site Passwords

THE ANNOYANCE: I hate having to type my username and password into my favorite web sites every time I visit them. Internet Explorer sometimes prompts me to save my password, but I still have to type my username. This is idiotic; why can't IE just log me in automatically?

THE FIX: IE's password-saving feature is not very well thought-out. By default, IE won't enter anything into login forms automatically, but will only fill in your password for you once you type in your username. Although you can turn this feature on or off by going to Tools→Internet Options, choosing the Content tab, and clicking the AutoComplete button, there's nothing else you can do to customize or improve it from within IE.

The Mozilla Firefox and Mozilla Suite browsers, both freely available from *http://www.mozilla.org*, do a much better job of remembering passwords than IE. Whenever you type a password into a web form, the Mozilla browsers ask you whether or not you'd like to save the password. (You can also choose "Never for this site" to turn off the prompt for a certain site without disabling the feature altogether.) Thereafter, the Mozilla browsers will automatically fill in your username and password each time you visit a saved site's login page (Figure 4-4)—no typing necessary! You can even view and edit your saved passwords: in Firefox, go to Tools→Options→Privacy→View Saved Passwords; in Mozilla Suite, go to Tools→Password Manager. You can also set a master password to protect your stored passwords from being viewed by uninvited guests (after all, remembering one password is easier than remembering fifty).

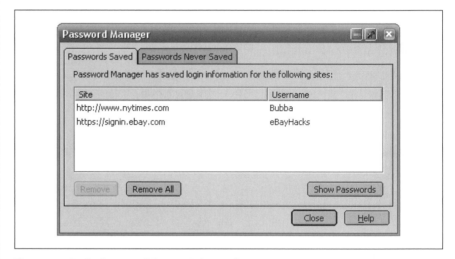

Figure 4-4. Firefox does a much better job than IE of automatically entering usernames and passwords into web forms.

Although Firefox and Mozilla Suite will do the typing for you, they won't press Enter or click the login button for you. For that, you'll need RoboForm (free, *http://www.roboform.com*). It works with IE out of the box, or with Mozilla Firefox and Mozilla Suite via a variety of special extensions. Among its many talents, RoboForm can not only remember and enter usernames and passwords automatically, but can click Login buttons for you as well. Like the Mozilla browsers, RoboForm can also automatically fill in long web forms, but it goes a step further by supporting complex JavaScript-based forms.

If RoboForm seems like overkill, try the free Google Toolbar, available for both Firefox and Internet Explorer from *http://toolbar.google.com*. It fills out forms for you—albeit without some of RoboForm's bells and whistles—but it also adds a language translator, a text field spell-checker, and, of course, quick links to Google's web search engine.

Living with Firefox in an IE World

THE ANNOYANCE: Some web sites (including Windows Update!) won't let me in because I'm using Firefox instead of Internet Explorer. But I loathe IE; I'd rather not open up my PC to spyware just to download my phone bill. What are my options?

THE FIX: Every browser has a *user agent* string—a text "signature" it sends to every web site you visit that identifies the browser name and version, and even the operating system version you're using. For example, Internet Explorer 6.0's user agent string looks like this:

```
Mozilla/4.0 (compatible; MSIE 6.0; Windows NT 5.1)
```

Firefox 1.5's looks like this:

```
Mozilla/5.0 (Windows; U; Windows NT 5.1; en-US; rv:1.7.10)
   Gecko/20050716 (No IDN) Firefox/1.5
```

If you use Firefox—or any non-IE browser, for that matter—you'll occasionally encounter a web site that won't let you in. The problem is usually caused either by lazy developers who haven't made their web sites standards-compliant, or by corporate licensing restrictions that forbid developers from supporting any non-Microsoft products. The good news is that you can fool 'em all!

The User Agent Switcher Extension for Mozilla Suite and Firefox (available for free from *http://chrispederick.com/work/useragentswitcher/*) allows both browsers to masquerade as any other browser, including Internet Explorer, Netscape 4, and even Opera. When you stumble upon an IE-only web site, just go to Tools→User Agent Switcher, and pick a browser, as shown in Figure 4-5. (Or click Options to edit the browser list or even type in a custom user agent string.)

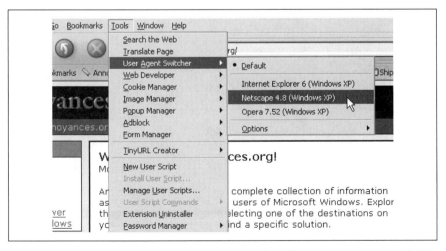

Figure 4-5. Use the User Agent Switcher to masquerade Firefox as IE to gain entry to sites that don't expressly support Firefox.

NOTE
When you find a site that doesn't work in Firefox or Mozilla Suite, send the webmaster a note and request that the site be made standards-compliant. A single email probably won't change the site owners' mind, but enough complaints may convince the webmaster to rethink the decision to support only Internet Explorer.

Of course, dressing up your browser as Internet Explorer doesn't necessarily mean the site will work like it's supposed to. Often, these sites require Internet Explorer because they employ proprietary IE features, such as ActiveX add-ons that can open the door to spyware (see "Lock Down Internet Explorer"). In these cases, you must either view the page in IE or abandon the site. If you take the former course, you'll appreciate the IE View extension for Firefox and Mozilla Suite (freely available from *http://ieview. mozdev.org*). When you encounter a site that won't work properly in Firefox, just right-click an empty area of the page and select "View This Page in IE," or right-click any link on the page and select "Open Link Target in IE."

Funny Symbols in Web Pages

THE ANNOYANCE: I see funny symbols in the text on some web pages, particularly where I'd expect to see hyphens or apostrophes. What's wrong?

THE FIX: You're viewing the site with the wrong code page. The code page is the assortment of characters your browser uses to render text, and it must match the code page that was used to create the site. Usually your browser picks the correct one automatically, but if you've previously changed the code page (or if another web site switched code pages on you), or if the web site doesn't specify the correct code page, the site won't display properly, as shown in Figure 4-6.

Figure 4-6. If a web site looks like this, you have the wrong code page selected.

In Internet Explorer, go to View→Encoding→Auto-Select. If there's already a checkmark next to Auto-Select, or if that doesn't help, go to View→Encoding→More, and choose the nationality that best matches the document you're viewing. The default code page for sites in English is *Western European (Windows)*.

In Firefox and Mozilla Suite, go to View→Character Encoding, and select *Western (ISO-8859-1)* for sites in English, or another nationalization that more closely matches the site you're viewing. If you find yourself returning to this menu often, go to View→Character Encoding→Customize to choose which code pages are displayed in the top-level menu. With either browser, some trial and error may be necessary before the site displays correctly.

Pictures Don't Show Up in Some Web Pages

THE ANNOYANCE: Recently, some icons, pictures, and photos appear to be missing from all sorts of web pages. Sure, these sites are loading faster, but porn sites aren't as much fun as they used to be.

THE FIX: There are a bunch of things that can cause this problem. First, clear your browser cache to remove any corrupt data that your browser might be using to display pages. In Internet Explorer, go to Tools→Internet Options, and in the "Temporary Internet files" section, click the Delete Files button. Check the "Delete all offline content" box, and click OK.

If you're using Firefox, go to Tools→Options, choose the Privacy category, and click the Clear button next to Cache. In Mozilla Suite, go to Edit→Preferences, choose the Advanced→Cache category, and click the Clear Cache button.

Some improperly configured firewall software—particularly Norton Internet Security and Norton Personal Firewall—can interfere with images in some web sites. Temporarily disable your firewall; if that helps, consult the firewall's documentation (specifically relating to the anti-hotlinking features) to fix the problem. (Note that neither the Windows Firewall nor most firewall-enabled routers typically exhibit this problem.)

Ad-blockers may also be suppressing content you want to see. By design, ad-blockers block images, animations, inline frames, and other content served up by certain sites, but your ad-blocker might be blocking more than just ads. Many sites also pull non-ad content from these same servers, sometimes for economic or technical reasons, but primarily in an attempt to thwart ad-blockers. Either way, turn off your ad-blocking software to see if that solves the problem.

Finally, bad proxy settings can break all sorts of things in web sites. If you're surfing from work, your employer may require you to go through a proxy server; turn it off and see if the problem stops. Likewise, if you're surfing from home and you're using a proxy server, you may have to turn it off to view sites reliably. In Internet Explorer, go to Tools→Internet Options, choose the Connections tab, and click the LAN Settings button to configure your proxy server. In Firefox, go to Tools→Options, choose the General category, and click the Connection Settings button. In Mozilla Suite, go to Edit→Preferences and choose the Advanced→Proxies category. See "Surf Anonymously for Free" for more information on proxies.

Improve Any Web Site

THE ANNOYANCE: I love Google's Gmail service, but because there's no Delete button it takes three clicks to delete unwanted messages. While I'm at it, there are some things I'd like to change about other web sites, too.

THE FIX: Use Greasemonkey to customize your favorite web sites. Greasemonkey is a free extension (available at *http://greasemonkey.mozdev.org*) for the Firefox and Mozilla Suite browsers that lets you add custom JavaScript code to any web page. The code then runs automatically as though it's part of the page itself and alters the page's appearance or changes its behavior.

By itself, Greasemonkey doesn't do much. To bring Greasemonkey to life, you must install *user scripts* that you download or write yourself. Most user scripts are designed to add features to individual web sites, but some were written to fix bugs. Visit *http://www.userscripts.org*, and you'll find plenty of gems. For instance, there's a user script that adds your requested Delete button to Gmail (see Figure 4-7); another script changes Google's image search results so thumbnails are linked to their full-size versions.

Figure 4-7. Use Greasemonkey to add features to web pages, such as this Delete button for Google's Gmail.

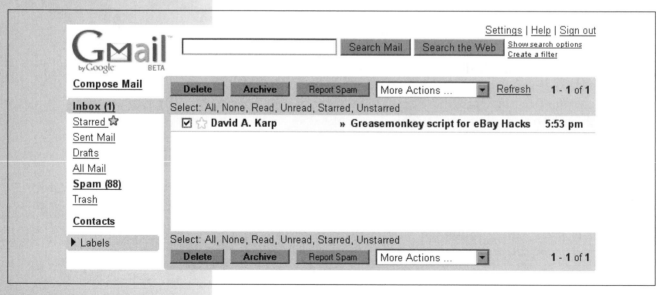

There are scripts for all sorts of web sites. In the eBay section, for instance, you'll find the "Show Only Negative Feedback" user script, which allows you to show only the complaints an eBay member has received (Figure 4-8)—something eBay won't let you do.

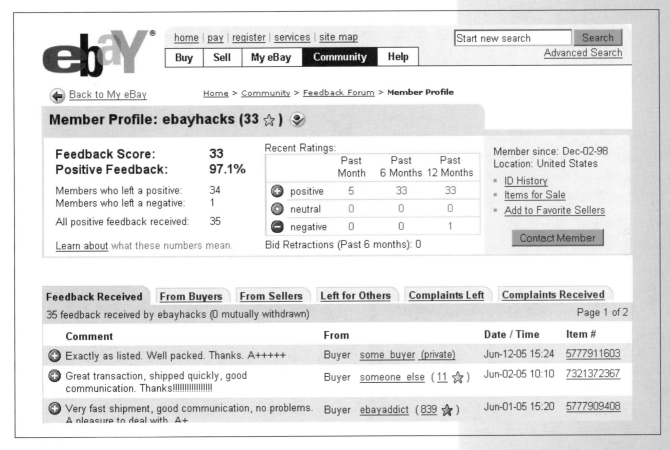

When you've found a user script you want, right-click the link to the script and select Install User Script. You can also click the link to display and examine the script in your browser, and then, if you like what you see, go to Tools→Install User Script. The script will be active immediately, but you'll have to reload any applicable pages to see the results.

Figure 4-8. Greasemonkey is also responsible for adding the Complaints Left and Complaints Received tabs to this eBay page.

Not all scripts are site-specific. The Linkifier script turns anything that looks like a URL—on any page—into an active link you can click. Similar scripts do the same thing for email addresses and even UPS and FedEx tracking numbers. The best part, though, is that with some knowledge of JavaScript, you can write your own user scripts and customize the Web to your heart's content! To get started authoring user scripts, visit *http://greasemonkey.mozdev.org/authoring.html* and pick up a copy of O'Reilly's *Greasemonkey Hacks* by Mark Pilgrim.

NOTE

Greasemonkey works only with Mozilla browsers (e.g., Firefox, Mozilla Suite, Netscape). If you're using Internet Explorer, try Trixie (http://www.bhelpuri.net/Trixie/), which runs Greasemonkey user scripts on IE. Given that nearly all Greasemonkey user scripts are written for—and tested with—Greasemonkey, there's no guarantee that they'll work as well (or at all) with Trixie and IE. But if you're stuck with IE, Trixie is your best bet.

Put an End to Pop-Ups

THE ANNOYANCE: There should be a law against pop-up advertisements. I hate having to close all those windows when I'm trying to get my work done.

THE FIX: Alas, I suspect anti-pop-up laws would be about as effective as anti-spam laws. But that doesn't mean you can't take matters into your own hands and stop the madness (more or less). In the old days, all you had to do was install a third party pop-up blocker, and you were set. Today, all major browsers come with built-in pop-up blockers (though some are better than others). The problem is that pop-ups are no longer limited to web sites, which means your anti-pop-up arsenal must grow to keep up.

To block web-based pop-ups in Internet Explorer, go to Tools→Pop-up Blocker→Turn On Pop-up Blocker. Of course, some sites use pop-up windows for purposes other than advertising, so you may decide to exclude sites from the blocker from time to time to allow their pop-ups to work. To do this, go to Tools→Pop-up Blocker→Pop-up Blocker Settings, type (or paste) the URL of the site into the "Address of Web site to allow" box, click the Add button, and click OK. Unfortunately, IE doesn't block all types of pop-ups, so a few windows may still poke through.

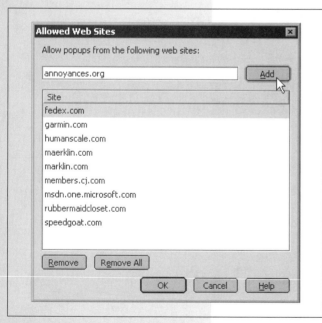

Figure 4-9. Mozilla Suite's pop-up blocker is particularly effective and makes it easy to allow pop-ups from certain sites

Both Firefox and Mozilla Suite block more types of pop-ups than Internet Explorer, but only Mozilla Suite makes it easier to add exclusions. In Mozilla Suite, go to Tools→Popup Manager→About Popup Blocking to turn on the feature. (You're also prompted to turn on the blocker the first time a web site tries to show a pop-up window.) When you want to allow a pop-up from a particular site, go to Tools→Popup Manager→Allow Popups From This Site, and click the Add button to exclude the site (see Figure 4-9).

Firefox is the only major browser to block pop-ups by default. To permit pop-ups from certain sites, go to Tools→Options, choose the Web Features category, and click the Allowed Sites button next to Block Popup Windows.

What if you have your browser configured to block pop-ups, but they're still occasionally showing up? If you see pop-ups when you're *not* surfing the Web, your PC may be infected with *spyware*, software designed to display advertisements and sometimes even monitor your surfing habits. Spyware, adware, and other types of malware (malicious software) come from some web sites, as discussed in "Lock Down Internet Explorer," and also piggyback on some downloadable applications (commonly P2P file-sharing programs and, strangely, many weather forecasting desktop applications).

Malware can be difficult to remove manually; the Add or Remove Programs control panel window is typically useless here. To get rid of these kinds of pop-ups, you'll need to install antispyware software. Among the best free antispyware tools are Spybot - Search & Destroy (*http://www.safer-networking.org*) and Ad-Aware (*http://www.lavasoft.com*). Also recommended is SpySweeper (*http://www.webroot.com*), which offers a free 30-day trial, and Microsoft's own AntiSpyware tool (*http://www.microsoft.com/downloads/*), which is free and worth a look.

> **NOTE**
>
> *Keep in mind that no antispyware program offers complete protection, so you may want to routinely scan your system with several of the antispyware tools listed here, as well as antivirus software, to keep your PC malware-free. Whatever package(s) you use, frequently run the tool's updater to make sure it's current on the latest threats.*

Stop That Browser Hijacker!

THE ANNOYANCE: I clicked a link on a web page, and I was suddenly transported to a search page I didn't recognize. The same thing happens on a bunch of different sites. Are these web sites broken, or is something else wrong?

THE FIX: Your PC is infected with a *browser hijacker*, a form of malware that redirects the links in web sites to special advertising sites that generate revenue for the person who wrote the hijacking program.

To get rid of the hijacker, use one or more of the up-to-date antispyware tools recommended in "Put an End to Pop-ups." If you don't have an antispyware program on your system, getting one after an infection can be difficult. Hijackers have a nasty sense of self-preservation and tend to block access to web sites offering antispyware tools.

One way to get around a browser hijacker is to open the Windows Control Panel. If you don't see the task pane on the left (see Figure 4-10), go to Tools→Folder Options, click "Show common tasks in folders," and click OK. (You can turn it off later by returning here and selecting "Use Windows classic folders.") In the See Also box that appears on the left, click the Windows Update link. The window that appears is a regular Internet Explorer window, but with a twist: this window is designed to download updates to Windows when IE has been disabled. It's typically unaffected by hijackers and other malware. From here, you can surf to any of the antispyware sites, download some utilities, and remove the hijacker.

> **NOTE**
>
> *If you know the exact URL of the .exe file to download, such as http://aspect1.tucows.com/files/spybotsd.14.exe, you can often get past a hijacker by typing the URL in your browser's address bar. With no links for the hijacker to redirect, the download should start right away.*

> **NOTE**
>
> *Firefox and Mozilla Suite also give you more control over JavaScript, the programming language used to facilitate most pop-ups and add some other annoying traits to web sites. To tweak the JavaScript settings in Firefox, go to Tools→ Options, choose the Web Features category, and click the Advanced button next to Enable JavaScript. In Mozilla Suite, go to Edit→Preferences→ Advanced→Scripts & Plugins. In either browser, you can prevent sites from moving or resizing windows, changing the text in the status bar, and more by simply turning off the respective options. See "Improve Any Web Site" for other ways to make sites less annoying.*

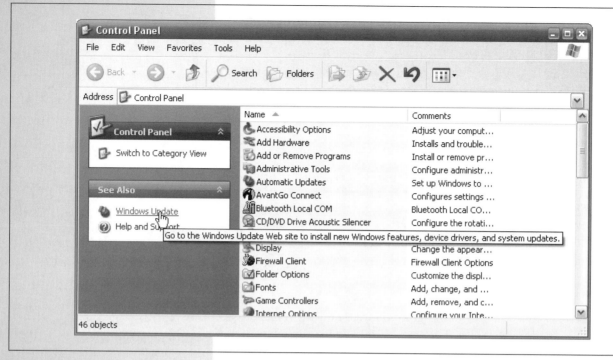

Figure 4-10. Use the Windows Update link in the Control Panel to open a safe Internet Explorer window.

Solve the Blank Form Mystery

THE ANNOYANCE: I filled out a form on a web page and clicked Submit, only to be told that there was something wrong with what I'd entered. When I clicked Back to return to the previous page, everything I typed was gone! What's wrong with the site?

THE FIX: This is caused by a bug in your web browser, and not the web site. All versions of Internet Explorer, and older releases of Netscape (Versions 4.x and earlier), are affected by this bug.

To date, no browser handles form data in previously visited pages perfectly, but there are a few workarounds.

For one, most web site designers are aware of the bug and have built their web sites accordingly. So, if you submit a form and then need to go back and change what you've typed, don't press your browser's Back button; rather, look for a Back button or Edit button right *on the page*, and click it to safely modify your text.

Next, make a habit of performing an impromptu backup *before* you submit any form. For instance, if you've written a long message, click in the text box, press Ctrl-A to highlight all the text, press Ctrl-C to copy it, open a text editor such as Notepad, and press Ctrl-V to paste it. (Repeat these steps for any long field in the form.) If you're later forced to return to the page by pressing your browser's Back button and the form is emptied as a result, you can simply paste your text back into the form.

> **NOTE**
>
> *Browsers based on the Mozilla engine, such as Firefox and Mozilla Suite, are better at saving form information, except under certain circumstances. For instance, if a form is generated on the fly, Mozilla browsers usually can't save the text you've typed into it.*

Finally, Mozilla Suite can pre-fill most types of web forms. Just before submitting a form, select Edit→Save Form Info. Then, if the form is blank when you return (or if you encounter a new form requiring similar data), select Edit→Fill in Form to restore your data.

Stop Annoying Animations

THE ANNOYANCE: The dancing hamster was cute at first, but now it's getting on my nerves. Everywhere I go on the Web, something is pulsating, flying across the screen, or playing music. How can I make this online circus stop?

THE FIX: Pressing the Esc key stops most animations, but this is a temporary fix and works only with animated *.gif* image files. If you want to permanently disable *.gif* animations altogether in Internet Explorer, go to Tools→ Internet Options, click the Advanced tab, and remove the checkmark next to the "Play animations in web pages" option (see Figure 4-11). You can also turn off sounds and videos with similar settings in the same section. Click OK when you're done.

> **NOTE**
>
> *RoboForm, which is discussed in "Remember Web Site Passwords," can also save form data, and it works with Internet Explorer and Firefox as well as Mozilla Suite.*

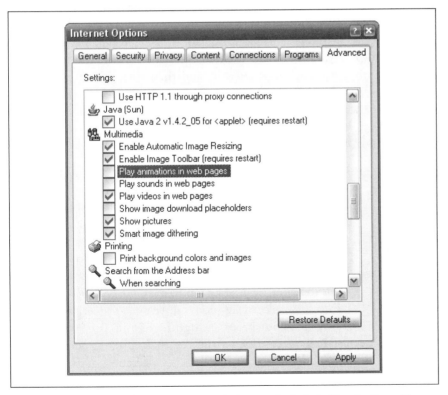

Figure 4-11. Use the Advanced tab in IE's Internet Options to selectively disable animations, videos, and sounds in web pages.

In Firefox and Mozilla Suite, type about:config into the address bar to show the staggering list of all available fine-tuning options for these browsers. Find *image.animation_mode* in the list (type something like anim in the Filter field to locate it quickly), double-click the option, and type none in the Enter String Value box. If you don't want to completely disable animations, you can type once here instead (normal is the default) to let sites play all animations only once, but never repeat (loop) them. Click OK when you're done.

Other types of animations require different strategies. If the animation, video, or sound is coming from a Java applet, the only way to stop it is to turn off Java support altogether. In Internet Explorer, go to Tools→Internet Options, click the Security tab, and click the Custom Level button. In the JavaVM section, select Disable Java, and then click OK in both boxes. In Firefox, go to Tools→Options, choose the Web Features category, remove the checkmark next to Enable Java, and click OK. In Mozilla Suite, go to Edit→Preferences, highlight the Advanced category, remove the checkmark next to Enable Java, and click OK.

JavaScript, not to be confused with Java, is often used to create flyovers (where a button or icon changes when you move the mouse over it) as well as cursor trails (the flying bits that follow your mouse pointer). To disable JavaScript in Internet Explorer, go to Tools→Internet Options, click the Security tab, and click the Custom Level button. In the Scripting→ Active scripting section, select Disable, and then click OK in both dialog boxes. In Firefox, go to Tools→Options, choose the Web Features category, remove the checkmark next to Enable JavaScript, and click OK. In Mozilla Suite, go to Edit→Preferences→Advanced→Scripts & Plug-ins, uncheck the Navigator box, and click OK.

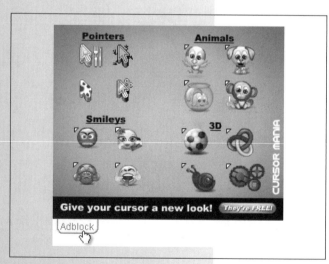

Figure 4-12. Use the Adblock Mozilla extension to hide annoying Flash animations.

Of course, none of this will disable plug-ins, such as Flash. To turn off Flash animations in Internet Explorer, you must uninstall the Flash player using Macromedia's elusive uninstaller tool, available at *http://www.macromedia.com/support/flashplayer/* (search the knowledge base for "uninstall"). But in Mozilla Firefox and Mozilla Suite, you can use the powerful Adblock extension, available for free at *http://adblock.mozdev.org,* to selectively hide animations. Once it's installed, restart your browser, and then go to Tools→Adblock→ Preferences. Open the Adblock Options menu, and if the Obj-Tabs entry doesn't have a checkmark next to it, click Obj-Tabs and then click Done. Thereafter, a little tab labeled Adblock will protrude from any Flash animation on a page (see Figure 4-12); just click the tab to show the address of the ad, and then click OK to begin blocking that particular Flash animation.

Adblock supports wildcards, so, for instance, you can block all Flash animations from a particular server, rather than having to do it manually for each one. The next time you click an Adblock tab, you'll see the address of the *.swf* file, like this:

```
http://advertising.server/ads/chipmunk.swf
```

Just replace the filename with an asterisk (∗), like this:

```
http://advertising.server/ads/*
```

to block all the files from the */ads/* folder on that server. Adblock will continue to hide these animations until you manually remove the corresponding rule from the Adblock Preferences window.

> ——— **NOTE** ———
>
> *Of course, Adblock can block all animations with the rule, *.swf. But since some sites use Flash exclusively, don't be surprised if you occasionally encounter completely blank pages.*

Open PDFs Outside the Web Browser

THE ANNOYANCE: If I double-click a PDF file on my desktop, it opens in Adobe Acrobat. But if I click a link to a PDF file on a web page, the PDF opens in my browser window instead of Acrobat. How do I get PDFs to open in Acrobat all the time?

THE FIX: When you view a PDF in a browser window, you're using an Acrobat plug-in that's installed automatically when you install Acrobat Reader (or the full version of Adobe Acrobat, for that matter). There's an option in Acrobat's Preferences dialog (go to Edit→Preferences and choose the General category in Acrobat 5.x and 6.x or the Internet category in Acrobat 7.x) called "Display PDF in Browser"; unchecking this box should disable the plug-in, but unfortunately this option often doesn't always work. In this case, you'll have to take matters into your own hands.

To bypass the plug-in, right-click links to PDF files and select Save Target As (Save Link As in Firefox or Save Link Target As in Mozilla Suite) to save them to your hard disk instead of opening them in the browser. (In Mozilla Suite, you can also hold Shift while clicking links to save their targets.)

To disable the Acrobat plug-in altogether, exit your browser, open a Search window (Start→Search→All files and folders), and, in the "All or part of the file name" field, type nppdf32. In the "Look in" list, choose Local Hard Drives, and then click the Search button. In a few minutes, you should see at least two (and possibly more) copies of the *nppdf32.dll* file. Delete all copies of *nppdf32.dll*, and close the Search window when you're done. (If you want to reinstate the plug-in, just reinstall Acrobat Reader.) The next time you click a link to a PDF file in any web page, your browser will prompt you to either save the file or open it with the default program (presumably Acrobat).

Control Tabbed Browsing

THE ANNOYANCE: I upgraded to Firefox some time ago, and while I like it, I can't say I've ever warmed up to the idea of "tabbed browsing." Every so often I open a link in a tab instead of a new window by accident, and I can't seem to close it fast enough. It's infuriating that I can't turn them off completely.

THE FIX: Some people like tabs because they reduce screen clutter, but if you like to view pages side by side, for example, tabs are just a nuisance. In Firefox, Ctrl-clicking a link opens it in a new tab, but Shift-clicking opens it in a separate window. (In Mozilla Suite, however, Ctrl-click opens new windows and Shift-click saves links.)

To disable all tabs in Firefox permanently, install the free Tab Killer extension (available at *http://extensionroom.mozdev.org/more-info/tabkiller*), and restart Firefox. Firefox will now ignore any attempts to open new tabs, instead opening links in the current window. To have Firefox open such links in new windows, go to Tools→Extensions, highlight Tab Killer, click the Options button, check the "Open new windows instead of new tabs" box, and click OK.

Conversely, Firefox users who despise the pileup of windows and will happily put up with tabs to keep the browser window tidy can install the free Single Window extension (*https://addons.mozilla.org/extensions/moreinfo. php?id=50*) or the free This Window extension (*http://extensionroom. mozdev.org/more-info/thiswindow*).

While you're at it, peruse both of these sites for dozens of other extensions that expand or tame this controversial feature. For instance, if you don't want to pick sides at all, you can install the free "Open link in..." extension (*https://addons.mozilla.org/extensions/moreinfo.php?id=379*). With this extension in place, right-clicking any link will display five different options: "Open Link in New Window," "Open Link in New Tab," "Open Link in New Background Tab," "Open Link in New Background Window," and "Open Link Here."

Faster Downloads Without the Hassle

THE ANNOYANCE: Downloading files from the Web takes forever, and sometimes the progress bar just stops! How can I kick-start downloads?

THE FIX: You need a *download manager* (sometimes called a download accelerator), a program designed to eliminate many of the inefficiencies in the download process. Unfortunately, most download managers are so cumbersome and poorly designed that you'll eat up a lot of time just setting them up before you begin each download.

One of the only decent download managers is Download Express, available for free from *http://www.metaproducts.com* (see Figure 4-13).

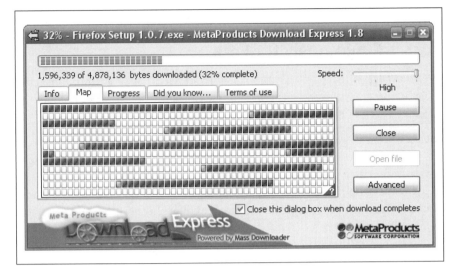

Figure 4-13. Use Download Express to accelerate downloads without filling in a page of options every time.

After installing Download Express, go to Start→All Programs→ MetaProducts Download Express→Download Express Options, and click the Integration tab. Check the "Use alternative integration method" box and click OK. (You'll need to exit and relaunch Internet Explorer for the change to take effect.)

Set Download Defaults in Mozilla Suite

THE ANNOYANCE: When I download files with Mozilla Suite, I'm often asked if I want to open the file or save it to my hard disk. Even when I check the "Always perform this action" box, Mozilla Suite keeps asking me. How can I stop this endless badgering?

THE FIX: This bug has been around for a long time in Mozilla browsers, although it was mostly fixed in Firefox. The solution is to install the free DownloadWith extension, available at *http://downloadwith.mozdev.org*, along with the Download Express download manager discussed in "Faster Downloads Without the Hassle."

Install both programs, restart Mozilla Suite, go to Edit→Preferences, and choose the DownloadWith category. Click the "Create new application" button, select MetaProducts Download Express from the list, and click OK. Then, choose the "Automatic download" tab, select the "All files" option, and choose MetaProducts Download Express from the Application drop-down list.

> **NOTE**
>
> *To integrate Download Express with Firefox and Mozilla Suite, install the MetaProducts Integration plug-in, which allows you to download any item with a right-click. Better yet, use the DownloadWith extension described in "Set Download Defaults in Mozilla Suite" to make Download Express your default downloader for any or all file types.*

NOTE

If you only want to automatically download certain file types, select "Specific files" instead of "All files." Then type a filename extension in the "File type" field, minus the dot (for example, enter zip for .zip files). Choose MetaProducts Download Express, from the Application drop-down list, and then click the Add/Update button to add your new entry to the list.

Click OK when you're done. From now on, to download a file from a web site, just click the link. Choose a folder to save the file in, and Download Express will handle the rest automatically.

Surf Anonymously for Free

THE ANNOYANCE: I visited some web site that showed my IP address and even the state where I live. This is freaking me out. How can I mask my identity when I'm on the Internet?

THE FIX: Use a proxy server to mask your IP address (and yes, your state) from the web sites you visit. As the name implies, a proxy server stands between your browser and the sites you surf, in effect "hiding" you from prying sites. Once you set up a proxy server, all information you send and receive with your browser goes through that server (email and other programs must be configured separately to use the proxy). Most large companies use their own proxy servers to help protect the data on company PCs from prying eyes, but you don't have to work at a big company to get the same protection.

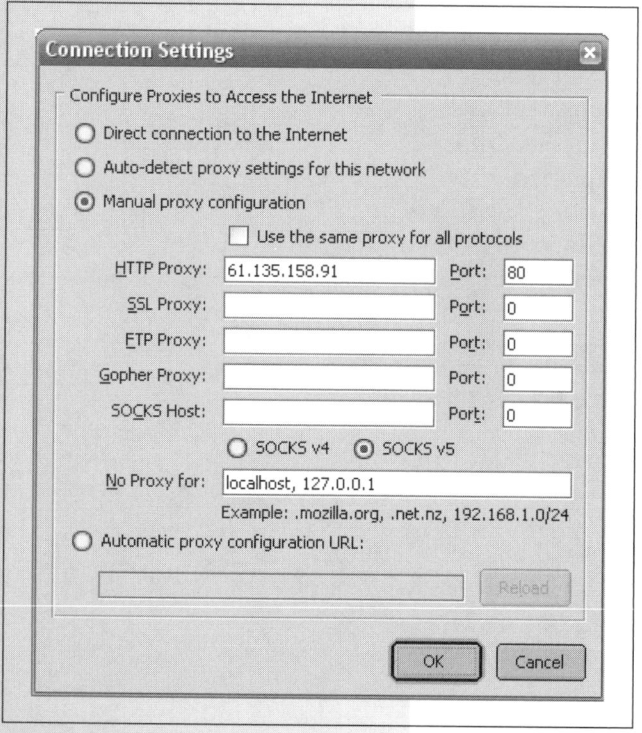

Start by visiting *http://www.annoyances.org/ip/* to view your IP address as web sites see it. Then, go to *http://www.proxy4free.com*, click "page 1" in the list on the left, and find any server marked "anonymous." Highlight its IP address and press Ctrl-C to copy it to the clipboard; also note the port number shown in the adjacent column. Next, configure your browser to use that proxy server.

If you're using Internet Explorer, go to Tools→Internet Options, choose the Connections tab, and click the LAN Settings button. Check the "Use a proxy server for your LAN" box, and then press Ctrl-V to paste the IP address into the Address field. Type the appropriate port number (usually 80 or 8080) into the Port field, and click OK when you're done.

The procedure is pretty much the same for other browsers. If you're using Firefox, go to Tools→Options, choose the General category, click the Connection Settings tab, and select "Manual proxy configuration" (see Figure 4-14). If you're using Mozilla Suite, go to Edit→Preferences→Advanced→Proxies, and select "Manual proxy configuration."

Figure 4-14. Configure a proxy server in your web browser to mask your IP address from prying web sites.

Now, go back to *http://www.annoyances.org/ip/*, and notice that your IP address has changed! (If you can't load the page, the proxy server is down; just choose another proxy server from Proxy 4 Free and try again.) From here on, until you disable the proxy, every site you visit will see your proxy server's IP address instead of yours.

What Can They Find Out About You?

Your IP address is sent to every web site you visit. While no one can determine your exact street address *directly* from your IP address, there are ways to infer this information with elaborate tracking schemes. Think of your IP address as a serial number, a unique identifier some web sites can use to identify you when you visit.

For instance, let's say you make a purchase from an online store that sells toasters. As soon as you pay for that new four-slicer, the store records your name, street address, credit card information, and IP address. Provided the toaster store keeps your private information private (and presuming its database isn't hacked into), you've got nothing to worry about. But can you say the same thing for that other site where you just signed up for a contest giving away free iPods?

This is where advertising comes in. Most ads on many web sites originate from only a handful of companies, and those companies track who's looking at their ads, even when you don't click them. If you view a page at a news web site that displays a banner ad hosted by, say, Adknowledge.com or Targetnet.com, and then you sign up to win a free iPod on another site that has another ad from the same agency, that ad server knows you've visited both sites. What's more, if the ad agency is in cahoots with the people who are giving away the iPods, they now have your email address, street address, shoe size, and anything else you typed into the sweepstakes signup page.

Now, most folks have dynamic IP addresses, which change every time they start a connection—but these connections can remain active all day (or, with a router, for

weeks at a time), which means your IP address can be used to track quite a bit of your online activity. What's more, many unscrupulous sites use so-called *tracking cookies* to do the same thing, tagging your PC with a unique serial number that can be read as you visit different sites.

So, how can you stop the snooping? Most antispyware software (see "Put an End to Pop-ups") is designed to scan your system and delete any tracking cookies it finds, but you may want to take it one step further and configure your browser not to accept any cookies from these sites. You can get a list of known tracking sites from *http://www3.ca.com/securityadvisor/pest/browse. aspx?cat=Tracking%20Cookie*. (If this feels like overkill, block only those sites responsible for the cookies your antispyware software finds on your PC.) To block cookies in Internet Explorer, go to Tools→Internet Options, choose the Privacy tab, and click the Sites button. In Firefox, go to Tools→Options, choose the Privacy category, expand the Cookies section, and then click the Exceptions button. In Mozilla Suite, go to Tools→Cookie Manager→Manage Stored Cookies.

Next, install ad-blocking software such as the Adblock extension described in "Stop Annoying Animations," and use a proxy server to mask your IP address as described in "Surf Anonymously for Free." Finally, get yourself a router, if you don't have one already, to protect your PC from other types of intrusions (see Chapter 5). For more strategies, pick up O'Reilly's *Computer Privacy Annoyances* by Dan Tynan and *PC Pest Control* by Preston Gralla.

Every byte of data you send and receive with your web browser will be sent through the proxy server. Unless you know—and trust—whoever is hosting that server, you should always disable the proxy before sending sensitive information (e.g., your home address, credit card details, etc.).

If setting up a proxy server sounds like overkill but you'd like to have protection on the odd occasions when you visit a site that you suspect may be harvesting information about you, an alternative is to use a free, single-serving proxy server, such as Proxify (*http://www.proxify.com*), The Cloak (*http://www.the-cloak.com/login.html*), or Anonymizer (*http://www.anonymizer.com*). Just type or paste the URL of the site you want to visit into the text box on any of these pages (at the Anonymizer site it's the Private Surfing box

NOTE

Anonymizer also has a free Privacy Toolbar (for Internet Explorer only, unfortunately), which does much the same thing as the web-based Anonymizer, albeit with a slicker interface.

in the upper-right corner), and press Enter. The proxy site will load up the page, allowing you to surf anonymously for this session. Click links in the page to continue surfing anonymously, or use your browser's address bar, bookmarks, or Internet Shortcuts to return to normal, non-proxy surfing.

If you want more flexibility than web-based proxies can offer, try Anonymizer's $29.95-per-year Anonymous Surfing tool or the $9.95 Anonymous Browsing Toolbar 3.3 (*http://www.amplusnet.com*). These programs, which run on your PC, perform pretty much the same function as the web-based proxies discussed above, but with more features and speed. All things considered, these software-based proxies are probably marginally safer than anonymous proxies and less of a hassle than web-based proxies.

Now, you might be thinking, why not just use a router? Well, routers—discussed in Chapter 5—offer terrific firewall production and indeed act as a layer between your PC and the rest of the Web. But when you surf from behind a router, web sites see your router's IP address, and thus can still collect all the same information about you and your geographical location. (See the "What Can They Find Out About You?" sidebar on the previous page for details.)

EMAIL

Pick the Default Email Program

THE ANNOYANCE: I use Eudora to read my email, but Outlook appears at the top of my Start menu. Can I put Eudora here instead, or does Microsoft want me to switch to Outlook?

THE FIX: Well, yes, Microsoft does want you to switch to Outlook. And they want you to use Word and Internet Explorer, rather than WordPerfect and Firefox. If they had their way, you'd be brushing your teeth with Microsoft Toothpaste. The good news is that you can have it *your way*; Sinatra would be proud.

To change the program that appears in your Start menu, right-click the Start button, select Properties, and choose the Start Menu tab. Make sure the "Start menu" option is selected, click the Customize button, and choose the General tab. Pick the desired program from the drop-down Email list in the "Show on Start Menu" section (see Figure 4-15), and click OK. (You can also remove the entry entirely by clearing the checkbox next to "E-mail.")

But the Start menu entry is only a small piece of the puzzle. What's particularly important is the *default* email program—the program that opens automatically when you click a *mailto:* link in a web page or email a file from within another application. To make your favorite email program the default, open the Internet Options control panel, click the Programs tab, and choose your program from the drop-down Email list. If you don't see your favorite email program here, see the "Add or Remove Email Clients" sidebar.

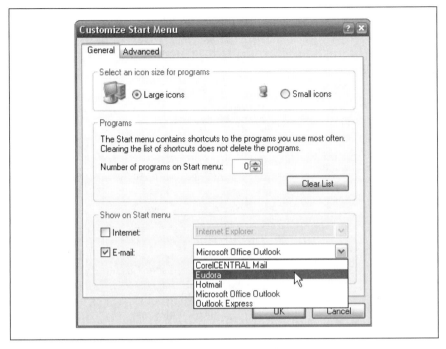

Figure 4-15. Choose your favorite email program to appear in the Start menu.

Stop Spam

THE ANNOYANCE: I downloaded my email this morning. Of the 873 messages in my inbox, only 4 were actually for me (my thinning hair and waning sex drive notwithstanding). Where are the other 869 messages coming from, and how do I stop them?

THE FIX: There is no perfect solution to the spam problem. Either you live with some junk mail in your inbox, or you employ a spam filter that occasionally deletes valid messages. Fortunately, a handful of steps can reduce your exposure to spam.

First, don't post your email address on web sites, in public forums, or in the backs of computer books. If you've already done this, you're already on every spam list on the planet.

If you're already getting tons of spam, now's the time to change your email address. Get your own domain name and create a bunch of different addresses for different purposes, such as *shopping@mydomain.com* for online shopping, *auctions@mydomain.com* for buying and selling on eBay,

Add or Remove Email Clients

If your favorite email program doesn't appear in either of the email client lists described in "Pick the Default Email Program," it doesn't mean that Microsoft specifically excluded it. Rather, it means that your application or email web site isn't properly registered with Windows.

The easiest way to fix the problem is to reinstall the program in question; if that doesn't help, check the vendor's web site for an update that fixes this problem.

If your program still doesn't show up, or if there are entries in the list you could do without, you can edit the list in the Windows Registry manually. Open the Registry Editor (go to Start→Run and type regedit) and navigate to *HKEY_LOCAL_MACHINE\SOFTWARE\Clients\Mail*. Here, you'll find a separate subkey for each program; to remove an entry from the list, just delete the corresponding subkey.

Adding entries is a little more involved. For starters, get the Gmail template I created for this task, available at *http://www.annoyances.org/downloads/gmail.reg*, and save it to your desktop. Double-click *gmail.reg*, click the Run button if asked, and then click Yes. A message will note that the Registry has been updated with this information. Now open the Registry Editor to view the new entry, located at *HKEY_LOCAL_MACHINE\SOFTWARE\Clients\Mail\Gmail*.

You can rename the Gmail key to whatever you like. To change the title that appears in Windows's Email list, double-click the (Default) value in the right pane, change the text in the "Value data" field, and click OK.

Next, go to *HKEY_LOCAL_MACHINE\SOFTWARE\Clients\Mail\Gmail\shell\open\command*, double-click the *(Default)* value in the right pane, and change the address of the program in the "Value data" field. If it's an application on your hard disk, type (or paste) the full path and filename of the program's *.exe* file (e.g., c:\Program Files\AcmeMail\acme.exe). If it's a web site, type the .exe filename of your browser, followed by the appropriate parameter (if any) and then the URL of the site. For example, if you're using Internet Explorer, type:

```
iexplore.exe -nohome http://gmail.com
```

If you're using Firefox, type:

```
c:\program files\firefox\firefox.exe http://gmail.com
```

If you're using Mozilla Suite, type:

```
c:\program files\mozilla\mozilla.exe -url http://gmail.com
```

Finally, set up your new Registry entry to respond to *mailto:* links you click in web pages. In this example, navigate to *HKEY_LOCAL_MACHINE\SOFTWARE\Clients\Mail\Gmail\Protocols\mailto\shell\open\command*, and double-click the *(Default)* value in the right pane. In the "Value data" field, type the address of the program or your web-based email site. This time, you'll need to add the %1 parameter so that Windows can pass the email addresses you click to your email program. Check the documentation for your program or email site for the correct syntax, but for programs it should look something like this:

```
c:\Program Files\AcmeMail\acme.exe /m %1
```

and for a web site (such as Gmail), you should type something like this:

```
iexplore.exe -nohome https://mail.google.com/mail/
?view=cm&tearoff=1&fs=1&to=%1
```

When you're done, test it out by clicking the Email entry in your Start menu and any *mailto:* link in a web page. If you run into trouble, just search Google for the word "mailto" and the name of your program (or email web site). You should find the information you need.

subscriptions@mydomain.com for newsletters, and *personal@mydomain.com* for personal correspondence, and have them all go to the same inbox. That way, if one of your addresses makes its way onto a spam list, you can take down the address without disrupting the email to your other accounts. Better yet, create a new email address for every site you visit, such as *amazon@mydomain.com*, *ebay@mydomain.com*, *nytimes@mydomain.com*, and *annoyances@mydomain.com*. That way, if an address starts getting spam, you'll know who sold you out.

Once you've got a "clean" email address, turn off image fetching for HTML messages in your email software. Some email messages have embedded pictures (as opposed to attachments); when you view one of these messages, your email program fetches the picture from the server, and that server records the event. (And voilà, your email address has been captured.) If you turn off image fetching, those servers are never notified, and you'll stay off more spam lists. Here's how to turn it off:

Microsoft Outlook

Go to Tools→Options, choose the Security tab, and, under Download Pictures, click Change Automatic Download Settings. Place a checkmark next to the "Don't download pictures or other content automatically in HTML e-mail" option, and then click OK in both boxes.

Microsoft Outlook Express

Go to Tools→Options, choose the Security tab, and, under Download Images, check the "Block images and other external content in HTML e-mail" box. Then click OK.

Eudora

Go to Tools→Options, and choose the Display category. Remove the checkmark next to the "Automatically download HTML graphics" option, and click OK.

Mozilla Thunderbird

Go to Tools→Options, and choose the Advanced→Privacy category. Select the "Block loading of remote images in mail messages" option, and click OK.

Next, install an independent, *passive* spam filter—one that marks potential spam as **Spam** instead of deleting it—such as SpamPal (free, *http://www. spampal.org*). Then configure your email program's filter to send all email containing the text **Spam** in the subject line to the Junk or Trash mailbox. That way, you can get the spam out of your face, but later peruse your Junk mailbox for valid messages before purging it.

Most email programs (e.g., Outlook, Thunderbird, and Eudora) have built-in spam filters that can likewise route spam into the trash, but third-party programs such as SpamPal are more configurable and update their spam lists and definitions frequently. Note: SpamPal works with any POP3- or IMAP4-based email program, which means it *doesn't* work with AOL or with web-based mail systems such as Gmail.

If your spam situation is particularly bad, and passive spam filters aren't cutting it, there are more drastic options. First, contact your ISP and request that they employ a server-based spam filter such as Postini (*http://www. postini.com*). The downside: some valid mail may never make it to your inbox.

> **NOTE**
>
> *All spam filters rely on up-to-date lists and definitions to block spam effectively, so make sure your spam filters are kept current. If you're using Outlook, you can get spam filter updates from http://office.microsoft. com/en-us/officeupdate/. Some other email programs, such as Eudora, include updates only with subsequent versions of the software; check your documentation for details.*

NOTE

If you're running an online business, think twice before you deploy one of these aggressive spam filters. The last thing you want is a spam filter deleting your customers' emails! And eBay users take note: spam filters are the number-one cause of negative feedback for both buyers and sellers.

You can also employ a more aggressive *interactive* spam filter, such as Cloudmark Desktop (*http://www.cloudmark.com*), which won't allow any email to reach your inbox unless the sender is on an approved-senders list. (Many ISPs, such as Earthlink, offer this type of service as well.) If a non-approved sender tries to send you a message, the program sends back an email requesting that the sender fill out a web form. This not only trips up spam (which is sent by machines), but lets you reject humans with whom you'd rather not correspond. Of course, you can also easily add any sender to your approved list. This approach can turn a flood of spam into a trickle, but it won't ever let through valid automated messages, such as newsletters, registration codes you've paid for, or order confirmation emails from online merchants. Also, these types of filters won't stop spoofed messages, wherein the sender is made to look like someone likely to be on your approved list (such as another user in your domain).

Don't Phall for Phishing

THE ANNOYANCE: I got a message from eBay telling me that my account would be suspended if I didn't update my information. When I got a nearly identical message from Wells Fargo, I got suspicious, seeing as I don't have a Wells Fargo account. What's the story?

THE FIX: Those messages aren't from eBay or Wells Fargo; they're spam. But unlike come-ons for weight loss and real estate schemes, this spam tries to trick you into revealing personal information.

The practice is called "phishing" (not to be confused with the musical group, Phish), and it works like this: you get an email that looks authentic (known as a *spoof*), and you're encouraged to click a link in the message. The link takes you to a web site that *looks* like eBay (or Wells Fargo, or whatever), where you're asked to log in. Type your username and password, and you'll unwittingly send your login information to the online thieves who created the fake site. Of course, your password isn't enough; often, you're asked to supply your credit card number, Social Security Number, mother's maiden name, and anything else they've thought of.

To avoid this trap, recognize the red flags. First, no reputable company will ever ask you to "verify" your information, and while many sites ask you to log in to access your account, you should never do so after following a link in an email. Instead, use a trusted bookmark or just type the URL into your browser's address bar by hand. Always examine your browser's address bar to make sure you're at a legitimate site, especially if you're about to type sensitive information into a web form. If you're not comfortable simply discarding the message, contact the company and ask if the email is legitimate.

Second, inspect any URLs in the message. Pass your mouse pointer over the link, and the address should pop up (assuming your email program supports this). Odds are you won't see something like *http://www.ebay. com*, but rather a long arcane URL with lots of symbols, or a numeric web address like *http://168.143.113.54*. This is a sure sign that you've gotten a phishing email destined for the circular file!

> **NOTE**
>
> *To further scrutinize a suspicious email, right-click the message body and select View Source to view the HTML source code of the message. Search for "http," and you'll find the real URLs tied to the links in the message.*

If you've configured your browser to save your login information (see "Remember Web Site Passwords"), you'll know you're not looking at the real site if your browser doesn't fill out the form for you; browsers save passwords for specific URLs, and your PC can tell the real thing even if you can't.

Finally, you can switch to an email program such as Eudora that warns you of potential spoof emails. When you get a message asking you to verify your account, for instance, Eudora will examine the URL inside the message and display a warning message (see Figure 4-16) if it suspects phishing.

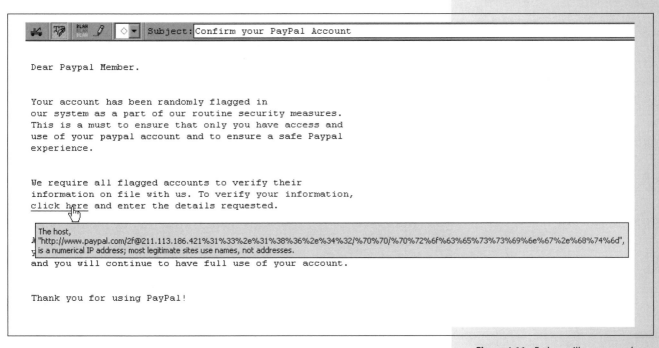

Figure 4-16. Eudora will warn you when you're looking at a message that appears to have been spoofed.

Send Large Files

THE ANNOYANCE: After several painful experiences, I've finally learned my lesson about sending large email attachments. But I really need to send photos of my newborn daughter to my family, and I don't know any other way.

THE FIX: Clogging your relatives' inboxes with 20 megabytes' worth of attachments is definitely a faux pas. Do it twice, and they may configure their spam filters to automatically dump all your emails in the trash.

If you want to share lots of photos, the best approach is to put the files on a web server somewhere, and then send out an email with the server's URL. Your message will go out in a flash, your recipients won't have any trouble opening it, and they'll be able to download the files they want at their leisure. If you have your own web space (often provided free by your ISP), you can FTP your files to the server, and then send your friends an address like this:

```
http://www.my-isp.net/~myusername/DSCN0165.JPG
```

where *my-isp.net* is your ISP's web site, *myusername* is your username, and *DSCN0165.JPG* is the name of a file you want to share. Contact your ISP for details.

Unfortunately, your ISP probably isn't interested in helping you host (and have your friends download) gigabytes' worth of data. If you don't have web space, or if your ISP restricts the types or size of files you can upload to it, visit YouSendIt (*http://www.yousendit.com*). You can upload any type of file to YouSendIt's servers, and they'll automatically email your recipients a link to your files. Your files are deleted after 7 days or 25 downloads, whichever occurs first. YouSendIt is free, requires no registration, and permits sharing of files up to 1 GB in size!

If you're only sharing photos, you have quite a few more options. For example, you can send your photos to a free photo printing/sharing service such as Shutterfly (*http://www.shutterfly.com*), DotPhoto (*http://www.dotphoto.com*), Flickr (*http://flickr.com*), or Kodak Gallery (*http://kodakgallery.com*). Anyone with whom you choose to share your albums can view your photos one at a time, or as pages of thumbnails; they can even order prints for scarcely more money than it costs to print them at home.

If you want your pals to be able to download the full-resolution pictures (something most printing services won't allow), send your photos to Putfile (*http://www.putfile.com*). After uploading your photos, Putfile supplies a URL to the files that you can send in an email. PutFile even generates HTML code you can reference on a web page, all for free.

NOTE

If you just need to send a few snapshots, emailing them is fine... as long you shrink them down first. Your 8-megapixel digital camera creates 4-MB files, but your friends don't need full-resolution photos unless they're going to print them. You can use Microsoft's free Image Resizer utility (see "Quickly Shrink Many Photos" in Chapter 3) to make your image files smaller before you email them. The total size of all the files you send should never be more than 400–500 KB.

Receive All Types of Attachments

THE ANNOYANCE: My clients email me attachments, and I can usually open them without a problem. But the other day, I received this message where the attachment should have been: "Outlook blocked access to the following potentially unsafe attachments: product list.mdb."

THE FIX: By default, Microsoft Outlook won't allow you to send or receive certain types of attachments, such as *.mdb* and *.exe* files; instead, you'll just get that error message. The rationale is that these files can contain viruses or other harmful code, but the fact that Outlook doesn't let you easily disable or at least customize this feature is just plain stupid. What's even more ridiculous is that Word (*.doc*) files, which are one of the most common transports of viruses, *aren't* blocked by default.

The simple fix is to have the sender resend the file, but with a different filename extension. (Better yet, have him zip up files to get them past the blocker, and make them smaller to boot.) I know what you're thinking: how secure is my system if Outlook can be so easily fooled by renaming *product list.mdb* to *product list.mda*? The answer: it isn't doing a good job, which is why spyware and viruses remain such a monumental problem in the PC world.

But what if the sender can't be reached, and you need the file right away? Or what if you need to be able to receive *.mdb* attachments every week?

To change the way Outlook works, you'll need to fiddle with the Windows Registry. Close Outlook and open the Registry Editor (go to Start→Run and type regedit). If you're using Office XP/2002, expand the branches to *HKEY_CURRENT_USER\Software\Microsoft\Office\10.0\Outlook\Security*. If you're using Office 2003, expand the branches to *HKEY_CURRENT_USER\Software\Microsoft\Office\11.0\Outlook\Security*.

Next, create a new string value by selecting Edit→New→String Value. In the right pane, type Level1Remove for the name of the new value. Double-click the new Level1Remove value to edit it, and type the filename extensions you'd like Outlook to allow in the "Value data" box. Extensions should be typed in lowercase, without the leading dots (.), and separated by semicolons (;). For example, type:

```
exe;mdb;vbs
```

to allow *.exe*, *.mdb*, and *.vbs* attachments, respectively. Click OK and then close the Registry Editor when you're done.

Now, restart Outlook and open that email with the error message. You should now be able to open those previously blocked attachments. (If an attachment is still blocked, you likely got the filename extension wrong.)

NOTE

Of course, receiving all attachments means you'll now be able to get potentially harmful files via email. Even though the majority of viruses are actually contained in files Outlook doesn't block by default, such as .zip files, exercise caution when opening any files you subsequently receive. Certainly make sure to scan all incoming attachments manually with your antivirus program, or, if you don't trust yourself to remember, have your antivirus program automatically scan all incoming files. When in doubt, contact the sender to make sure they actually sent you the attachment in question before you open it.

Hide Old Email Recipients

THE ANNOYANCE: When I start to type the name of a recipient in an outgoing email message, my email program shows me a long list of matching names and addresses. Where did all these names come from, and how can I clean out the list?

THE FIX: Email programs build these lists by culling names you've typed previously, names of people in your In and Out mailboxes, and names in your address book. Unfortunately, this can include misspelled and obsolete names as well as valid ones.

To remove a single name or address from the history list in Outlook or Eudora, type the first few letters and, when the history list appears, highlight the errant entry (see Figure 4-17) and press the Delete key.

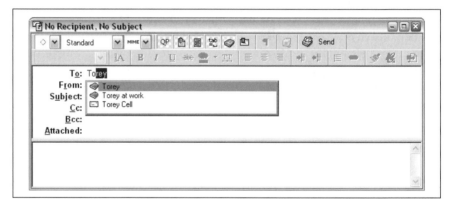

Figure 4-17. You can delete individual entries from your email program's history list.

You can also disable the history list completely. In Outlook, go to Tools→ Options, choose the Preferences tab, click the E-mail Options button, and then click the Advanced E-mail Options button. Uncheck the "Suggest names while completing To, cc, and bcc fields" box, and click OK in each dialog box.

In Eudora, go to Tools→Options, choose the Auto-completion category, and uncheck the boxes next to all the options under the "Auto-complete items in recipient fields with data from" heading. If you don't want to disable the feature but you want to make it harder to accidentally select the wrong name, check the "Don't auto-complete, just list matches" box and click OK when you're done.

Back Up Stored Email

THE ANNOYANCE: Ever since my hard disk crashed last year, I've been paranoid about backing up my important data. Most of my files are easy enough to find in the *My Documents* folder, but I'll be darned if I can figure out where my email is located.

THE FIX: Backing up your email is as simple as making copies of the mailbox files. Their locations depend on the email software you're using.

Eudora typically stores its email in either the application folder (usually *\Program Files\Qualcomm\Eudora*) or your user data folder (*\Documents and Settings\{username}\Application Data\Qualcomm\Eudora*). Each mailbox is stored in two files: messages are stored in a plain-text *.mbx* file, and a corresponding "table of contents" is stored in a binary *.toc* file. So, to back up your Out mailbox, you'd need to copy both *out.mbx* and *out.toc*. Mailboxes in folders are stored in actual folders (e.g., *Business.fol* contains the *.mbx* and *.toc* files for your *Business* folder). Your best bet is to back up the entire *Eudora* folder and all of its subfolders, which will catch all your email, your address book, your personalities, and all your account settings.

Outlook, on the other hand, stores all your email, contacts, and even your calendar in a single binary *.pst* file located in your *\Documents and Settings\ {username}\Local Settings\Application Data\Microsoft\Outlook* folder. (The exception is Outlook in a networking environment using Exchange Server, where your *.pst* file is stored on a file server somewhere; in this case, contact your administrator for help.)

> **NOTE**
>
> *Since all of Outlook's data is bundled up in such a tidy package, there's no simple way to merge it with the Outlook data on another computer (say, if you quit your job and wanted to take your email home). Of course, you can overwrite one .pst file with another, but then you'll lose all your email on the target system. One solution is the Message Vault ($49, http://www.comaxis. com/mv.htm), which, among other things, can extract the mailboxes from a .pst file and export them to Eudora .mbx files. Also available is Microsoft's own Personal Folders Backup add-in for Outlook 2003, freely available from http://www.microsoft.com/downloads/.*

If you're using Outlook Express, your email is stored in separate *.dbx* files—one for each mailbox—in the *\Documents and Settings\{username}\ Local Settings\Application Data\Identities\{some long string of characters}\ Microsoft\Outlook Express* folder. Just back up the entire folder, and you're set.

> **NOTE**
>
> *Eudora's .mbx files share the same format as Unix mailbox files, so if you want to import a few years' worth of mail you've been reading with Pine, it's as simple as FTPing the file into your Eudora folder (in ASCII mode) and renaming the file with the .mbx extension. Restart Eudora, and the imported mailbox will show up in the Mailbox menu!*

Email Long URLs

THE ANNOYANCE: Whenever I send an email containing a long web address, my recipient complains that it doesn't work. I finally realized that the long address was being broken apart somewhere along the way, but it's a hassle telling people that they need to reassemble broken URLs.

THE FIX: You've discovered the evils of word wrap. Your typical computer displays lines 80 characters wide. If you send someone a mondo URL, her email program will break it up into separate lines.

Since email vendors have yet to fix this glitch, one neat fix is to shrink the URL before you send it. For example, TinyURL (*http://tinyurl.com*) can take any horrendously long URL, such as:

```
http://maps.google.com/maps?ll=37.826870,122.422682&spn=0.007197,0.009
112&t=k&hl=en
```

and turn it into a tidy, easy-to-email URL like:

```
http://tinyurl.com/cfpmc
```

TinyURL is fast and free, and the URLs it makes never expire. Also available is SnipURL (*http://www.snipurl.com*), which does pretty much the same thing but adds tracking features.

So, what do you do when someone *sends* you a long URL? Well, you can highlight it, copy it to the clipboard (Ctrl-C), and then paste it into Notepad (Ctrl-V), where you can then proceed to manually reassemble the URL onto one line. (Take care to remove extraneous characters, such as spaces and punctuation, while leaving in the stuff that belongs.) Then, copy it again and paste it back into your web browser's address bar. Or, if you're using Firefox or Mozilla Suite, you can streamline this process with the free Open Long URL extension (*https://addons.mozilla.org/extensions/moreinfo.php?application=firefox&id=132*). Install the extension, restart your browser, and then select File→Open Long URL. Paste the long, broken URL into the box and click OK, and the extension will reassemble the URL for you and open the page. See? Much easier than fixing our email software.

NOTE

Find yourself making TinyURLs often? For a shortcut, just go to http://tinyurl.com/#toolbar, and drag the TinyURL! link onto your browser's Links toolbar. Thereafter, just click the button to create a TinyURL from the current page.

If you use Firefox, try the free TinyURL Creator (https://update.mozilla.org/extensions/moreinfo.php?id=126, or better yet, http://tinyurl.com/574q9). To use the tool, right-click an empty area of the current page and select "Create Tiny URL for this Page." A shortened URL is created on the spot and copied to the clipboard for your immediate use.

Wireless and Networking

5

A network connects two or more computers, allowing users to exchange files, collaborate on projects, share printers, share an Internet connection, and more. All you need to set up a network is a broadband connection (for the Internet part), one or two hundred dollars' worth of equipment, and a little patience. But wait... it gets better. You don't even have to rip apart the walls to lay cable. If you're ready to cut the proverbial cord, you can build a wireless network (or expand your existing wired setup with wireless technology) and surf the Internet from your back porch.

That's the good news. The bad news is that while setting up home networks isn't too difficult, you'll likely face a whole slew of annoyances as you attempt to share your Internet connection, printers, drives, and folders. Of course, you'll also need to tackle knotty logon, password, and security issues with your network. Ready? Let's dig in....

Network Two Computers

THE ANNOYANCE: I want to set up a home network, but I can't figure out what I need to make it work. I thought *Gosford Park* was confusing, but this is ridiculous!

THE FIX: Well, to start with you need at least two computers, and a way to connect them. If you're assembling a wired Ethernet network, you're in luck: almost every PC manufactured after 1998 or so has a built-in Ethernet Network Interface Card (NIC). (Many newer PCs—and nearly all laptops produced after 2003—also include wireless cards.)

For the most part, network cables have gone the way of the dinosaur, because of the convenience offered by wireless networking. But cables still offer a fast, hassle-free connection that's susceptible to neither interference (see "Increase Range and Improve Reception") nor intruders (see "Surf Safely at the Coffee Shop"). If you decide to go the cable route, you'll need category-5 *patch* cables to connect each PC to your router. (If you're setting up a wireless network, you'll also need one of these cables to connect the wireless router to your DSL or cable modem, as discussed later in this chapter.) Or, for a quick-and-dirty two-PC network without a router, a single category-5 *crossover* cable will do in a pinch.

Of course, you'll also need a router, which serves as a hub for the aforementioned cables. (If you want to connect any computers wirelessly, you'll need to get a wireless router that includes a built-in access point.) Routers let you share an Internet connection among any number of computers, and even offer protection from the outside world by way of a built-in firewall (for more on firewalls, see "Set Up a Wireless Network").

After you've properly installed the drivers for your network adapters (wireless or otherwise), Windows should do the rest without much help from you—but unfortunately, it doesn't always work out that way. (If you run into trouble installing the network adapters or other hardware, turn to Chapter 6.)

You can fix most simple configuration problems by completing the cumbersome Network Setup Wizard on all PCs in your network. Open the Network Connections control panel, and click the "Set up a home or small office network" link on the left side. (Or, if you don't see the Network Tasks pane, double-click the Network Setup Wizard icon.) Click the Next button on the first few pages, and then answer the questions as follows:

- If you're asked about disconnected network hardware, place a checkmark next to the "Ignore disconnected network hardware" option, and click the Next button.

- On the "Select a connection method" page, choose Other, and click the Next button.

- On the "Other Internet connection methods" page, choose the "This computer connects to the Internet directly..." option, and then click the Next button.

- When asked for a computer name, choose a unique, one-word name for your PC (each computer must have a different name), leave the description field blank, and click the Next button.

- On the "Name your network" page, Windows will automatically name your network "MSHOME," even if you've previously typed a different network name. Type a new name if you want, but make sure all the other PCs on your network share the same network name. Click the Next button.

- On the "File and printer sharing" page, choose the "Turn on file and printer sharing" option if you want to exchange files over your network (see "Share Files with Other Computers"), and then click the Next button.

Proceed through the following (mostly pointless) screens by clicking the Next button, and when you arrive at the "You're almost done" page, choose "Just finish the wizard." Click the Next button, and then click the Finish button. Whew!

Back in the Network Connections window, select View→Details to show the pertinent information. Right-click the "LAN or High-Speed Internet" connection you're using, and select Properties. Then, select Internet Protocol (TCP/IP) from the list and click the Properties button to show the Internet Protocol (TCP/IP) Properties dialog box (see Figure 5-1).

Figure 5-1. You may have to manually configure TCP/IP properties to get your PC noticed on your network.

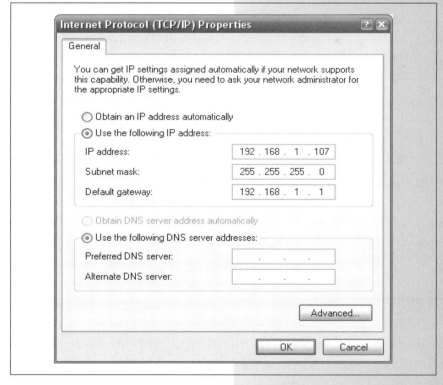

In most cases, selecting the "Obtain an IP address automatically" and "Obtain DNS server address automatically" options will suffice. If, however, you can't get your network to work with automatic addressing, try the following settings:

1. Choose the "Use the following IP address" option.

2. In the IP address field, type 192.168.1.100. (When you configure the second PC on your network, type 192.168.1.101 in the IP address box. For the third PC, type 192.168.1.102, and so on.)

> ── **NOTE** ──
>
> *Often, networks don't work because Windows and your router fail to negotiate the correct addresses automatically. The first three numbers in each PC's IP address (e.g., 192.168.1.) must exactly match the first three numbers in the IP address of your router—usually 192.168.1.1 or 192.168.0.1—which you can get from your router's documentation. Only the last number (e.g., 100, 101, 102) must be different for each PC.*

3. In the Subnet mask field, type 255.255.255.0.

4. In the Default gateway field, type the IP address of your router (usually 192.168.1.1 or 192.168.0.1).

5. In the "Preferred DNS server" and "Alternate DNS server" fields, type the IP addresses of your ISP's primary and secondary DNS servers, respectively. Contact your ISP or visit your ISP's web site for this information.

6. Click OK in both boxes when you're done.

> ── **NOTE** ──
>
> *The addresses you type for the subnet mask, gateway, and DNS servers should be the same for all PCs on your network.*

These "static IP" numbers will help ensure that all the PCs on your network can communicate reliably with each other. For best results, set static IP addresses on all the PCs on your network.

Return to the Network Connections window when you're done. The Status column shows whether or not a connection has been established (e.g., "Connected" or "Network cable unplugged").

If it says "Acquiring network address," it means Windows is in the process of establishing a connection; if you see this for more than, say, 10 seconds, it means your router isn't automatically assigning your PC a proper IP address. If you're connecting wirelessly, this error typically appears when you haven't supplied the necessary WPA or WEP security key (see "Connect to a Wireless Network"). For wired networks, this error could indicate a problem with the router, the cabling, or the NIC and its drivers. If the "Obtain an IP address automatically" option is selected in the TCP/IP Properties dialog box for your network connection, try specifying a static IP address, as described earlier, to fix this problem.

If the status column says "Limited or no connectivity," it usually means a connection has been established but your IP address is incorrect; make sure that the first three numbers in your PC's IP address match the first three numbers in your router's IP address, and that the fourth is different from any other PC on your network.

Share Files with Other Computers

THE ANNOYANCE: I need to access a bunch of documents on my office desktop PC from my laptop. I want to open the files over the network and avoid the whole CD/floppy/USB drive shuffle, but I can't get it to work.

THE FIX: There are a handful of steps you need to take to configure your PCs before you can exchange files between them on your network:

1. Complete the Network Setup Wizard on each PC on your network (see "Network Two Computers"), and make sure you enable file sharing when prompted.

2. If you're using Windows XP Professional or Windows XP Media Center Edition, open Windows Explorer, select Tools→Folder Options, and choose the View tab. Remove the checkmark next to the "Use simple file sharing (Recommended)" option, and click OK. (This option is not available in Windows XP Home Edition.)

3. The next step is to formally *share* the appropriate folder on the main PC. Open Windows Explorer and navigate to the folder containing the files you want to open remotely. Right-click the folder, select Properties, and choose the Sharing tab.

   In Windows XP Home, check the "Share this folder on the network" box. In Windows XP Professional and Media Center Edition, select the "Share this folder" option (see Figure 5-2). (If Windows asks whether you understand the "risks," confirm that you indeed wish to enable file sharing.)

   Enter a descriptive name in the "Share name" field. This is the name used for your folder when you view it over the network.

   > ─ **NOTE** ─
   > *If you're using Windows XP Home Edition and the "Share this folder on the network" option is grayed out, remove the checkmark next to the "Make this folder private" option. If that option is grayed out as well, click the "another folder" link at the bottom of the window, remove the checkmark next to the "Make this folder private" option on the window that appears, and click OK. Then return to the folder you want to share and try again.*

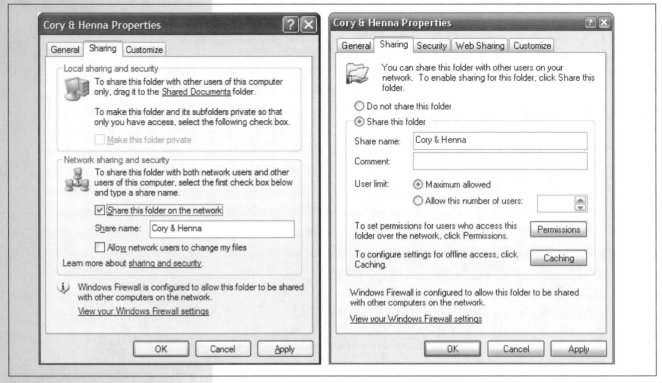

Figure 5-2. To allow the exchange of files over a network, use the "Share this folder on the network" option in XP Home Edition (left) or the "Share this folder" option in XP Professional/MCE (right).

NOTE

If you're using Windows XP Professional and you want to share the entire drive (not just the folder), see "Share an Entire Drive," later in this chapter.

4. If you want to be able to remotely modify, delete, or create new files in this folder, you must set the permissions accordingly. In XP Home, just place a checkmark next to the "Allow network users to change my files" option. In XP Professional, click the Permissions button and follow the steps in "Protect Shared Files,"

5. When you're done, click OK. A little hand icon will appear over the yellow folder icon to identify it as shared.

But you're not finished yet! For the sake of security, the desktop computer holding the files you want to share must have a password associated with the owner of the files, as described in "Protect Shared Files." (By default, user accounts don't have passwords in Windows XP.) What's more, users trying to access those files remotely must be able to provide the same username and password. This user validation may be transparent or may require a login, depending on who owns the files:

- When you first connect to the PC with the shared files, Windows will check to see if the usernames of the owner of the shared files and the one using the remote PC are the same. If the usernames are different, Windows will ask for a username and password. For example, if "Jane" on one computer tries to read the files on a computer belonging to "Rutiger," Jane will be required to type Rutiger as well as Rutiger's password in order to access the shared files.

- If the username is the same on both PCs, the passwords must match. For example, if "Rutiger," while logged into one computer, tries to access files belonging to "Rutiger" on another computer, and each Rutiger account has precisely the same password, Windows will grant access to the files without any prompt at all. But if the passwords on both accounts don't match exactly, Windows may not let you in, even if you type the correct username/password combination into the login box. The solution: just change one of the passwords so they match.

Once you have the user accounts and passwords straightened out on all your PCs, open Windows Explorer on the remote computer—the one accessing the files on that desktop PC—and navigate to the *My Network Places* folder, shown in Figure 5-3.

NOTE

Once you choose a password, Windows will ask you for it every time you power up your PC. To skip this step, see "Log in Automatically."

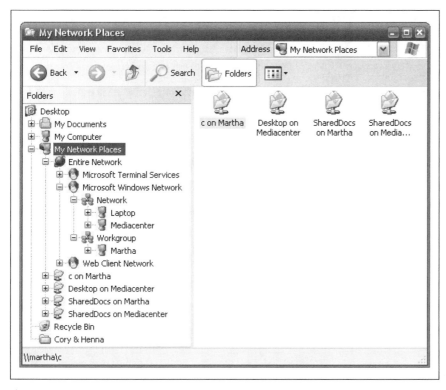

Figure 5-3. Use the My Network Places folder to access shared folders on other PCs.

You may see several familiar-looking folders in *My Network Places*, such as *My Documents on Laptop* or *C on Desktop*. Windows Explorer automatically creates these folder shortcuts to provide easy access to frequently accessed shares. If you don't see the folder you want here, don't panic; just open the *Entire Network* folder, then *Microsoft Windows Network*, then the name of your workgroup (e.g., *MSHOME*), and finally the name of the PC with the files you want (e.g., *Desktop*).

NOTE

Want to share bits of data without hassling with files? The Copycat utility, free from http://www.r2.com.au, automatically transfers the contents of your clipboard (used to hold data that you cut or copy) to all the PCs on your network. Just highlight some text on one machine, and press Ctrl-C; then, on another PC, press Ctrl-V to paste it anywhere you like!

NOTE

If you don't see the other PC in your workgroup, see "Find Missing Computers in My Network Places." If you get an "Access is denied" error at any point, it means the owner of the files on the other computer has set permissions to keep you from messing with his data. If you have control over the other PC, see "Protect Shared Files" for help.

Inside the folder, you'll find a listing of the folders, printers, and (for some reason) scheduled tasks shared on that PC. Open any shared folder to access the files therein as though they were stored on your own hard disk: copy or move via drag and drop, rename, delete, or just double-click to open the files in place.

Find Missing Computers in My Network Places

THE ANNOYANCE: I'm trying to open a file on another PC on my network, but it doesn't show up in *My Network Places*. This is driving me crazy!

THE FIX: This is a really common problem, and one that is not always easily solved.

First, a remote computer may not appear in *My Network Places* if it doesn't have any files or printers shared. See "Share Files with Other Computers" to set up file sharing or "List All Your Shared Folders" to see what's being shared on any PC.

Shared folders on remote PCs can show up in two places in the *My Network Places* folder: shortcuts to previously accessed folders sometimes appear right in the *My Network Places* folder itself, but for a complete list, navigate to *\Entire Network\Microsoft Windows Network*, open your network (e.g., *MSHOME*), and then open any PC to show its shared folders and printers.

Also, you may or may not see a PC that is in another workgroup in the *Microsoft Windows Network* folder in *My Network Places*. If you don't see the other workgroup, and you have control over the other PC, change its workgroup name to match the rest of the PCs on your network. Open the System control panel (or right-click My Computer and select Properties), and then choose the Computer Name tab. The name of your PC, as well as the workgroup to which it belongs, is shown here (see Figure 5-4); click the Change button to rename the PC or join a different workgroup. All the PCs on your network should belong to the same workgroup, but no two PCs should share the same computer name.

Figure 5-4. Use System Properties to change your PC's computer name and workgroup.

If the workgroup matches but the PC still doesn't show up, one trick that often works is to type the name of the PC directly into Windows Explorer's address bar. (If you don't see the address bar, select View→Toolbars→ Address Bar.) Erase the text in the address bar, and type two backslashes followed by the missing PC's name, like this:

```
\\misterx
```

where *misterx* is the name of the remote PC. Press Enter, and with luck—and about 5–10 seconds of patience—Windows should list the shared folders on the remote computer.

If you still can't see the PC, make sure the network is functioning on both the remote computer and the local PC (the one you're sitting in front of). If they're both connected to a router that provides a shared Internet connection, for instance, open a web browser on each PC to test the connection. If you can load a web site, the network is working.

Often, you can force stubborn computers to show up by setting a static IP address for each PC on your network, as described in "Network Two Computers." Then use the ping command to test connectivity. Select Start→ Run, type cmd, and click OK to open a Command Prompt window, and then type:

```
ping 192.168.1.107
```

In this example, 192.168.1.107 is the IP address of the remote PC; replace this with the appropriate address. If you get a reply like the following from the remote machine, it means your computer can see and successfully communicate with that machine on your network:

```
Reply from 192.168.1.107: bytes=32 time=3ms TTL=64
```

If, on the other hand, you see a timeout message like this, the connection is broken:

```
Request timed out.
```

File sharing will not work as long as ping returns this error, so your best bet is to check your hardware and IP address settings instead of toiling with the *My Network Places* folder.

If the network checks out but you still can't see the remote PC, try restarting both computers and resetting your router (refer to your router's instructions for the reset procedure).

If one of the PCs is running an older operating system (particularly Windows 95 or 98), see "Connect to a Windows 9X/Me PC."

If all else fails, it's likely a problem with the hardware. Try replacing the cables if you have a wired network, or see "Increase Range and Improve Reception," later in this chapter, if you have a wireless network. For help with updating drivers, replacing network adapters, and resolving hardware conflicts, see Chapter 6.

Protect Shared Files

THE ANNOYANCE: I want to share a bunch of files with other PCs on my network, but I'm worried that doing so will allow anyone to see them. How do I protect my data?

THE FIX: Any computer connected to your PC over a network—including the several billion machines on the Internet—may be able to access the files in your shared folders. Thus, the best way to protect your data is to not share it in the first place. If you need to share files, exclude folders that contain particularly sensitive data. See "List All Your Shared Folders" for a comprehensive list of shared folders on your PC, and then take advantage of XP's security features, such as they are, to protect the rest of your files.

The first thing you need to do is set a password for your user account. Open the User Accounts control panel, select your account from the list, and then click "Create a password." Type your password twice, followed by a clue to act as a reminder down the road (you may well need it), and then click the Create Password button when you're done. Thereafter, anyone wanting to access your files from another computer on your network will have to supply the password (with some exceptions for Windows XP Professional).

Now, unless you employ some sort of firewall anyone outside your local network—namely, everyone on the Internet—can access your data (and yes, no matter how uninteresting you may think the contents of your PC are, this *can* happen to you). Windows XP comes with the "Windows Firewall," a feeble software-based solution, but nothing beats a hardware firewall placed between you and the rest of the world. If you don't have one already, get yourself a router for this purpose, as described in "Set Up a Wireless Network."

> **WARNING**
>
> *If you're using a wireless network, anyone within range may be able to join your network and access your files, unless you follow the steps in "Surf Safely at the Coffee Shop."*

For any more protection, you'll need to use *permissions*, which are special settings that control precisely who can do what to your files. Permissions are available only in Windows XP Professional (and Media Center Edition); if you're using Windows XP Home, your ability to protect your data effectively stops here.

On an XP Pro system, every file, folder, and drive has two sets of permissions you can set: permissions for local users (other people sitting at your PC), and permissions for anyone accessing your files through a shared folder. To set the permissions for a shared folder, right-click the folder, select Properties, choose the Sharing tab, and then click the Permissions button.

What About Encryption?

Windows XP Professional also has some built-in data encryption features, but encryption offers no more protection than restrictive permissions when using shared folders. Rather, encryption is designed to protect your data from those who use your PC directly, either by sitting in front of it or by remote control using Terminal Services (a.k.a. Remote Desktop). For more information about the ins and outs of encryption, as well as Remote Desktop, see O'Reilly's *Windows XP Annoyances for Geeks, Second Edition*, by David A. Karp .

The Share Permissions window, shown in Figure 5-5, shows a list of configured users in the top list, and the specific things the selected user is allowed to do down below.

First, make sure your own username appears in the upper list; if it doesn't, or if it merely shows "Everyone" (like the one in Figure 5-5), click the Add button. Type your username—or the username of the person you want to be able to access your stuff—in the "Enter the object names to select" field, and then click the Check Names button. If Windows underlines what you've typed, the username is okay; otherwise, you'll get a "Name not Found" message. Click OK when you're done adding names.

Next, highlight your username in the "Group or user names" list, and place checkmarks in the boxes in the Allow column below as you see fit. Want others to be able to read the files in this folder but not change any of them? Put a checkmark in the Read box, but not in the Full Control or Change boxes.

> **NOTE**
>
> *In most cases, you won't have to bother with the checkboxes in the Deny column unless you start messing with "groups" of users. Permission to carry out a given action is implicitly denied as long as there's no checkmark in the corresponding Allow box.*

If you want to deny any user access to your files—particularly the self-explanatory "Everyone"—highlight the username, and click the Remove button. Now, any user who is not expressly listed here (or included in any groups listed here) will not have access to your shared files.

When you're done, click OK. The changes take effect immediately and apply to the selected folder share, as well as to all subfolders and files contained therein.

Share an Entire Drive

THE ANNOYANCE: I looked at the Sharing tab for my *C:* drive, and the "Share this folder" option is selected, meaning the drive is currently being shared. However, I don't see it in *My Network Places*. What's going on?

THE FIX: In Windows XP Professional (and Media Center Edition), all drives are shared automatically. For instance, the Sharing tab for drive C: on your PC probably looks like the one shown in Figure 5-6. (None of this applies to Windows XP Home.)

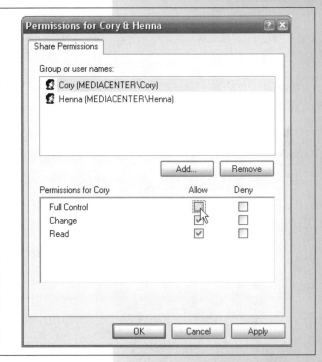

Figure 5-5. Set sharing permissions to protect your data from intruders (or just to keep the kids from accidentally messing up your stuff).

> **NOTE**
>
> *By adding someone else's username to the Permissions window, you can protect your data without handing over your username and password. If your PC is part of an NT domain (typical in a corporate environment), you can add users from your domain or even another domain by clicking the Locations button to change the scope of the user validation. But on a home network, you'll need to create a new user account on your PC (using the User Accounts control panel) before you can type it into the Permissions window.*

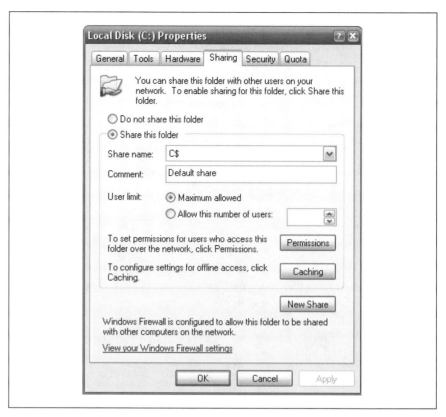

Figure 5-6. Each hard disk on your PC may already be shared.

Microsoft calls this an *administrative share*, and it's enabled by default so that tools such as the Computer Management utility (accessed by going to Start→Run and typing compmgmt.msc) running on a remote computer can operate on your PC. The dollar sign at the end of the share name (e.g., *C$*) identifies it as a hidden share, which means it won't ever show up in *My Network Places*. All it takes to view a hidden share is to type the share name into Windows Explorer's address bar, like this:

    mycomp\c$

In this example, *mycomp* is the name of your computer. Provided there aren't any password or permission restrictions (see "Protect Shared Files"), anyone can access the files in this shared folder as readily as any non-hidden share. (For more on hidden shares, see "List All Your Shared Folders.")

> — **WARNING** —
>
> *Yes, administrative shares indeed constitute a potential security risk, as they allow access to any files on your hard disk, whether they're in folders you've specifically shared or not. If you want to remove administrative shares for good, see "Turn Off Administrative Shares."*

Now, you can use these administrative shares to access your drives remotely, as explained earlier, but if you want to share your drive so that it shows up in *My Network Places*, just click the New Share button at the bottom of the window. In the New Share dialog box, type a share name (e.g., C), set any permissions, and click OK.

List All Your Shared Folders

THE ANNOYANCE: I know a folder is being shared when I see that little hand icon on top of the yellow folder icon. But all it takes is one forgotten share to leave my private files open to prying eyes. Can I get a comprehensive, reliable list of everything being shared on my PC?

THE FIX: You can simply open the *My Network Places* folder in Windows Explorer and navigate through *Entire Network* to find your PC and a list of all its shared resources, but this listing doesn't necessarily show *everything* that's being shared. Specifically, any *hidden* shares are, well, hidden.

To view all your network shares—including the hidden ones—select Start→ Run, type compmgmt.msc, and click OK to open the Computer Management tool. In the System Tools branch on the left, click the [+] icon next to *Shared Folders* to expand it, and then highlight the *Shares* folder, as shown in Figure 5-7.

NOTE

Concerned about security? Instead of sharing the entire drive, just share the individual folders you need to access across your network.

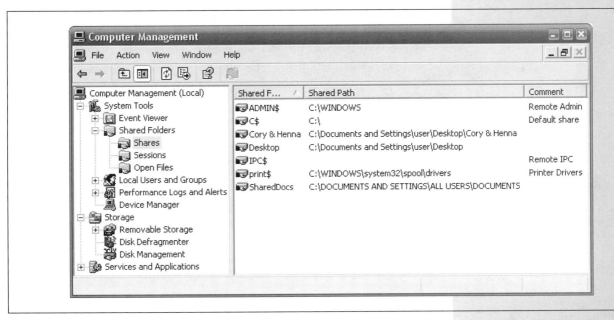

Figure 5-7. The Computer Management tool lists all the shared folders on your PC, including hidden ones you probably didn't even know existed.

Any share with a dollar sign at the end of its name (e.g., *C$*) is hidden. While hidden shares don't show up in *My Network Places*, you can access them just as readily as non-hidden shares, as explained in "Share an Entire Drive."

From here, you can right-click any share and select Stop Sharing to turn it off, making this window a very convenient place to quickly tighten up security on your system. If you add or remove any shares in Windows Explorer, press the F5 key or click the Refresh button on the toolbar to update the list.

Although you can stop sharing any hidden share (such as *C$*) in this window, Windows will recreate all administrative shares the next time you start your computer, in effect sharing every file on your PC whether you want it to or not. To stop this from happening, see "Turn Off Administrative Shares."

Turn Off Administrative Shares

THE ANNOYANCE: Windows insists on sharing my entire hard disk, despite the fact that I've only elected to share specific folders. What are administrative shares, and why can't I turn them off?

THE FIX: Hmm... it's almost as though Microsoft cares more about corporate strategy than the personal security of their customers. Funny, that.

If you're using Windows XP Professional (or Media Center Edition), your entire hard disk is indeed being shared on your network whether you like it or not (see "Share an Entire Drive" for details). If you open Windows Explorer, right-click drive *C:*, and select Sharing and Security, you'll see that the drive is already shared as *C$*. This is called an *administrative share*, and although the *$* suffix makes it hidden in *My Network Places*, users on your network can still browse the share—thereby gaining access to all the files on your drive—by typing the following path into Windows Explorer's address bar:

    mycomp\c$

where *mycomp* is the name of your PC. Combine this with the fact that user accounts don't have passwords by default, and you'll see how insecure Windows XP can be. (See "Protect Shared Files" for further steps you should take to secure your system.)

Administrative shares allow network administrators to install software, run Disk Defragmenter, or perform other maintenance on your PC remotely. But unless you're in a corporate environment, you have nothing to gain by leaving this back door open... and everything to lose.

To patch this hole, open the Registry Editor (go to Start→Run and type regedit), and navigate to *HKEY_LOCAL_MACHINE\SYSTEM\ CurrentControlSet\Services\lanmanserver\parameters*. In the right pane, double-click the *AutoShareServer* value, type 0 in the "Value data" field, and click OK. Then double-click the *AutoShareWks* value, type 0 in the "Value data" field, and click OK. Close the Registry Editor when you're done.

Next, go to Start→Run, type compmgmt.msc, and click OK to open the Computer Management tool. In the System Tools branch on the left, click the [+] icon next to Shared Folders to expand it, and then highlight the *Shares* folder (see Figure 5-7 in "List All Your Shared Folders"). To manually remove the administrative shares, right-click each one (e.g., *C$*, *D$*, *E$*) and select Stop Sharing. Go ahead and remove any hidden share (anything with a dollar sign in the name), with the following three exceptions:

- *IPC$*, which stands for Inter-Process Communication, is used for remote administration of your computer, something very few people need outside of a corporate environment. Although it has been proven that the *IPC$* share can be exploited, the only way to disable it permanently is to turn off file sharing altogether. You can stop sharing *IPC$* temporarily, but Windows will recreate the share the next time you restart.

- *print$* is used to exchange printer driver files when you share a printer. You should leave this share intact.

- *wwwroot$* will be present if Microsoft's Internet Information Server (IIS) software is installed. Leave this share intact if you want to use your computer as a web server or a web software development platform.

When you're done, restart your computer, and then reopen the Computer Management tool to check your work.

Speed Up Network Browsing

THE ANNOYANCE: It seems to take forever to browse the folders on the other PCs on my network. How can I speed things up?

THE FIX: The *Scheduled Tasks* folder, which appears in *My Network Places* along with your shared folders and printers, is responsible for much of the slowdown. Since the shared *Scheduled Tasks* folder takes so long to load, and has very little value to most Windows users, you can just turn off the share to speed things up.

Open the Registry Editor (select Start→Run and type regedit), and navigate to *HKEY_LOCAL_MACHINE\SOFTWARE\Microsoft\Windows\ CurrentVersion\Explorer\RemoteComputer\NameSpace*. Inside the *NameSpace* key, you may see one or several subkeys, each responsible for a special shared folder. To see what any one of these subkeys does, select it and look at the *(Default)* value in the right pane.

To stop sharing *Scheduled Tasks*, just delete the *{D6277990-4C6A-11CF-8D87-00AA0060F5BF}* key.

While you're here, you can further improve performance by turning off the *Printers and Faxes* share. If you don't plan on sharing any printers, delete the *{2227A280-3AEA-1069-A2DE-08002B30309D}* key.

Close the Registry Editor when you're done. The change should take effect immediately.

> ─── **NOTE** ───
>
> *If, for some reason, you want to re-enable the Scheduled Tasks share, just recreate the subkey. Select Edit→New→Key and type {D6277990-4C6A-11CF-8D87-00AA0060F5BF} for its name.*

Connect to a Windows 9X/Me PC

THE ANNOYANCE: I have an old Windows 98 system I need to network with my Windows XP machine, but I can't seem to get the two PCs to communicate.

THE FIX: Getting XP to happily communicate with Windows 9x machines over a network can be a bit of a chore. Fortunately, there are two tactics that usually solve the problem.

First, assign a static IP address to each PC on your network, regardless of the Windows version being used; see "Network Two Computers" for instructions.

Second, Windows 95 and Windows 98 (and occasionally Windows Me) install a driver called NetBEUI by default. NetBEUI is not compatible with Windows NT–based systems (such as Windows XP and 2000), and it can cause problems if installed on any system on your network. To remove NetBEUI from a Windows 95/98/Me system, open the Network control panel and choose the Configuration tab. If you see NetBEUI in the list, highlight it, and click the Remove button. Remove all instances of NetBEUI from this window, and then click OK when you're done. You'll probably have to restart your PC.

Find Missing Remote Printers

THE ANNOYANCE: I need to print to a printer that's physically connected to another PC on my network, but when I browse for the printer in the Add Printer Wizard, it never shows up. I also tried typing the printer's network address into the wizard without any luck, and the printer manufacturer is absolutely no help.

THE FIX: The traditional way to use a printer installed—and shared—on another PC is to open the Printers and Faxes control panel and then click Add Printer. On the "Local or Network Printer" page, choose "A network printer, or a printer attached to another computer," and on the next page, choose "Browse for a printer." Unfortunately, a variety of problems can cause the printer to be absent from this screen.

First, make sure the PC to which the printer is connected is turned on, the network is working for all PCs involved, and the printer is indeed shared. On the remote PC (the one with the printer), open the Printers and Faxes control panel. Right-click the printer you'd like to share, select Properties, and then choose the Sharing tab. Select the "Share this printer" option, and then click OK.

If the printer is shared, and you're sure its driver supports network sharing, there's a quick workaround that usually works (although it won't solve the underlying problem, whatever that might be). Open Windows Explorer on a PC not directly connected to the printer, and click the *My Network Places* folder. Open *Entire Network*, then *Microsoft Windows Network*, then your workgroup (e.g., *MSHOME*), and then the PC to which the printer is attached. Inside, you'll find a *Printers and Faxes* folder, and inside that, you'll see all the printers shared on that PC. Right-click the printer you want to use, and select Connect.

If all goes well, the printer will show up in the Printers and Faxes dialog in 10–20 seconds, and you should be able to print to it immediately thereafter.

PC Slows When Accessed over the Network

THE ANNOYANCE: My PC slows to a crawl when someone reads a shared file on my hard disk over the network. I need to keep those shared folders active, but the performance slowdown interferes with my work. What can I do?

THE FIX: Although heavy network traffic can bog down a PC, it may indeed be nothing more than a hardware problem. Specifically, your network adapter may conflict with another hardware device in your system.

If you're using a desktop PC, shut down Windows, unplug the power cable, and crack open the case. Locate your network adapter—the card into which you plug your network cable—remove the screw, pull out the card, and pop it into a different slot. Reassemble and turn on your PC and see if the problem goes away.

If, on the other hand, your NIC is integrated on the motherboard, it probably shares an IRQ with one of the PCI slots, and thus the PCI card in that slot may be causing the problem. Remove all nonessential PCI cards from your system, and start up Windows. If the problem persists, you may have to shuffle the remaining, essential PCI cards until you resolve the problem. If, on the other hand, the problem vanishes after you remove the PCI cards, shut down your PC and reinsert the cards one by one, reassembling and restarting your system after each insertion, until you find the culprit. If the culprit is a troublesome PCI slot, cover it with a piece of masking tape to remind yourself to keep it unoccupied.

> **NOTE**
>
> *Note that some printers can't be shared (this problem may come up if the manufacturer sells a more expensive "network-ready" printer that they'd rather have you buy). Review your printer's documentation and check the manufacturer's web site for driver updates if you can't get sharing to work. Typically, printers suffering from this limitation do show up in the "Browse for a printer" list but display an error when you try to install the drivers or print remotely.*

If you're still stuck, you may need to update your network drivers or even replace your network hardware (see Chapter 6 for other hardware annoyances).

Log in Automatically

THE ANNOYANCE: I added a password to my Windows user account to protect my shared data, but now I have to type it every time I turn on my PC. Isn't there a way to skip this step?

THE FIX: It may seem ironic to create a password for your PC and then immediately override it with an automatic logon, but it's a perfect solution for a single-user PC on a home network. As described in "Protect Shared Files," your user account needs a password if you want to share files with other PCs on your network, particularly if you want to protect your data from intruders. But unless those intruders routinely walk by your computer, you can forgo having to type that password every time you start Windows.

To do this, go to Start→Run, type control userpasswords2, and then click OK to open the alternate User Accounts window shown in Figure 5-8. (The standard User Accounts window in the Control Panel isn't sufficient for this task.)

Figure 5-8. Use the alternate User Accounts window to do things you can't do with the standard User Accounts window.

Remove the checkmark next to the "Users must enter a user name and password to use this computer" option, and click OK. In the Automatically Log On dialog box, type your username, enter your password twice, and click OK. The next time Windows starts, you'll skip the Welcome screen and go straight to your desktop.

Use the Administrator Account

THE ANNOYANCE: When I installed Windows, I had to choose an Administrator password and then create a separate user account for myself. Can I delete the superfluous account and simply use the Administrator account as my primary login?

THE FIX: You can, but only in Windows XP Professional and Media Center Edition. (Note: in MCE, the Administrator account is named "Media Center" by default.) In Windows XP Home, the Administrator account is restricted and can be used only when you start your PC in Safe Mode.

To log in as the Administrator, go to Start→Log Off, and click the Log Off button. Once you see the Welcome screen, press Ctrl-Alt-Del twice to show the old-fashioned "Log On to Windows" dialog box. Type Administrator for the username, enter the Administrator password below, and click OK.

Once you've logged on as the Administrator, you can delete the superfluous user account from the User Accounts control panel. Of course, you'll lose all the settings from that account, so it may not be worth it if you've been using the account for some time.

To show the Administrator account on the Welcome screen, open the Registry Editor (go to Start→Run and type regedit), navigate to *HKEY_ LOCAL_MACHINE\SOFTWARE\Microsoft\WindowsNT\CurrentVersion\ Winlogon\SpecialAccounts\UserList*, select Edit→New→DWORD Value, and type Administrator for the name of the new value. Double-click the new *Administrator* value in the right pane and type 1 in the "Value data" field. When you're done, close the Registry Editor and restart Windows for the change to take effect.

INTERNET CONNECTIONS

Get Your PC Online

THE ANNOYANCE: I just signed up for a broadband Internet connection in my home. Everything seems to be plugged in correctly, but I can't get to any web sites.

THE FIX: Modern broadband connections are pretty simple, until they stop working. Most of the time, the solution involves nothing more than unplugging your cable or DSL modem (and router, if you have one), leaving the devices unplugged for at least two full minutes, and then plugging them back in. If that doesn't work, you'll have to do a little digging.

> **NOTE**
>
> *If you don't yet have a router, consider getting one as part of the solution to this problem. As described in "Set Up a Wireless Network," routers offer better firewall protection than Windows can; they also take care of a lot of the problems that commonly plague broadband connections, such as finicky dialers.*

Examine your DSL or cable modem's port lights, which will tell you whether or not a particular service is working. One should be lit (green, usually) when your PC is connected, and another should be lit when your broadband is connected. These lights typically flash to indicate that data is being transferred. If they're off, or perhaps red or orange, something is wrong with your modem or your connection, and no amount of wrangling in Windows will fix it. To see if your modem is to blame, reset it (see your modem's documentation for details) and try again; replace your modem if

> **NOTE**
>
> *Don't know the Administrator password? Provided you're logged in as a user with administrator privileges (not the same as the Administrator account), you can choose a new password for the Administrator account in the alternate User Accounts window (go to Start→Run and type* control userpasswords2*). Just highlight any user in the list other than Administrator, and then click the Reset Password button.*

Troubleshoot Your Dialer

If you're still using the software that came with your router, see "Get Rid of Third-Party Dialers" for an alternative that may work.

Whether you use a router, XP's own Point-to-Point over Ethernet (PPPoE) dialer, or your ISP's dialing software to connect, the way your dialer behaves when you try to connect should tell you what's wrong. If it tells you that your login is incorrect, either your username or your password is wrong. The most common mistake involves the username, which often resembles an email address (e.g., *username@myisp.net*) instead of just a bare name. Check your documentation for details, or call your ISP to have them reset your password.

If you have to wait a long time before the dialer gives you any error at all, your IP settings may be incorrect; see "Network Two Computers" for the fix. If, on the other hand, you get an error right away, it's probably a configuration problem with your dialer software, such as the wrong network adapter selected.

If your dialer indicates that there was no response from the server (or something similar), it usually means your service is down. Check your cables, and contact your ISP for status.

it won't respond even after a reset. If your modem checks out, your connection might be down; give your ISP an hour or two to bring your service back up, and contact them if it takes any longer.

Does your broadband connection require special dialer software? See the "Troubleshoot Your Dialer" sidebar for dialer-specific help. Otherwise, you likely have an always-on connection, one that uses either a dynamic (randomly assigned) IP address or a static (always the same) IP address. In this case, refer to the paperwork that came with your broadband connection, and change Windows's TCP/IP settings accordingly, as described in "Network Two Computers." Specifically, choose the "Obtain an IP address automatically" option if you're using a dynamic address, or the "Use the following IP address" option for a static address.

Get Rid of Third-Party Dialers

THE ANNOYANCE: My ISP gave me this CD when I signed up for Internet service. Not knowing any better, I installed it, and now my PC is littered with ads and junk software. Do I need any of this stuff?

THE FIX: In most cases, the software that comes with broadband service is unnecessary, providing little more than branded web software and links to your ISP's various marketing partners. The exception is the "dialer" program required by certain types of broadband connections, which is used to send your username and password to your ISP in order to connect to the Internet. Such software is typically flaky and the cause of all sorts of Internet connection problems. Fortunately, you can usually dump your ISP's proprietary software in favor of either Windows XP's built-in dialer or the auto-connect capabilities of a router.

> **NOTE**
>
> *There are a few exceptions. If you're using a USB modem, such as the SpeedTouch 330, it may require special drivers in order to work. If you have one of these, you may be better off replacing it with a combination modem and wireless router, such as the SpeedTouch 580, than trying to get it to work with anything other than the software that comes with it. Another exception is a wholly proprietary Internet connection provider such as AOL, which isn't compatible with anything other than the provided connection software.*

First, remove the superfluous software provided by your ISP: in the Add or Remove Programs control panel, highlight your ISP's software, and click the Remove button. If your ISP installed more than one software package, you may have to uninstall several entries from this list.

The best alternative to a software-based dialer is a wireless router, which will dial your connection automatically, keep you online all the time, protect your PC with its built-in firewall, and even provide wireless access to boot (see "Set Up a Wireless Network" for details).

Although routers are hard to beat, you can use Windows's built-in PPPoE dialer to connect to the Internet without any added hardware. Open the Network Connections control panel and click the "Set up a home or small office network" link on the left (or double-click the Network Connection Wizard icon). Answer the questions as follows:

1. Click the Next button to skip the introductory page, choose the "Connect to the Internet" option, and then click Next again.

2. Choose the "Set up my connection manually" option, and click Next.

3. Choose the "Connect using a broadband connection that requires a user name and password" option, and click Next.

4. Type a name for this connection, and click Next. A good choice is the name of your ISP, or just "DSL" or "cable."

5. Enter your username and password (see Figure 5-9), choose the desired options underneath (if you're not sure, turn them all on), and click Next.

6. Click the Finish button to complete the wizard.

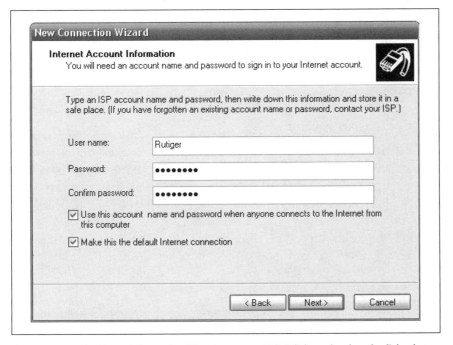

Figure 5-9. Use the Network Connection Wizard to set up a PPPoE dialer and replace the dialer that came with your broadband modem.

To initiate the connection, double-click the icon you just created in the *Network Connections* folder. If you elected to create a desktop shortcut in the wizard, you can also double-click the new desktop icon. By default, a Connect dialog will appear, at which point you can click the Connect button to dial and connect your PC to the Internet.

Normally, you'll have to dial this connection before you can go online. To have Windows connect automatically, first right-click the connection icon and select "Set as Default Connection." Next, open the Internet Options control panel, choose the Connections tab, and select the "Always dial my default connection" option.

To skip the Connect dialog, right-click the new connection and select Properties (or click the Properties button in the Connect dialog box). Choose the Options tab, and remove the checkmark next to the "Prompt for name and password, certificate, etc." option. This is particularly useful if you want Windows to connect automatically when you first start your computer; just drag the PPPoE connection icon from the *Network Connections* folder into your *Startup* folder in your Start menu.

Share an Internet Connection

THE ANNOYANCE: I have three PCs in my house, but only one Internet connection. How can I access the Web from all three PCs at the same time?

THE FIX: There are several approaches, but the best solution is to use a router (preferably one with wireless support). Essentially, you take the cable that goes from your modem to your PC, unplug it from your PC, and plug it into the back of the router. Then you connect all your PCs to your router, either wirelessly or with cables, and then configure your router, as described in "Set Up a Wireless Network." The router also protects the PCs on your network with its built-in firewall, a must-have in an era of viruses, spyware, and bored teenage hackers.

The alternative to a router, useful only if you need a quick-and-dirty solution or can't use a router for some reason, is to use Windows XP's built-in Internet Connection Sharing (ICS) feature. The trick, basically, is to connect one PC (called the "host") simultaneously to the Net and to your local network. Then you set up your other PCs to piggyback, so to speak, on the host PC's Internet connection. Since the host PC needs two network cards, (one for the local network and one for connecting to the Internet), this approach likely won't save you any money—or time, for that matter—over using an inexpensive router.

To set up ICS on the host PC, open the Network Connections control panel and select View→Details. You should have at least two connections listed: one for your Internet connection and one for your workgroup. If not, your network is not ready.

Find your connection for the Internet. In most cases, this connection will be the network adapter connected to your DSL or cable modem. (For connections that require a username and password, use the PPPoE broadband connection you set up in "Get Rid of Third-Party Dialers.") Right-click the connection icon, select Properties, and choose the Advanced tab. Check the "Allow other network users to connect through this computer's Internet connection" box, and click OK. Back in the *Network Connections* folder, it should now say "Enabled, Shared" in the Type column.

The next step is to configure each of the other computers on your network to use the shared connection. On each of the other "client" PCs, open the Network Connections control panel, right-click the connection icon corresponding to the network adapter plugged into your workgroup, and select Properties. Choose the General tab, highlight the "Internet Protocol (TCP/IP)" entry in the list, and click the Properties button. In most cases, you'll want to select the "Obtain an IP address automatically" option. If, however, you need static IP addresses, choose the "Use the following IP address" option, and fill out the fields as instructed in "Network Two Computers". For the "Default gateway," type the IP address of the PC hosting the shared Internet connection.

That's it! Test your connection on each PC by loading a web page. Of course, for this to work, the host computer must be turned on and connected to the Internet—a requirement that makes the router a much better choice for the long haul.

Measure Your Internet Connection Speed

THE ANNOYANCE: I'm not sure I'm getting the best speed from my Internet connection, but the Connection Status window in Windows XP doesn't give me any useful information. And while I'm at it, are the ads I've seen for "faster" Internet connections mostly hype, or is there something I can do to improve my connection speed without spending any extra cash?

THE FIX: *Throughput* is the practical measurement of bandwidth: the quantity of data you can transmit over a connection in a given period of time. The simplest way to measure your throughput is to visit one of the many bandwidth-measuring web sites, such as Broadbandreports.com (*http://www.dslreports.com/stest/*) or Bandwidth Place (*http://bandwidthplace.com/speedtest/*).

For the most accurate results, make sure you close all superfluous programs before running the test. In addition to calculating your bandwidth and reporting the results, these services typically ask for your Zip Code and connection type to compile statistics on typical connection speeds in your area. The results should look something like Figure 5-10.

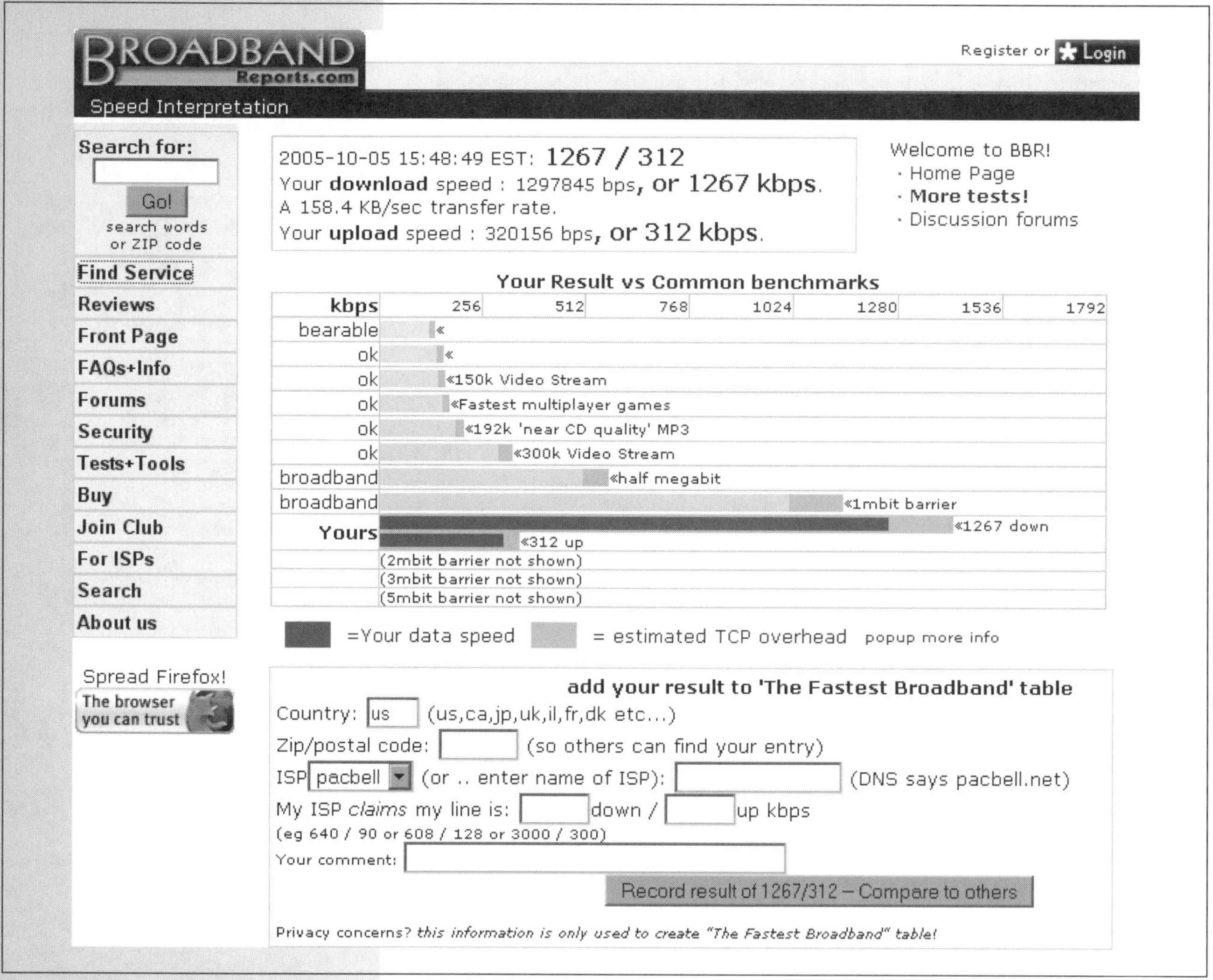

Figure 5-10. Use Broadband Reports's speed test page to measure the speed of your Internet connection.

Now, according to the results in Figure 5-10, the download speed is a respectable 1267 kbps (kilobits per second), which means, in practical terms, that it should take about 6.5 seconds to download a 1-MB file under ideal conditions.

However, ideal conditions are rare; real-life transfers are often much slower, due to overburdened servers and busy networks. Since your connection speed (or lack thereof) is most noticeable during file downloads (compared with web surfing or emailing), you can overcome some of these conditions by using a download manager, as described in "Faster Downloads Without the Hassle" in Chapter 4.

So what do you do if your connection seems too slow? First, close all open windows, and turn off all background programs (such as the ones that show up in the System Tray in the lower-right corner of the screen, near the clock). Do the same for any other PCs using your Internet connection. Next, examine the lights on your router or broadband modem; if they're flashing, it means that some program is still running on your PC, possibly consuming bandwidth. This is a possible sign that a virus, worm, Trojan horse, or some sort of spyware has made its way onto your PC (see "Put an End to Pop-ups" in Chapter 4), but see the "Overcome a Bandwidth Limit in SP2" sidebar for another possibility.

> **NOTE**
>
> *For real-time monitoring of your connection's throughput, try a desktop bandwidth monitor. The slickest tools are widgets, fancy plug-ins for the free Kapsules script engine (http://www.kwidgets.com) For instance, Bandwidth Watcher, Simple Bandwidth Monitor, Mr. Network, and KapMule, all available at http://www.kwidgets.com/forge.aspx, provide pretty graphical displays and up-to-the-second measurements of the amount of data being transferred via your Internet connection.*

Of course, it's also possible that you're hitting the upper limit of your broadband connection. But whether or not an upgrade from your ISP is worth the money depends on the bandwidth you're getting now and the amount of cash your ISP is demanding for the faster service. If your connection measures more than one megabit per second (1024 kbps), it's unlikely you'll notice a huge difference in real-world speed with a faster connection. On the other hand, more expensive connections sometimes offer substantially higher *upload* speeds, which may be worth the added cost if you spend a lot of time sending files to web servers, or even if you want to host a web site on your PC.

> **NOTE**
>
> *If you're using a router, visit the manufacturer's web site for a possible firmware update that might fix some performance problems and may even add new features to your router.*

Make Peer-to-Peer File Sharing Work

THE ANNOYANCE: My peer-to-peer (P2P) file-sharing program stopped working when I installed Service Pack 2. Is Microsoft trying to put an end to P2P, or can I fix this?

THE FIX: Most large companies would like to see P2P disappear, mostly because nobody has found a respectable way to make money off it. But the problem you're experiencing is almost certainly caused by the new Windows Firewall software built into SP2, which is blocking your file-sharing program from establishing a connection to its server.

Overcome a Bandwidth Limit in SP2

There's a little-known change in Service Pack 2 that limits the number of concurrent open TCP/IP connection attempts to 10. This may adversely affect programs that use multiple TCP/IP connections, such as some download managers, port scanners, and P2P software (and, by design, viruses).

To see if this is happening on your system, open the Event Viewer (select Start→Run and type eventvwr.msc), and highlight the System entry in the left pane. In the right pane, click the Event column header to sort the list by event code, scroll through the list, and look for 4226 errors. If you see any 4226 events, you can fix the problem by downloading a patch for your *tcpip.sys* file (sorry, no Registry change here) by going to *http://www.lvllord.de/?url=tools#4226patch*. Note that only advanced users should attempt this.

NOTE

Microsoft frequently releases updates and bug fixes for its firewall. If you decide to use the Windows Firewall, make sure you download all available updates using the Windows Update feature.

A *firewall* is a layer of protection that permits or denies network communication based on a predefined set of rules. These rules restrict communication so that only certain applications are permitted to use your network connection. This effectively closes back doors to your computer that viruses, hackers, and other malicious parties or applications might otherwise exploit. The Windows Firewall (see Figure 5-11) replaces the nearly worthless Internet Connection Firewall (ICF) found in earlier versions of Windows XP. While it's better than its predecessor, it also acts more aggressively and closes more back doors by default. (See "Set Up a Wireless Network" for more information about firewalls.)

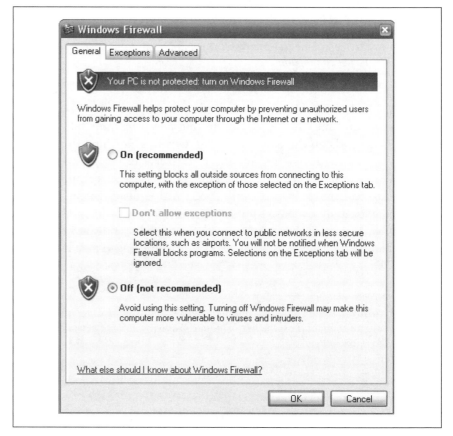

Figure 5-11. The Windows Firewall, which is turned on by default in Windows XP Service Pack 2, is known to cause problems.

NOTE

If you're using a router with a built-in firewall and you don't need to protect your PC from the other computers in your local network, you can safely turn off the Windows Firewall for good.

To see if the Windows Firewall is to blame, disable it temporarily. Open the Security Center control panel, click Windows Firewall, select the "Off (not recommended)" option, and click OK.

If your P2P software now works, the firewall software is clearly the culprit. (If it still doesn't work, the problem lies elsewhere; consult your P2P software documentation for details.) Go ahead and return to the Windows Firewall window, and select the "On (recommended)" option to re-enable it. Next, choose the Exceptions tab, click the Add Program button, and find your P2P application in the list (if you don't see it, click Browse to locate the .exe file on your hard disk). Highlight the program and click OK in both boxes. The Windows firewall should now let your P2P program do its thing without interference—the change will take effect immediately. (If you're using a third-party firewall program, check the software's documentation for help creating exceptions.)

If creating this exception doesn't work, return to the Exceptions tab of the Windows Firewall window and create another exception. This time, instead of basing the exception on the program filename, configure the firewall to allow all communication over the port used by your software. Click the Add Port button, type a name for the exception (for example, P2P), and type the port number (e.g., 6699). If you don't know the port number used by your P2P software, consult the software documentation. Click OK in both boxes, and give it a whirl.

Use MSN Messenger Behind a Firewall

THE ANNOYANCE: I want to use MSN Messenger at work, but my company's firewall blocks instant-messenger software. How can I get around this?

THE FIX: The last thing you should be forced to do when you're at work is your job. To that end, several web-based versions of popular IM programs have been designed that can sneak through firewalls quite easily. (Such programs operate over TCP port 80, and are thus indistinguishable from web sites in the eyes of the firewall.) In the case of MSN Messenger, just go to *http:// webmessenger.msn.com* and click "Start MSN Web Messenger" to log in.

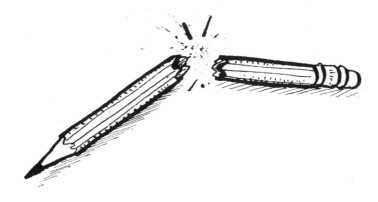

WIRELESS CONNECTIONS

Set Up a Wireless Network

THE ANNOYANCE: I can't get my wireless network off the ground. I want to use the Internet, share files, and so on, but none of it seems to work. I thought this was going to be easy!

THE FIX: Wireless networking *is* easy! (Unless it's not.)

Wireless networking can be extremely convenient when it works but an absolute headache when it doesn't. The good news is that if you take the time to set up your router correctly, update your firmware, and install Service Pack 2, most wireless problems will disappear.

A router lets you connect your PC (or all the PCs in your workgroup) to the Internet, as well as connect multiple PCs to each other. Routers also include built-in firewalls, offering much better protection than software-based firewalls such as the Windows Firewall built into Service Pack 2. But most importantly, a wireless router acts as an access point, a central hub to which all wireless devices in your home or office can connect. To set up a wireless network, you'll need a wireless router (preferably one that supports the 802.11g standard), and at least one PC with a wireless network adapter.

Connect your PC directly to your wireless router with a cable; that's right, a cable! You'll need to communicate with your router to set it up properly for wireless access—something you won't be able to do wirelessly throughout the whole process. Connect one end of a category-5 patch cable to your PC's Ethernet port, and the other end to one of the numbered LAN ports on the back of the router. Then plug in the router's power cable.

Your router probably came with setup software on a CD; in most cases, you don't need this and can use the router's more flexible web-based setup instead. Open a web browser on your PC, and type the router's IP address (usually 192.168.1.1, but check the router's manual) into the address bar. The router's built-in web server should show you a setup page like the one in Figure 5-12.

If you can't connect to your router, your computer is probably not on the same subnet as the router. The first three numbers of your computer's IP address must match the first three numbers of your router's IP address, but the fourth number must be different. For instance, if your router's address is 192.168.0.1, you may not be able to connect to it until you manually change your PC's address to 192.168.0.xxx, where xxx is any number between 2 and 255 (see "Network Two Computers" for further instructions). If all else fails, reset the router, following the instructions in the documentation, and try again.

NOTE

If you don't have Service Pack 2 yet, use the Windows Update feature now to get it (open Internet Explorer and select Tools→Windows Update). See Chapter 6 for more information about SP2 and Windows Update.

On the setup page, choose your Internet connection type from the list. If your Internet connection requires a username and password, select PPPoE. If your ISP has provided an IP address for your connection, select Static IP. Otherwise, choose Automatic Configuration - DHCP. (Naturally, the options for your router may be slightly different.)

Click the Apply or Save Settings button at the bottom of the page when you're done. Within a few seconds, you should have Internet access; go ahead and test it by opening a second browser window (press Ctrl-N) and visiting any web site.

Once your Internet connection is working, visit the router manufacturer's web site and download any available firmware updates. (You can usually find your router's current firmware version on the Status page in the router's

Figure 5-12. Configure your router via its web-based setup page.

—— NOTE ——

If you select PPPoE, the router should prompt you for a login. Type the username and password for your broadband connection, not your login for Windows, your email account, or anything else. If you choose Static IP, enter the IP addresses of your ISP's DNS servers. Your ISP should provide this information to you.

web-based setup.) Firmware updates include essential bug fixes, performance enhancements, security patches, and occasionally new features. Consult your router's documentation for firmware update instructions.

Next, go to your router's wireless setup page (see Figure 5-13): this is either a link in the main menu or a tab across the top of the page. Choose a new SSID (the name for your wireless network), and turn off the Wireless SSID Broadcast option to keep your wireless network private (see the sidebar "The Evils of SSID Broadcast" for details). Click the Apply or Save Settings button at the bottom of the page when you're done.

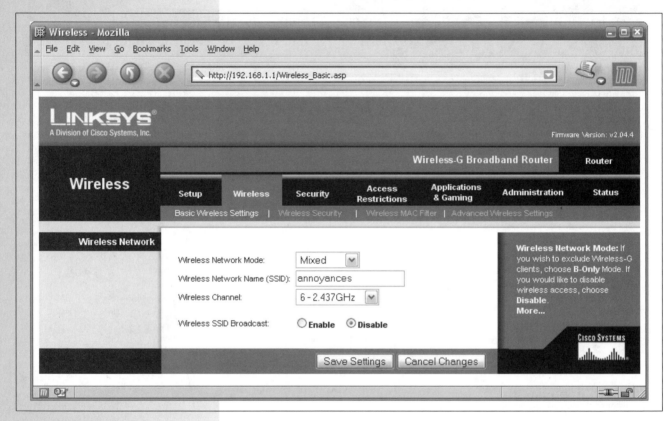

Figure 5-13. Choose a private SSID in your router's wireless setup page.

NOTE ────────

If you're using a Wireless-G router (a faster sibling of the 802.11b standard, capable of 54 Mbps), avoid the temptation to select the "G only" option on the wireless setup page. This feature prevents slower Wireless-B devices from joining your WiFi network—a fact you'll likely have forgotten when a visiting relative tries to connect to your home network to check her email a few months from now.

You should also enable encryption for the best wireless security. This setting will be accessible either through a button on the current page, or on a separate tab entitled WEP, WPA, Encryption, or simply Wireless Security, like the one in Figure 5-14. WEP, the Wireless Encryption Protocol, prevents anyone without your secret WEP key from connecting to or spying on your wireless network. Some routers also support WPA, or WiFi Protected Access, which provides a slightly higher level of security.

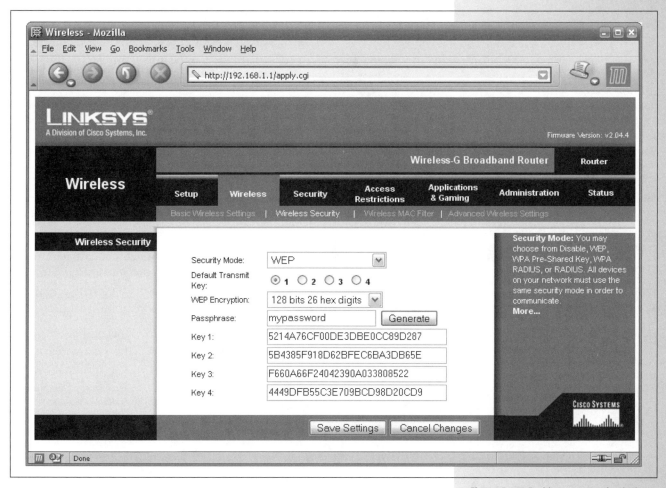

Figure 5-14. Enable encryption for the best wireless security.

On your router's encryption page, enable WEP, and then choose the highest WEP encryption level supported by your router (in this example, 128-bit). Higher levels provide better protection, but also mean longer (and harder to type) WEP keys.

Some routers have you choose a *passphrase*, which is a word your router uses to generate the WEP keys. In the example shown in Figure 5-14, I typed the word "annoyances" and clicked the Generate button to create four 26-digit WEP keys (the first one, Key 1, is the only one that is used). Generally, all of the computers on your wireless network will have to use the same key.

The Evils of SSID Broadcast

Your SSID is the back door into your wireless network. If you broadcast your SSID, anyone with an SSID sniffer will be able to find it in a matter of seconds, connect to your network, and use your Internet connection (or even snoop around your shared folders).

The same danger exists if you continue to use your router's default SSID; probably a million people around the globe are using "linksys," which makes it a good guess for anyone trying to gain access to your network. Choose an SSID like you'd choose a password, and your wireless network will stand a better chance of remaining private.

The only time you'll likely want to enable SSID broadcast, other than for testing purposes, is if you're setting up a public WiFi access point, say in a coffee shop or bed and breakfast, and you want to make it easy for your patrons to connect.

Figure 5-15. The Wireless Network Connection dialog shows all WiFi access points within range (except the hidden ones).

NOTE

Before you save your changes, take this opportunity to record your key in a file to simplify the subsequent setup of your PCs. Highlight the first key (Key 1), and press Ctrl-C to copy it. Then open your favorite text editor (e.g., Notepad), and press Ctrl-V to paste it into a new, empty document. Save the file on your desktop.

When you're done, click the Apply or Save Settings button at the bottom of the page, and then remove the cable connecting your PC to your router.

The next step is to enter one of the keys into each computer connected to your wireless network, as described in "Connect to a Wireless Network."

If you have trouble connecting to the router wirelessly, you probably entered the WEP key incorrectly. To fix the problem, either reconnect using a cable and change the settings or, as a final resort, reset the router as described in your router's documentation.

Connect to a Wireless Network

THE ANNOYANCE: I think I set up my wireless router correctly, but my PC doesn't see it.

THE FIX: You probably turned off your router's SSID broadcast feature, as instructed in "Set Up a Wireless Network." While this means that strangers using WiFi sniffers (described below) won't "discover" your network, it also means that your network won't show up when *you* scan for it, either.

To test this, open the Network Connections control panel and double-click your unconnected wireless connection to open the "Choose a wireless network" dialog box shown in Figure 5-15.

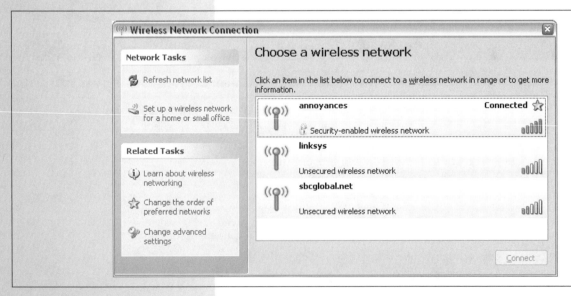

(You can also right-click the wireless connection icon in your System Tray or in the Network Connections window and select View Available Wireless Networks.) This window, Windows XP's built-in "sniffer," scans for WiFi access points within range and displays the results, typically in less than five seconds. (See the "Drive-by Sniffing" sidebar for more uses for this window.)

To connect to any visible network in the list, highlight it and click the Connect button. If your wireless network doesn't show up, simply click the "Set up a wireless network for a home or small office" link on the left to start the Wireless Network Setup Wizard (also accessible directly in the My Network Places folder). Click the Next button on the first page. On the "Create a name for your wireless network" screen, type your wireless network's SSID in the "Network name (SSID)" field (see Figure 5-16). If you've enabled WEP or WPA encryption for your router, select the "Manually assign a network key" option. If you selected WPA encryption in your router's setup, place a checkmark by the "Use WPA encryption" option; otherwise, for WEP, leave it unchecked. Then click Next.

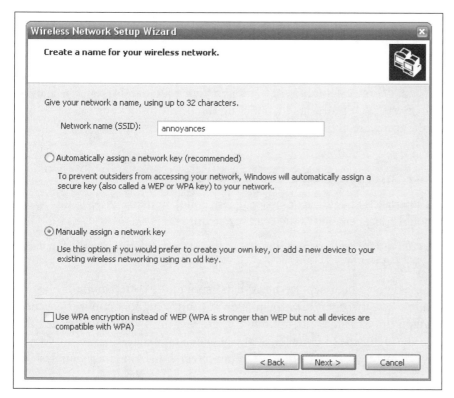

Figure 5-16. To connect to a hidden wireless network, type its SSID into the Wireless Network Setup Wizard.

On the next page, turn off the "Hide characters as I type" option to make the text fields here easier to deal with. Now, if you've saved your WEP key from the router setup page (see "Set Up a Wireless Network"), you can open

The Ethics of WiFi

Thanks to Windows XP's built-in WiFi sniffer, it's easy to detect and connect to any unsecured wireless network—including the network of an unsuspecting neighbor, which raises the thorny issue of ethics.

There are countless personal wireless networks around the globe, and most of them, you'll find, are unsecured. This means that if you walk down the street in a populated area, you'll probably find a working wireless Internet connection before you reach the end of the block. Some will have been left open intentionally, but most will be unsecured merely because their owners don't have the benefit of the advice in this chapter.

Now, just because you can connect to these networks, does it mean you should? Are you taking advantage of someone else's ignorance by breaking into their private network, or are you simply making use of a public resource that you'd be equally eager to share?

I'm not about to try to solve this dilemma in these short pages; I only wish to raise the question, and to suggest that if you do ever decide to utilize someone else's wireless network, you make sure to do no harm. Think about your impact, both on the bandwidth of the foreign network and the privacy of those who operate it. And then tread lightly.

—From *Windows XP Annoyances for Geeks, 2nd Edition*

the file, highlight the key, press Ctrl-C to copy the text, and then click in the "Network key" field and press Ctrl-V to paste in the text. Otherwise, you'll have to type in the key from your router setup page manually. Unless you feel like typing this long key twice, just copy and paste it into the second field, and then click the Next button.

Finally, the wizard gives you the opportunity to save your settings to a USB flash drive, theoretically making subsequent setups easier (why no option exists to save settings to a CD writer, floppy drive, or simply a file on your desktop is a mystery). If you don't have a USB flash drive handy, or if you don't need to set up any more computers, choose the "Set up a network manually" option. Click Next and then Finish when you're done.

From now on, your wireless network will show up in the "Choose a wireless network" list on this PC (as long as it's in range), even if you've chosen not to broadcast your SSID. You probably won't see it right away, though; just wait a few seconds and then click the "Refresh network list" link on the left. Your network should appear at the top of the list, proudly signifying that it has established a connection. You can now open a web browser and test your new wireless connection.

If you don't see the network, you either mistyped the SSID, or your wireless router isn't properly set up. If the network shows up but Windows can't connect, you likely mistyped the encryption key. If, after repeated attempts, you can't connect, disable encryption in your router and try again. You can usually fix such problems by updating the firmware in your router, as well as the firmware and drivers for the wireless card in your PC.

Surf Safely at the Coffee Shop

THE ANNOYANCE: I like to sit at my local coffee shop with my wireless laptop, sip a double decaf soy latte, and read my email. Is this safe?

THE FIX: Good question, and not one that occurs to a lot of people. Soy lattes can be risky if you don't take proper precautions.

Now, when you connect to the WiFi hotspot at the coffee shop (or on some random street corner downtown), you're connecting to a public, unsecured workgroup. This may not seem like a problem until you consider the other PCs that also may be connected, any of which may share a virus or two with you, or merely serve as a conduit for an intruder hacking into your system.

To improve your security, first turn off any and all shared folders (see "List All Your Shared Folders"). And if you haven't done so already, set up a password for your user account, as described in "Protect Shared Files." This will go a long way toward protecting your data from casual intrusions, but you shouldn't stop there.

To be on the safe side, enable the Windows Firewall (see "Make Peer-to-Peer File Sharing Work") or install more competent third-party firewall software, such as ZoneAlarm Pro ($49.95, *http://www.zonelabs.com*). The best solutions allow you to easily switch between a relaxed state, permitting all your programs to work while you're safely behind your router's firewall at home, and a heightened state of security when you're on the road.

Of course, mind what you do on the Net while you're at that coffee shop, too. As long as you're using someone else's network, nothing you do should be considered private. Although secure SSL-protected web sites do provide better privacy than insecure sites, you're probably better off visiting financial web sites only when you're at home.

Increase Range and Improve Reception

THE ANNOYANCE: My laptop connects to the Internet without any problem as long as I'm in the same room as my wireless router. But once I change rooms or move too far away from my router, the connection drops in and out. What's the deal?

THE FIX: Interference is the name of the game. The tiny WiFi transceiver in your PC should be capable of picking up any wireless network within about 300 feet under ideal conditions—namely, outdoors with a clear line of sight. Indoors, the range can be quite a bit lower; typically, the signal won't go through more than two or three walls, and perhaps one floor or ceiling.

Drive-by Sniffing

Every WiFi-equipped PC is capable of WiFi sniffing: scanning the area immediately surrounding it and listing any hotspots (wireless network access points) it finds. Of course, only those networks that are broadcasting their SSIDs will show up, which is why you'll probably want to turn off SSID broadcast on your own router (see the "The Evils of SSID Broadcast" sidebar).

The "Choose a wireless network" dialog box is Windows XP's built-in WiFi sniffer, and it is particularly handy when you're trying to find an Internet connection away from home. Whether you're in a coffee shop, in a hotel, or just driving through some residential neighborhood, you can use the sniffer to list any available WiFi networks within range. The closest networks (or rather, the ones with the strongest signals) are listed first, followed by the weaker, more distant hotspots.

A yellow padlock icon indicates secure hotspots—wireless networks requiring WEP or WPA security keys—so highlight the unsecured network with the strongest signal, and click the Connect button. With any luck, Windows should connect to the network in 10–15 seconds, and you should be able to start surfing normally soon thereafter.

If you're concerned about your own privacy when using someone else's hotspot, see "Surf Safely at the Coffee Shop."

The placement of your wireless router and the arrangement of nearby obstacles will have a significant effect on the strength and range of your WiFi signal. Of course, your router will need to be within spitting distance of your DSL or cable modem, but with a sufficiently long cable, you should have some leeway with the router's placement. Use the signal strength indicator in the "Choose a wireless network" window (right-click the wireless connection icon in the System Tray or Network Connections window and choose View Available Wireless Networks) to test various configurations (see Figure 5-15 in "Connect to a Wireless Network").

> **NOTE**
>
> *Place your wireless router out in the open; don't put it under your desk, in a drawer, or behind a metal file cabinet. If you're feeding several PCs, place your router in a central location. Consider cabling any stationary computers to optimize the placement of the router for your portable (wireless) ones.*

Now, other technology in your home or office may also interfere with your wireless network, limiting its range, speed, and reliability. Both the popular 802.11b and newer 802.11g standards operate over the 2.4-GHz band, which is also inhabited by many cordless phones and all microwave ovens. (The black sheep of the family, 802.11a, solves this problem by using the 5-GHz band, but its short range and limited compatibility make it an unpopular choice.) This means that you'll get better results if you move the router away from any cordless phone base stations, televisions, radios, security systems, or TV dinners. (Better yet, replace your aging 2.4-GHz portable phone with a WiFi-friendly 5.8-GHz cordless phone.)

If, after adjusting the placement of your router, you still need more range, consider either a repeater (range extender) or an aftermarket antenna (provided your router has an antenna port to accommodate one). If you need a lot more distance (possibly at the expense of some versatility)—and you fancy yourself a tinkerer—a Pringles "cantenna" (*http://www.oreillynet. com/pub/wlg/448*) can extend your wireless range by a mile or more!

> **NOTE**
>
> *Like to stay mobile? Keep an eye on your wireless reception with the free Wireless Strength widget (http://www.widgetforge. com/?w=58), a graphical signal strength meter that sits on your desktop. (This tool requires the Kapsules scripting engine, freely available from http://www. kwidgets.com.)*

Turn Off "Not Connected" Messages

THE ANNOYANCE: Every time I turn on my PC, a little yellow balloon pops up in the lower-right corner of my screen and says that my network cable is unplugged. I'm not using a network cable at all, and my wireless connection works fine. Does this error mean anything?

THE FIX: Not really. It's kind of like the flight attendant who wakes you up during a long flight to ask if you want a pillow (no offense intended to flight attendants... or pillows).

Windows XP is designed to notify you whenever one of your network connections isn't connected, even when another connection is working fine. Common sense would tell you to open the Network Connections control panel, right-click the connection in question, choose Properties, and uncheck the "Notify me when this connection has limited or no connectivity" box. However, this seemingly apt option has no effect on this error.

Unfortunately, the only way to permanently do away with this useless message is to disable the offending connection entirely. Open the Network Connections control panel, right-click the connection, and select Disable. You'll notice that both the message and the icon in your Tray disappear, never to be seen again (unless you re-enable the connection).

Connect PCs Wirelessly Without a Router

THE ANNOYANCE: My sister and I both have wireless laptops, but we're traveling and nowhere near a wireless router. Can we connect to each other anyway?

THE FIX: Yes you can, using something called an *ad-hoc* wireless network, a little-known feature specifically designed to connect two PCs to one another wirelessly.

On one of the PCs, open the Network Connections control panel, right-click your wireless connection, and select Properties. Choose the Wireless Networks tab, and click the Add button to display the Wireless Network Properties dialog box shown in Figure 5-17.

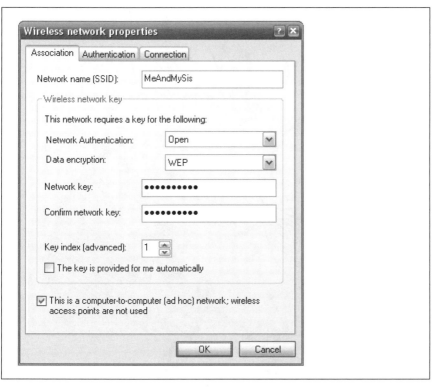

Figure 5-17. Create an ad-hoc network to connect two PCs wirelessly without a router or nearby WiFi hotspot.

Type a name for your ad-hoc network in the "Network name (SSID)" field. From the Network Authentication drop-down list, choose Open, and from the Data encryption list, choose WEP.

Next, remove the checkmark next to the "The key is provided for me automatically" option, and then make up a key to type into both the "Network key" and "Confirm network key" fields. The key can be any combination of numbers and letters from A–F; for the sake of simplicity, use a 10-character (64-bit) key.

Finally, place a checkmark next to the "This is a computer-to-computer (ad hoc) network; wireless access points are not used" option at the bottom of the window, and then click OK. The new network should show up in the "Preferred networks" list, along with the word "(Automatic)," signifying that Windows will connect to this network automatically when it is in range.

Now, repeat these steps on the other PC, and then open the "Choose a wireless network" dialog box on both PCs (see "Connect to a Wireless Network"). With any luck, and a few clicks of the "Refresh network list" link, the two PCs should connect and form a private workgroup. To set it up so you can exchange files between the two PCs, see "Share Files with Other Computers."

Setup and Hardware

Installing and setting up an operating system is akin to dental surgery (without anesthesia), sitting in traffic on a hot day (without A/C), or cleaning the cat litter box (without—never mind). Surprisingly, and to Microsoft's credit, Windows XP's installation and hardware detection procedures are a lot better than those of previous versions of Windows. However, they're a long way from being effortless.

Hassling with Microsoft's registration system, dealing with restore CDs, sorting out drivers, and worse are still unenviable tasks, but once you know how to deal with these annoyances you can make Windows run more smoothly...at least, until the next version of the operating system comes out!

SETUP

Boot with the Windows CD

THE ANNOYANCE: My PC got hit with a pretty nasty virus, and the damage was so severe that I had to wipe my hard disk clean (see "Wipe Your Hard Disk Clean"). Now I'm trying to reinstall Windows, but my PC won't boot off the CD. How else can I install this thing?

THE FIX: Normally, you're supposed to install (or reinstall) Windows from *within* Windows. With Windows running, pop the CD into your drive, and Setup should start automatically. This is the method of choice if you're upgrading to a newer version of Windows or simply reinstalling your existing version to fix some problems, since Setup is able to preserve your settings (desktop icons, colors, etc.), as well as installed applications and data.

Of course, on a PC without any working copy of Windows, you'll have to do a "clean install," which typically requires that you boot your computer directly off the Windows CD. However, for this to work your PC must be configured to check your CD drive for bootable discs before booting off the hard disk, and most PCs aren't set up this way by default.

To change the default boot device for this and all subsequent boots, restart your computer. Immediately before the Power On Self Test (POST) "beep," press the key on your keyboard (usually Del, F1, F2, or Esc) used to enter your PC's BIOS setup screen. Refer to your computer's manual for details about your system's BIOS setup.

Once inside Setup, navigate to the "Boot" or "Startup" section (see Figure 6-1) with the cursor keys. Using the keys indicated on the screen (usually in a legend at the bottom), move your CD or DVD drive so that it is listed before your hard disk (a.k.a. HDD). Setup screens vary widely, so consult your manual for specific instructions. When you're done, save your settings and reboot (usually by pressing Esc, F10, or the End key).

When your PC reboots, it should poll your CD drive and check for a bootable CD. If the XP CD is in the drive, you'll be asked to "Press the spacebar to boot off CD." Press the spacebar, and in a few seconds you should see a series of unfriendly messages (white text on a black screen) that indicate that Windows Setup is loading.

If your PC won't boot off the XP CD, chances are that your CD or DVD drive is one of the astonishingly large percentage of drives that don't properly support bootable CDs. If you can't get yours to work, try a different drive. Another possibility is that your PC didn't come come with a real Windows CD, but rather something called a *restore disc*—see "Create a Usable Restore Disc" for details.

NOTE

On some modern PCs, you can press F12 at startup to show a list of possible boot devices; from here, choose your CD drive to boot off the Windows CD for this session.

NOTE

When you've successfully installed the operating system, follow the above procedure to change your BIOS settings again, reinstating the hard disk as the default boot device.

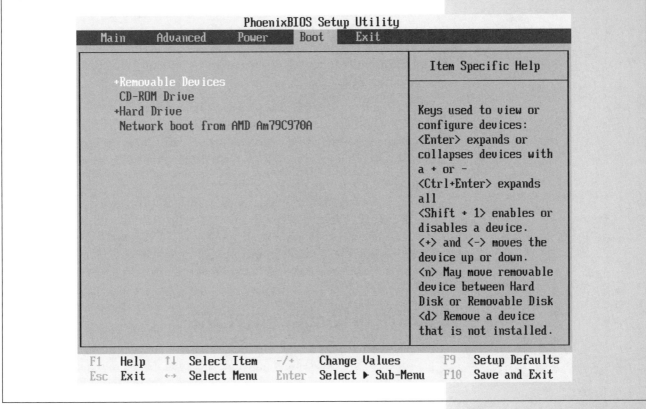

Figure 6-1. Use the BIOS setup to instruct your PC to boot off your CD drive.

Setup Hangs Before It's Finished

THE ANNOYANCE: I'm in the middle of installing Windows, glaring at the slowly moving progress bar, when all of a sudden the bar stops moving. Against my better judgment I wait patiently, and seconds later the screen goes black. The computer reboots and I have to start over. What now?

THE FIX: This is usually caused by a hardware problem, more often than not involving the video card. If you're using a desktop PC with a removable video card (as opposed to one that's built into the motherboard, as in most laptops), replace it with one you're certain is compatible with Windows XP. There are compatibility lists on Microsoft's web site, and there's even an Upgrade Advisor on the XP CD; while hardly comprehensive (and occasionally even inaccurate), these can be used to confirm that your video adapter or other component is specifically incompatible with Windows XP. If replacing the video card doesn't help or is impractical, remove all nonessential cards and try Setup again.

If your video card isn't the problem—or if your PC's video card is built into the motherboard—the culprit is often an out-of-date BIOS (updatable software stored on a chip on the motherboard). Visit your PC manufacturer's web site and look for a BIOS update for your model. (The version number of your BIOS is usually shown onscreen immediately after your PC is turned on, and just before the Windows logo appears.) In most cases, the update comes in the form of a downloadable file and accompanying updater software; carefully follow the instructions to update your BIOS, and then try Windows Setup again.

Don't rule out your CD drive, either. Older drives—particularly ones that have accumulated several years' worth of dust and cat hair—can be unreliable when transferring large amounts of data. If Setup keeps failing and you've ruled out everything else, try replacing your CD drive.

Of course, there are a host of other—admittedly more obscure—problems that can cause Windows Setup to hang, such as mismatched or faulty RAM, incorrect CPU voltage settings, or an incompatible hard disk controller. If you're using a nonstandard RAID, SATA, or SCSI controller, you may have to either press F6 at the beginning of Setup to load custom drivers, or temporarily remove the controller to complete Setup.

Reinstall Windows over SP2

THE ANNOYANCE: After being battered by a virus and my meager attempts to eradicate it, my PC is essentially nonfunctional. I need to reinstall Windows XP without erasing my hard disk and all my data. But when I pop in my XP CD and try to run Windows Setup, I'm told that I can't install Windows over a newer version. It doesn't make sense: I'm installing XP over XP!

THE FIX: The problem is that you're not using Windows XP, you're using Windows XP Service Pack 2 (or SP2), which Microsoft considers a newer version of the operating system. If you're like most of us, the service pack—a bundle of patches and updates assembled by Microsoft—was installed automatically as part of the Windows Update service.

Does this mean your old XP CD is useless? Not necessarily. If you need to reinstall Windows, you have two options. First, you may be able to uninstall SP2 via the Add or Remove Programs control panel, and then reinstall XP. Alternatively, you can use your existing Windows CD to create a new Windows disc that includes SP2 and then use the new disc to reinstall Windows. This second process is called *slipstreaming*, and while somewhat arduous, it's worth the trouble, particularly if you want to be prepared for future PC emergencies (if your PC won't boot you won't be able to remove SP2, which means you won't be able to reinstall Windows, and your remaining option will involve crushing your PC with a large, blunt instrument).

To start, you'll need a real, original Windows XP CD; if you only have a restore disc (see "Create a Usable Restore Disc") or an XP CD with SP1 already installed, you can't use this fix. You'll also need a CD writer, a blank disc, and a full-blown CD burning application, such as Roxio Easy Media

> **NOTE**
>
> *Okay, I lied. There are other options—see "Windows Won't Start."*

Creator ($99.95, *http://www.roxio.com*) or Nero Ultra Edition ($79.99, *http://www.nero.com*). Windows Explorer's built-in CD burning feature won't cut it.

First, open Windows Explorer and create two new folders in the root folder of your hard disk: *c:\xp* and *c:\sp2*. Pop your original XP CD in your drive, highlight everything in the root folder of your CD (press Ctrl-A), and copy (drag) all the files on the CD into the *c:\xp* folder you just created.

Next, download the "Full Network Install" release of Service Pack 2. The filename is *WindowsXP-KB835935-SP2-ENU.exe*, and it's available at *http://www.annoyances.org/sp2/*. Save this 270+ MB file to the *c:\sp2* folder on your hard disk, and when it's finished downloading, rename the file to *sp2.exe*.

Open a Command Prompt window (go to Start→Run and type cmd.exe), and type:

```
c:\sp2\sp2.exe /integrate:c:\xp
```

If you get an error stating "This Service Pack cannot be integrated into a destination that also has integrated Software Updates," it means your CD is not a true, original Windows XP CD and thus can't be slipstreamed. If you get a "not a valid Win32 application" error, the patch you downloaded is corrupt; you'll need to delete it and download it again. If you get the cryptic "file too big for memory" error, you're short on disk space—you need at least 1 GB of free space *after* you've copied the setup files.

You'll need one more thing from your original Windows CD. Download IsoBuster from *http://www.isobuster.com* ($25.95, free working demo), and run the program. In the main IsoBuster window, select your CD drive from the list and highlight the *Bootable CD* folder on the left. On the right, you should see an *.img* file (e.g., *Microsoft Corporation.img* or possibly *BootImage.img*). Drag this file into the *c:\sp2* folder on your hard disk.

Next, open your CD burning software, and start a new "Bootable Disc" project (in Roxio) or "CD-ROM (Boot)" project (in Nero). When prompted, specify these settings:

- Bootable disc type: no emulation

- Boot image data/image file: specify the *.img* file you extracted with IsoBuster

- File system: Joliet

- Sector count (boot section): 4 sectors

- Load segment: 0x7C0

- Volume label: use the same CD volume label as your original XP CD

In most CD-burning programs, you'll be prompted for this information in a piecemeal fashion via a series of dialog boxes once you start the CD project. (Consult your application's documentation for additional settings necessary to create bootable CDs.) When given the opportunity, add the entire contents of the *c:\xp* folder to your project, and then burn the CD.

When the burn is complete, you should have a bootable Windows XP SP2 CD, which can be used just like your original XP CD. You can test the CD by using it to boot your system, as described in "Boot with the Windows CD." Once you're sure the CD works, you can delete both the *c:\xp* and *c:\sp2* folders.

To use the CD to reinstall Windows, you have two options: insert the new CD while Windows is running, or—if you can't get into Windows—boot off the CD (as described in "Boot with the Windows CD"). In either case, choose the option to upgrade Windows rather than performing a fresh install, so that Setup can retain your installed applications and all your settings. Then, just follow the onscreen prompts to complete installation.

Unless you choose to format your hard disk, as described in "Wipe Your Hard Disk Clean," all your data will remain intact.

Wipe Your Hard Disk Clean

THE ANNOYANCE: I had a pretty serious virus invasion recently, and rather than trying to recover my data—none of which I care about—I want to wipe my hard disk clean and start over. How do I do this?

THE FIX: You'll typically find it much easier to destroy data than to create it. Nonetheless, there's no direct way to wipe your hard disk clean from within Windows, and understandably so.

If you wipe your hard disk using either of the following methods, and you have no recent backup, you will lose all your personal data with no reliable means of retrieving it.

The easiest way to wipe your hard disk clean is to use the "restore disc" that came with your PC (see "Create a Usable Restore Disc"). Not only will it erase your hard disk, but it will reinstall Windows, all your drivers, and even much of the software that originally came with your PC. Just insert the CD and follow the instructions.

Don't have a restore disc, or want more control? Just boot your system off an original Windows XP CD, as described in "Boot with the Windows CD." Wait for a few minutes while Setup loads the drivers it needs and completes initiation, and then press Enter to "Set up Windows XP now." Press F8 to agree to the silly license, and moments later you'll see a list of drives and partitions on your system, like the one in Figure 6-2.

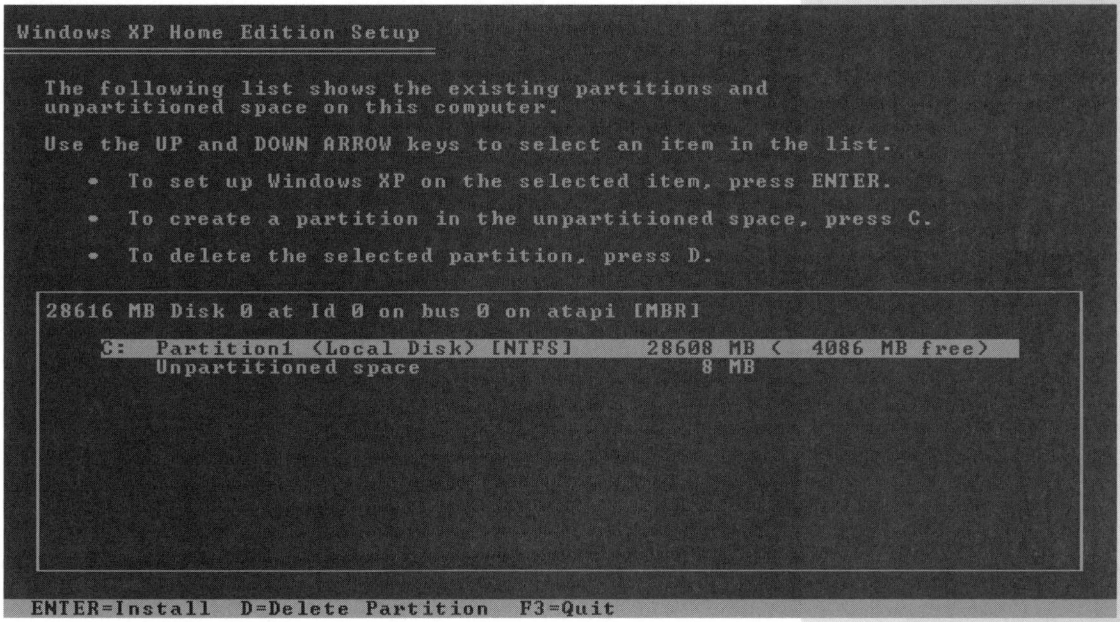

```
Windows XP Home Edition Setup

    The following list shows the existing partitions and
    unpartitioned space on this computer.

    Use the UP and DOWN ARROW keys to select an item in the list.

        •  To set up Windows XP on the selected item, press ENTER.

        •  To create a partition in the unpartitioned space, press C.

        •  To delete the selected partition, press D.

    28616 MB Disk 0 at Id 0 on bus 0 on atapi [MBR]

        C:  Partition1 <Local Disk> [NTFS]      28608 MB < 4086 MB free>
            Unpartitioned space                     8 MB


    ENTER=Install   D=Delete Partition   F3=Quit
```

How you proceed at this point is up to you, but assuming there's no valuable data on your system, use the cursor keys to select partitions on your drive and then press the D key to delete them. (Deleting a partition instantly erases all data on it.) When there are no partitions left (all you see is "Unpartitioned space"), press the C key to create a new partition, type the maximum size for the partition (in MB), and press Enter. Then, highlight the new partition and press Enter to install Windows on it. Complete the setup by following the instructions onscreen.

Figure 6-2. Use the partition editor in Windows XP Setup to quickly erase your hard disk and prepare a fresh XP installation.

Create a Usable Restore Disc

THE ANNOYANCE: I've read that only reinstalling Windows can resolve some problems, and I'm wondering whether or not I have a Windows CD. All I can find is something called a "restore disc." Is this the same thing?

THE FIX: Probably not. Due to licensing restrictions, and in order to save a few cents, many PC manufacturers do not include original Windows CDs with their computers. The good news is that some manufacturers will send you a Windows CD if you ask; you did pay for it, after all. Some companies require a modest shipping fee; others, not so modest. But odds are that your PC vendor will refuse your request outright. In this case, eBay is a good source for inexpensive XP CDs, or, if you want to pay full price, you can go to any software retailer. Just make sure you get a valid, legal copy—complete with an official certificate of authenticity and CD key—whether it's used or new.

In most cases, the recovery CD included with your PC is good for one thing: wiping your hard disk clean and filling it with all the software that was included with the machine when it was new. Unless you're preparing to sell your computer, this isn't usually a practical choice. (See "Wipe Your Hard Disk Clean" for other circumstances that might make this a more attractive option.)

Recovery CDs do typically have a few things your ordinary Windows XP CD lacks, though: namely, drivers for all the hardware that came with your PC, along with the crummy applications that came preinstalled on your system. You probably haven't given much thought to these drivers, since they were preinstalled on your computer, but unless you want to wipe your hard disk each time you need to solve a hardware problem you'd be wise to build yourself a separate driver CD from which you can easily install individual drivers.

First, visit your PC manufacturer's web site, and download all the latest drivers for your PC. Make sure you get your video, network, wireless, sound, and chipset drivers, as well as drivers for any products you've added after purchasing the PC.

If any drivers are encapsulated in ZIP files, unzip them into separate folders; that way, you'll be able to install them directly from your CD later (without having to manually unzip them first). When you have everything in hand, burn all the drivers to a CD, write "Drivers" and today's date on the disc with a Sharpie pen, and put it in a safe place. This disc and your original Windows XP CD (and regular backups of your precious data) are all you need to recover your PC from a serious crash.

Set Up a Dual-Boot System

THE ANNOYANCE: I'm a holdout, still using good ol' Windows 98 on my every-day PC... but I'm finally getting tired of the crashing, and I'd like to try Windows XP without committing to it. Can I install Windows XP on my machine without losing Windows 98?

THE FIX: Absolutely—just use the dual-boot feature built into Windows XP. With a dual-boot (or multiboot) setup, you can install multiple operating systems side by side on the same computer and simply choose which one to use each time you boot.

Windows 98 doesn't explicitly support a dual-boot configuration, but it doesn't have to. The key is to install Windows XP *last*, so that its boot manager (installed automatically with Windows XP) can accommodate both your existing operating system and the new one.

Setting up a dual-boot system is easy, but it's not necessarily intuitive. First, you must install XP into a different folder or drive than the one your current version occupies. So, if Windows 98 is installed in *c:\windows*, you'll

---

> **NOTE**
>
> *Having your network drivers on disc is particularly important, because without them you probably won't be able to connect to the Internet and download other drivers later on, when you really need them.*

A Word About Filesystems and Dual-Boot

Windows XP supports both the NTFS and FAT32 filesystems. If you need to set up a dual-boot machine with Windows 9x/Me and Windows XP, you'll need to use FAT32 on any drives that you want to access from the older Windows, as only Windows 2000, NT, and XP support NTFS.

—From *Windows XP Annoyances for Geeks, 2nd Edition*

need to put Windows XP in something like *c:\winxp* or *d:\windows*. (If you're installing XP over another OS that has its own boot manager, such as Windows 2000 or Unix, you'll have to use a different drive for each operating system.)

Note: don't install Windows XP from *within* your current version of Windows, or Setup will perform an upgrade, and you'll lose Windows 98. Instead, boot off your XP CD, as described in "Boot with the Windows CD," and follow the instructions onscreen to complete the installation. When Setup detects your existing Windows installation, it will give you the option of upgrading it or installing XP into a different folder or drive.

If, at the end of the installation, Windows XP is the only operating system on your computer, it will boot automatically without giving you a choice. Otherwise, you'll see a menu of installed operating systems each time you boot, from which you can choose the OS you wish to use for that session.

STARTUP AND SHUTDOWN

Windows Won't Start

THE ANNOYANCE: I turned on my computer this morning, and all I got was a black screen and the rather unhelpful message "Operating system not found" in little white letters. Is my PC trying to tell me that my hard disk has crashed?

THE FIX: When you turn on your PC, the first thing it does after completing its Power On Self Test (POST) is to scan your hard disk for something called a *master boot record* (MBR), a pointer to a program on your hard disk that tells your PC which partition contains your operating system. This error message means that your PC can't find Windows XP's boot information, because the MBR is corrupt, the entry for Windows in the MBR is absent or corrupt, or any of a half-dozen other reasons. But don't panic—the solution is often a simple one.

First, eject any disks from your PC's floppy and CD drives, and then reboot. Some computers check these drives for boot information before moving on to your hard disk, and display the above error message if no boot records are detected.

If that doesn't help, determine whether your PC is detecting your hard disk at all. During the self-test, your PC displays a bunch of information about your system, including details about the processor, memory, and hard disks. (Many new PCs display a large logo while this is happening, but you can usually hide the logo and display this information by pressing the Esc key.) If the screen blows by too quickly, or you don't see any hard disk information, enter your system BIOS setup screen, as described in "Boot with the Windows CD," and peruse the information there.

> **NOTE**
>
> *Already using Windows XP, and want to try out Windows Vista? When setting up any multiboot PC, always install earlier operating systems first, followed by more recent versions. Typically, the boot manager included with the last operating system installed is the one that is used.*

> **NOTE**
>
> *If you don't want the hassle associated with a dual-boot sytem, or if you want to install many different versions of Windows, you can use a program like Microsoft VirtualPC. Instead of separate partitions, you create multiple hard disk images (resizable files on your hard disk), and then launch VirtualPC and install the operating sytems to those images from within your version of Windows. Although there's a performance hit, it's the only way to run multiple versions of Windows on the same PC simultaneously.*

If your hard disk—typically identified by manufacturer and model number—is not listed, your PC is not detecting it. There are about 50 things that can cause this problem, but it's often nothing more than a bad data cable. Crack open your PC's case, and make sure the IDE, SATA, or SCSI cable connecting your hard disk to the motherboard is firmly attached at both ends. If the problem persists, replace the cable with a brand new one. You could also unplug every drive other than your hard disk (e.g., CD and DVD drives, Zip and tape drives, etc.) to see if one of them is causing the problem.

If your PC *is* detecting your hard disk but Windows still won't load, fire up the Windows Recovery Console (WRC) and attempt repairs there. To get into the WRC, insert your Windows XP CD in your CD drive and turn on your computer (see "Boot with the Windows CD" if this doesn't work). After Setup loads all of its drivers, press the R key to start the Windows Recovery Console.

When the WRC starts, you'll see a screen titled "Windows NT™ Boot Console Command Interpreter." If you're asked "Which Windows installation would you like to logon to," type the number next to your Windows XP folder (usually 1...c:\Windows), and then type your administrator password (see Chapter 5). Once you've logged in, the WRC looks and feels a lot like the Windows Command Prompt (a.k.a. DOS), but it supports only a handful of DOS commands.

At the prompt, type dir and press Enter to display a listing of the files and folders in the root folder of your hard disk (usually *c:*). If you see a bunch of garbage characters or you get a strange error, stop immediately and take your hard disk to a data recovery expert.

Otherwise, if the listing looks normal (i.e., you see the *WINDOWS* and *Program Files* folders), type fixmbr and press Enter. Then type fixboot and press Enter. When the two commands finish, press Ctrl-Alt-Del to restart your computer and see if Windows loads properly.

If Windows still won't boot, your hard disk needs more help than I can provide in these pages. If your drive contains any valuable data, try a recovery utility such as SpinRite ($89.00, *http://www.grc.com*) or, if you don't want to risk doing more damage, take it to a data recovery expert and hope for the best.

> **WARNING**
>
> *Checking your hard disk for signs of corruption is a crucial step. If you continue and attempt repairs on a corrupt drive, you may irreparably damage data that otherwise might be recoverable. Windows Setup actually provides another, easier-to-use feature (an alternative to the WRC) entitled "Repair an existing installation," but it's a poor choice because it doesn't let you check for corruption before effecting repairs.*

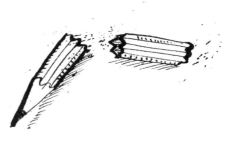

Desktop Never Appears

THE ANNOYANCE: Windows just won't finish loading. I stare at the Windows logo for what seems like an eternity, and then the pulsating progress bar stops pulsating. That's it; Windows never loads. What's going on?

THE FIX: When Windows boots, it loads all of its drivers, initializes its network connections, and loads its high-level components (Explorer, fonts, etc.) into memory. These things are loaded in order; if one task cannot complete—because of a corrupted file or network error, for instance—the next task cannot begin and the boot process stalls.

If the problem started happening as soon as you added a new hardware device, check the device manufacturer's web site for a driver or BIOS update. Otherwise, first unplug your network cable and try again. If Windows loads, there's something wrong with your network connection, Internet connection, router, or whatever else is on the other end of that cable.

Still stuck? Unplug all the USB and FireWire devices connected to your PC. If Windows loads, reconnect them one by one, restarting Windows after each reconnection, until you find the culprit that hangs the system. Really stuck? Start disconnecting any non-USB peripherals (e.g., keyboard, mouse, parallel printer) attached to your PC and, if necessary/applicable, PCI or PCMCIA cards and any other nonessential devices inside your PC.

If the above steps don't work, there may be a problem with your hard disk—but if you're getting as far as the Windows logo, it's probably not too serious. To investigate, restart your computer, and just after the beep but before the Windows logo appears, press the F8 key. From the Windows Advanced Options Menu, use the arrow keys to highlight Safe Mode, and press Enter.

Safe Mode allows Windows to load without network support, hardware drivers, some services, and a handful of other components that can sometimes cause this problem. If Safe Mode works, open Windows Explorer, right-click your hard disk (e.g., drive *c:*), select Properties, and choose the Tools tab. In the "Error-checking" section, click the Check Now button. Check the boxes next to both options in the "Check disk" section and click the Start button, and ScanDisk will open and check your drive for errors. When it's finished, restart Windows normally.

> **NOTE**
>
> *If you're running off a battery, plug your laptop into its charger and wait for about 20 minutes for the battery to accumulate sufficient charge to start Windows.*

Chapter 6, Setup and Hardware ————————————————————————

Un-Hobble the Windows Recovery Console

THE ANNOYANCE: There's a virus-infected file on my hard disk that I can't delete, so I'm trying to use the Windows Recovery Console to excise it. But the WRC apparently will only let me delete files in the root directory and in *c:\Windows*. What gives?

THE FIX: The WRC does more than repair master boot records (see "Windows Won't Start"); it provides access to the files on your hard disk when Windows isn't running, allowing you to copy, delete, or rename them as you see fit. However, it won't let you do this until you release a restriction that's in place by default.

Return to Windows, go to Start→Run, type secpol.msc, and press Enter to start the Local Security Settings editor. Navigate to *\Security Settings\ Local Policies\Security Options* in the tree on the left, and double-click the "Recovery Console: Allow floppy copy and access to all drives and all folders" entry on the right. Select Enabled, and click OK.

Next, return to the WRC and type:

```
set AllowAllPaths = true
```

Make sure to include the spaces before and after the equals sign, and press Enter. Thereafter, you can delete any file in any folder. Although the change you made in the Local Security Settings is permanent, you'll have to issue the above set command once each time you use the WRC.

You may have noticed a Catch-22 of sorts in this fix. If Windows won't boot and you're using the WRC to effect repairs, you won't be able to release the Local Security Settings restriction. In this case, you'll either have to live without the ability to delete files in other folders, or install a second copy of Windows XP on another partition (see "Set Up a Dual-Boot System") and delete the file from there.

Windows Won't Shut Down

THE ANNOYANCE: When I try to shut down Windows, it hangs at the "Saving Settings" screen. Why can't Windows even handle a simple shutdown?

THE FIX: Every time you shut down your PC, Windows attempts to close all running applications, stop all active services, and unload all drivers in memory. If just one of these components stops responding, Windows will wait until it can be closed successfully. As you can probably guess, all it takes is one crashed program or one stubborn driver to prevent Windows from shutting down.

The most common culprit is a power management bug found in many PCs. If you ever put your PC to "sleep" by pressing the power switch or closing the laptop lid, Windows may not be able to complete a formal shutdown

---

NOTE

There are some other settings you can change in the WRC. To use wildcards (and ?) when typing commands, type:*

```
set AllowWildcards = true
```

and press Enter. To access files on floppies and CDs, type:

```
set AllowRemovableMedia
= true
```

and press Enter.

NOTE

If all you want to do is delete an in-use file, see "Delete an Udeletable Folder" in Chapter 2.

---

thereafter. Unfortunately, there's not much you can do about this, other than checking your PC manufacturer's web site for a BIOS update (see "Setup Hangs Before It's Finished").

If you never hibernate or sleep your PC, the problem may be spyware—which can be adequately described as "stubborn"—that refuses to be unloaded. (See "Put an End to Pop-ups" in Chapter 4 for tips on how to rid your system of such parasites.)

If an antispyware scan doesn't solve the problem, the errant program is likely a legitimate software component, and it may take a bit of sleuthing to track it down. Close all open applications, and then right-click an empty area of the Windows Taskbar. From the menu that appears, select Task Manager. Then choose the Processes tab to see a list all the programs running on your PC, including those running in the background; click the Image Name column header to sort the list alphabetically (see Figure 6-3).

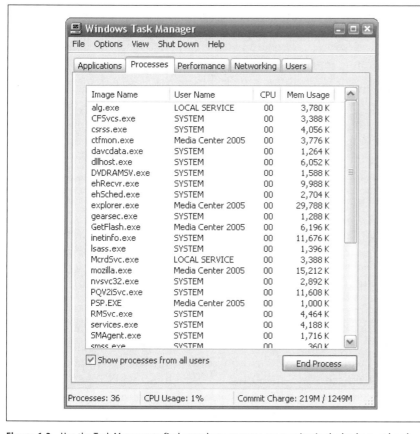

Figure 6-3. Use the Task Manager to find out what programs are running in the background and mucking up your system.

Your goal: find the programs that are causing your shutdown problem. Although the Task Manager won't give you this information directly, it will let you close almost any running program, one by one. Any program that you close with the End Process button in the Task Manager won't be running when you shut down, and thus can't prevent Windows from shutting down properly. (This isn't foolproof, but it works pretty well most of the time.)

Most of the programs listed in the Task Manager's Processes tab are Windows components necessary for the operating system to function (e.g., *csrss.exe*, *inetinfo.exe*, *rundll32.exe*, *svchost.exe*, *winlogon.exe*, etc.); the rest are either applications you've started or malware (viruses, spyware, etc.). A few processes will be self-explanatory, such as *explorer.exe* and *firefox.exe*, but odds are that you'll recognize very few others. So how do you tell the difference between the good processes and the bad?

The best way to research a particular process is to look up the filename in an online database of "known" processes, such as *http://www.neuber.com/taskmanager/process/*. If you need more information, search for the filename with Google. However, there are two big complications that make identifying your running processes more difficult.

First, some forms of malware use the same filenames as common Windows components to disguise themselves. For instance, *csrss.exe* is the main executable for the Microsoft Client/Server Runtime Server Subsystem, a Windows component, but it also can be a virus (the W32.Netsky.AB@mm worm or the W32.Webus Trojan, specifically). The good news is that such ambiguities are almost always chronicled in the online process databases.

> **NOTE**
>
> *Rather than trying to painstakingly distinguish valid processes from Trojan horses, just scan your system with trusted antivirus and antispyware utilities, as described in "Put an End to Pop-ups" in Chapter 4. If the shutdown problem persists once that's out of the way, odds are that the culprit is nothing more than a valid yet misbehaving driver or application.*

The other complication is that some entries in the Task Manager's Processes list are simply loader programs for background processes. Case in point: each instance of *svchost.exe* corresponds to a running service, but the Task Manager won't tell you which ones are which; all you'll see are multiple entries labeled *svchost.exe*. To see which services are running, and to stop, restart, or configure any services on your system, go to Start→Run, type `services.msc`, and click OK.

When you've closed a handful of suspect programs, go ahead and shut down (or restart) Windows. If Windows shuts down normally, one of the programs you just closed was indeed the cause of the problem. Try updating or uninstalling the offending program or driver, and your shutdown problems should vanish.

> **NOTE**
>
> *For an alternative to the Task Manager that allows you to see the full paths of the processes in memory, fire up the System Information tool (go to Start→Run and type* `msinfo32.exe`*), expand the Software Environment branch on the tree, and select Running Tasks.*

> **NOTE**
>
> *If you want to stop a program from loading every time Windows boots without uninstalling it, see "Faster Windows Boot."*

Unattended Shutdown

THE ANNOYANCE: I thought I shut down my computer before leaving the office, but when I got back the next day I saw that it was still running. On the screen was a window that said an application had stopped responding. Why didn't Windows just close the program and shut off my PC?

THE FIX: As noted earlier in "Windows Won't Shut Down," Windows tries to close all running applications, stop all active services, and unload all drivers each time it shuts down. Often, Windows just sits and waits if one of those programs won't cooperate and close. All it takes to grease the wheels and change how Windows treats hung applications is a few quick changes to the Windows Registry.

Open the Registry Editor (go to Start→Run and type regedit), and navigate to *HKEY_CURRENT_USER\Control Panel\Desktop*. Double-click the *AutoEndTasks* value in the right pane, type 1 (one) in the "Value data" field, and click OK. Next, double-click the *WaitToKillAppTimeout* value, type 1000 in the "Value data" field, and then click OK. Close the Registry Editor when you're done, and restart Windows so the changes can take effect. Thereafter, Windows will close stubborn programs automatically and with all due haste (whenever possible) when it's time to shut down.

Faster Application Startups

THE ANNOYANCE: Sometimes it seems to take an eternity for programs to load. I stare at an hourglass while listening to the hard disk thrash about, and then the application's window finally appears. There's got to be a way to speed this up.

THE FIX: Before Windows can load an application, it must set aside enough room in your PC's memory. If you have a lot of applications already loaded, you'll probably run out of memory, at which point Windows will use part of your hard disk called *virtual memory* to make up for the deficiency. Since hard disks are much slower than RAM, this technique (called *swapping*) slows down your computer considerably. You can temporarily alleviate this problem by closing unneeded programs before opening any new ones, but a better long-term solution is to install more memory (RAM) in your PC.

Of course, no matter how much memory you have, Windows will still use your hard disk to some extent. To keep your hard disk—and thus your system—running optimally, run Disk Defragmenter routinely (go to Start→ Run and type dfrg.msc). Also, the more space you set aside for virtual memory, the more efficiently Windows can utilize it. At a bare minimum, make sure you have half a gigabyte (500 MB) of free hard disk space at all times.

> **NOTE**
>
> *Another problem that may cause an interminable delay when shutting down is an inability to "save settings" in a timely fashion. The fix, which is perplexingly not offered by the Windows Update service, is to apply the User Profile Hive Cleanup Service, available at http://www.microsoft.com/downloads/.*

> **NOTE**
>
> *See "Stop Heavy Hard Disk Usage" for tips on how to configure Windows to use virtual memory more efficiently.*

Faster Windows Boot

THE ANNOYANCE: Why does Windows take so long to load? Is there anything I can do to speed it up?

THE FIX: All the software and hardware devices you add to your PC eventually take their toll, creating more for Windows to load each time it boots. The most effective way to combat this bloat is to routinely format your hard disk (see "Wipe Your Hard Disk Clean") and reinstall the operating system and all your applications. Unfortunately, reinstalling can be a time-consuming and frustrating process, and when all is said and done, it'll only be a matter of time before Windows once again becomes bogged down. Instead, optimize a few key areas of your PC to effect a more permanent performance increase.

First, add more memory (RAM) to your system. You should have a minimum of 384 MB of RAM to run Windows XP, but 512 MB or even 1 GB is better. The more memory you have (up to a point), the easier it will be for Windows to find space for all those drivers and programs during boot time. The rest of the time, that extra RAM means Windows will use slower virtual memory less often (see "Faster Application Startups").

One of the biggest contributors to a slow bootup is the long list of programs configured to load at boot time. Not only do these programs take time and processor cycles to load, but they eat up memory and even more processor cycles while they're running, further sapping your PC's performance. Most of the startup programs you can control are listed in your *Startup* folder and in the Registry.

The *Startup* folder (Start→All Programs→Startup) is merely a collection of shortcuts to programs that load every time Windows boots. This folder is empty by default; anything you see in your own *Startup* folder has been added—presumably by you or by an application you installed—since Windows was installed, and thus none of them are actually required by Windows. To stop a startup item from loading with Windows, just drag it into another folder for safekeeping (or straight into the Recycle Bin if you want to delete the shortcut).

So how do you tell what belongs and what doesn't? The names of most of the shortcuts in your *Startup* folder should be self-evident; the Microsoft Office Startup Assistant, for instance, is a component of Microsoft Office that's supposed to help Office applications start faster. Delete the Startup Assistant from your *Startup* folder, and you likely won't notice any difference... except that Windows will load slightly faster. Deleting other shortcuts here may disable some (typically noncritical) features, so be sure to check the program's documentation for the purpose of the shortcut.

NOTE

Startup Delayer, available for free at http://www.r2.com.au, allows you to have your proverbial cake and eat it, too. Instead of deleting startup programs, Startup Delayer simply staggers when they're loaded, allowing you to begin using Windows more quickly.

Programs configured in your Registry to start with Windows are typically listed in *HKEY_CURRENT_USER\Software\Microsoft\Windows\CurrentVersion\Run* and *HKEY_LOCAL_MACHINE\SOFTWARE\Microsoft\Windows\CurrentVersion\Run*. (Use the Favorites menu in the Registry Editor to bookmark these locations, making it easy to return to each key and clean out any unwanted programs as they appear.)

To remove an unwanted program from either Registry key, just highlight it and press the Delete key. You'd be wise to back up both keys before making any changes, though: to create a backup, just highlight a key, select File→Export, and type a filename for the *.reg* backup file. Then, if you need to reinstate a deleted value, just double-click the *.reg* file to merge its contents with the Registry.

Programs listed in these Registry keys are typically less self-descriptive than their counterparts in the *Startup* folder, so you may need to do some research before you remove anything (the research processes is described in "Windows Won't Shut Down").

While you're at it, open the Services list (go to Start→Run and type services.msc) to see some other programs Windows loads at startup. Any service that says "Automatic" in the Startup Type column is set to load when Windows starts, and ones that say "Started" in the Status column are currently running. (Click either column header to sort the list to make these services easier to find.) If you double-click a service, you can stop it by clicking the Stop button, or prevent it from loading the next time Windows starts by selecting Manual or Disabled from the "Startup type" drop-down list. Be warned, though: most services listed here are essential Windows components. Read the description shown to learn more about any particular service.

Aside from startup programs, sometimes having too many files in your *Temp* folder can not only slow Windows startup but, in extreme cases, prevent Windows from loading at all. Windows and your applications use this folder to temporarily store data, usually from documents you have open. When you close applications (or when applications crash), temporary files are often left behind, and these files can proliferate faster than rabbits in spring. To clean out this folder, open Windows Explorer, navigate to *\Documents and Settings\{username}\Local Settings\Temp*, and delete any files with modification dates earlier than the last time you started your PC. (You can use Creative Element Power Tools, available at *http://www.creativelement.com/powertools/*, to clean out this folder automatically.)

If you have hundreds of fonts installed on your system, they may be adding to boot time as well. If you can survive without 400 different decorative typefaces (especially if all you ever use is Times New Roman), thin out

> **NOTE**
>
> *If you want to see all your startup programs in one place, whether they're listed in the Registry or your Startup folder, open up the System Information tool (go to Start→Run and type* msinfo32.exe*), expand the Software Environment branch, and select Startup Programs.*

your fonts to speed Windows bootup. Open the Fonts control panel and uninstall any unwanted fonts by dragging them to another folder (or to your Recycle Bin to delete them permanently). Be careful not to delete any Windows fonts, though, such as Marlett, Fixedsys, MS Sans Serif, or any other fonts that start with "Microsoft" or "MS" (you can find a list at *http://www.kayskreations.net/fonts/fonttb.html*). If you do delete a system font by mistake, don't sweat—XP's Windows File Protection system will restore it.

If you periodically need a lot of fonts, invest in font-management software such as Adobe Type Manager, which can remove and reinstall fonts in groups at the click of a button.

Keeping an Eye on Prefetch

Prefetch is a feature in Windows XP that stores specific data about the applications you run, in order to help them start faster. Prefetch is an algorithm that helps anticipate cache misses (times when Windows requests data that isn't stored in the disk cache), and stores that data on the hard disk for easy retrieval.

This data is located in *Windows**Prefetch*, and theoretically, periodically clearing out the data in this folder (say, once a month) will improve performance. As new applications are subsequently started, new Prefetch data will be created, which may mean slightly reduced performance at first. But with older entries gone, there will be less data to parse, and Windows should be able to locate the data it needs more quickly. Any performance gains you may see will be minor, but those wishing to squeeze every last CPU cycle out of their computers will want to try this one.

Note that deleting Prefetch data may increase boot time slightly, but only the next time you boot Windows. Each subsequent boot should proceed normally, since the Prefetch data will already be present for the programs Windows loads when it boots.

If you want to disable Prefetch, open the Registry Editor, navigate to *HKEY_LOCAL_MACHINE**SYSTEM**CurrentControlSet**Control**SessionManager*\\ *Memory Management**PrefetchParameters*, and change the EnablePrefetcher value to 0. (Other supported values: 1 to Prefetch applications only, 2 to Prefetch boot processes, and 3 to Prefetch both.)

—From *Windows XP Annoyances for Geeks, 2nd Edition*

WINDOWS UPDATE

Is That Update Safe?

THE ANNOYANCE: I maintain a bunch of PCs for a small company, and I've turned off the Automatic Updates feature on every machine, mostly for my own sanity. The last thing I need is for Microsoft to deliver a "fix" to all the employees that ends up causing more problems than it solves. Is there an easy way to keep these PCs up to date while excluding the more troublesome patches?

THE FIX: Ever feel like an unpaid beta tester for Microsoft? If so, join the club.

The problem with being too conservative about the updates is that many of them fix serious security holes in Windows—and we all know how common those are. If you're an experienced user and take the proper precautions (see "Lock Down Internet Explorer" in Chapter 4), you can probably forgo most updates and be perfectly safe. But when you're administering PCs for an office full of people who can't tell the difference between virus-infected attachments and letters from their mothers, you may be better off installing many of those updates.

Still, there's no rule that says you have to install updates right away. Instead, wait a few weeks to see what ugly problems the press and users report. First, disable the Automatic Updates feature: open the System Properties control panel, choose the Automatic Updates tab, and then select "Turn off Automatic Updates." Click OK when you're done.

As they become available, research new patches. Sites such as *http://www.patchmanagement.org* and *http://www.annoyances.org* are full of stories, complaints, and solutions relating to Microsoft's "fixes." (See "Remove a Windows Update" for an example.)

Once you've decided to install an update, visit the Windows Update Catalog at *http://windowsupdate.microsoft.com/catalog/* (Figure 6-4) and click the "Find updates for Microsoft Windows operating systems" link. Select your Windows version from the list of operating systems, and then click the Search button to reveal all the updates released to date. Select the desired category (such as "Critical Updates and Service Packs"), and in the "Sort by" drop-down menu, sort the listings by "Posted date" to group together the most recent updates. Click the Add button below any update to add it to your download queue.

> **NOTE**
>
> *One advantage to using the Windows Update Catalog is that you'll get a self-contained installer that you can use repeatedly without having to download the update for each PC, saving you time and bandwidth.*

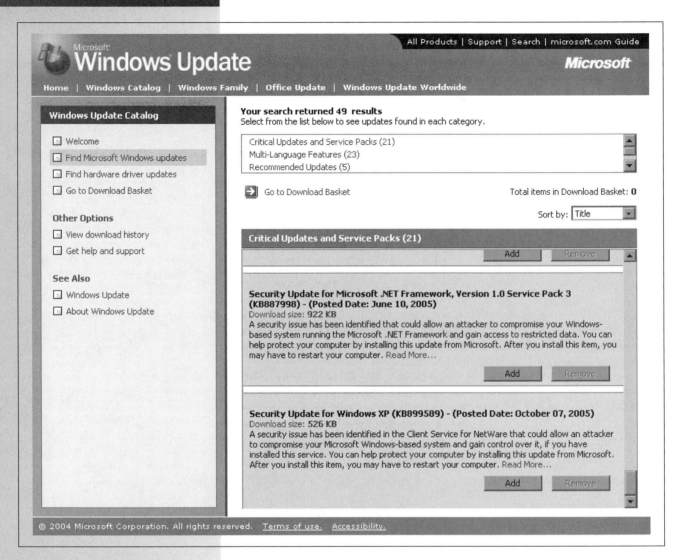

Figure 6-4. Use the Windows Update Catalog to download individual updates.

--- **NOTE** ---

To install SP2 on multiple computers remotely, download the Windows XP SP2 Deployment Tools for Advanced Users package from http://www.microsoft.com/downloads/.

It's especially important to install service packs manually, as opposed to letting the Automatic Updates feature do it. These über-updates are enormous and can require several hours per PC to install. The last thing you want is a new service pack tying up all the PCs in your office. Instead of allowing these to be installed automatically, wait a few months for the bugs to be ironed out (in the form of subsequent updates) before you install any Microsoft service pack. When you're ready, pick a weekend or a day when everyone is in a meeting, and download the "Network install" version of the service pack directly from Microsoft's web site (go to *http://www.annoyances.org/sp2/* for a shortcut to the SP2 network install). Put the installer on a network share or burn it to a CD, and run it directly on each PC.

Remove a Windows Update

THE ANNOYANCE: I've been getting an obscure error message that says, "The instruction at 0x30303731 referenced memory at 0x30303731. The memory could not be 'read'." I searched Google for the message and came upon an article that tied it to Hotfix Q328310, which I gather is an update from Microsoft. Will removing the update fix the problem? If so, how do I do it?

THE FIX: Well, it's worth a shot. If you suspect that a Windows update is causing a problem, you can uninstall it by opening the Add or Remove Programs control panel and placing a checkmark next to the "Show updates" option at the top of the screen. Scroll down to the "Windows XP – Software Updates" section shown in Figure 6-5, select the update from the list, and click the Remove button. (Of course, if this doesn't fix the problem, you can always go to the Windows Update site and reinstall the update, as discussed in "Is That Update Safe?".)

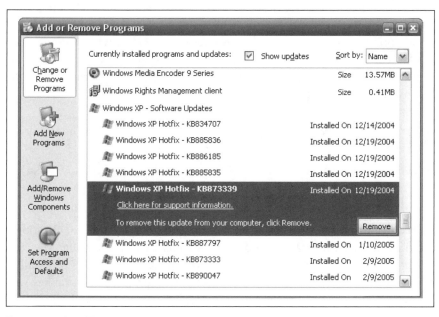

Figure 6-5. Use Add or Remove Programs to uninstall unwanted Windows updates.

But what happens if Add or Remove Programs says "This update cannot be removed," or if the update isn't in the list at all? First, it's possible your article got the number wrong—to confirm it, search Google or the Microsoft KB at *http://support.microsoft.com/search/* for the update number (e.g., Q328310). It's also possible that the hotfix was installed along with a service pack and thus might not show up in Add or Remove Programs.

If you're sure you have the right number for the installed update but it doesn't show up in Add or Remove Programs, there's another place you can look. Open Windows Explorer and navigate to the Windows folder (usually *C:\WINDOWS*). Make sure Explorer is configured to show hidden files (see "Find a File Where Search Doesn't Look" in Chapter 2), and locate the subfolder that begins with a "$" character and corresponds to the hotfix you want to remove. In the case of Q328310, you'd want the *\WINDOWS\$NtUninstallQ328310$* folder; use Explorer's Search feature (Ctrl-F) if you can't find it.

When you've located the correct folder, open it, go to the *spuninst* subfolder, and double-click the *spuninst.exe* file inside to uninstall the update.

Update Internet Explorer Safely

THE ANNOYANCE: According to the Windows Update site, there's a new version of Internet Explorer, but I'm afraid to install the update lest it overwrite a bunch of settings without asking. What are my options?

THE FIX: You're right to be suspicious; if you install IE via Windows Update, it will almost certainly overwrite your file types and make itself the default browser, whether you want it to or not. Fortunately, you can download a standalone installer from *http://www.microsoft.com/ie/*, which will let you choose the installation options. Make sure you click any "Advanced" or "Custom" buttons you encounter during installation so you can customize IE's installation to suit your needs.

Get Past the Validity Check

THE ANNOYANCE: I recently tried to use Windows Update, but I got a "Validation Failure: Product Key Failed Validation" error. What does this mean, and how do I get past it?

THE FIX: Microsoft has shipped millions and millions of copies of Windows XP since its release in 2001, and each one has a unique product key: the 25-digit series of letters and numbers you had to type when you installed XP. Of course, if your PC came with Windows XP preinstalled, that key was entered when your machine left the factory, but it's in there nonetheless.

In an attempt to combat software piracy, Microsoft has taken further steps to ensure that every copy of Windows XP that is installed is installed with a valid, legitimate license. To that end, Microsoft added a new component to the Windows Update service that checks to see if you have a valid product key. The problem is that quite a few (we're talking millions here) product keys that were once valid—such as the one printed on the hologram sticker on the bottom of your laptop—have become invalidated for one reason or another. In theory, all you need to do is contact Microsoft (or perhaps your PC vendor) and request a new key. Whether you get one, however, is a different matter.

However, you can get your Windows updates without spending hours on the phone with Microsoft technical support. First, note that the Automatic Updates feature doesn't (at the time of this writing) require the same validation as the standard Windows Update web site. To use the Automatic Updates feature, open the System control panel, choose the Automatic Updates tab, and select either "Automatic (recommended)" or "Download updates for me, but let me choose when to install them," and click OK.

If you'd rather use the Windows Update web site and manually select which updates to install, open Internet Explorer, go to Tools→Internet Options, choose the Programs tab, and click the Manage Add-ons button. Highlight "Windows Genuine Advantage" in the list, select the Disable option below, and click OK. Then, go to Tools→Windows Update to get your update without the validation hassles.

HARDWARE

Add a New Hard Disk

THE ANNOYANCE: I'm running out of disk space, and given how cheap new hard drives are, I figured I'd upgrade. But I don't know where to start; do I just crack open my PC's case and plug it in, or is there more to it?

THE FIX: It all depends on whether you want to replace your current hard disk or simply augment it with a second drive. If your PC has an unoccupied drive bay and your old hard disk isn't an antique, it's much easier to install the new drive as a second hard disk. But if you're using a laptop, for instance, and there's only room for one drive, or if your current drive is so old that its capacity is measured in megabytes instead of gigabytes, you'll want to replace the old drive with the new one. The course you choose also determines whether or not you'll need to move all your data to the new drive, a process that can be a bit of an ordeal.

Whether you're replacing or augmenting, you'll need to connect both drives to your PC at the same time. Doing so means fussing with cables and changing tiny jumpers. Consult the documentation that came with your PC and drives for details, or visit the drive manufacturer's web site for instructions.

So that Windows will still boot, connect the new drive such that your old unit is still configured as the primary hard disk. When adding a new IDE/PATA drive, for instance, you can configure it as a "master" or "slave" device: for now, leave the old drive as the master and configure the new drive—typically by setting a jumper on the back of the unit—as a slave. (The master and slave designations are used to prevent conflicts; a single IDE cable should never have more than one master or slave.)

NOTE

Make sure the controller to which you connected the new drive is set to "Auto detect" in your system BIOS. Otherwise, your PC won't see the drive, and neither will Windows. See "Windows Won't Start" for more information, and consult your PC's documentation for specific details.

NOTE

If you have a laptop or a micro desktop PC, odds are you won't find any free slots or drive bays. In this case, your best bet is to temporarily install your new drive in an external enclosure and connect it to your PC with a USB 2.0 or FireWire cable.

If you're installing an SATA drive, just connect it to a free SATA port. If you're adding a second SCSI drive, leave the old drive set to SCSI ID 0 and set the new drive to ID 1. (Depending on your setup, you may have to temporarily disconnect your CD drive to make room for the new hard disk on the IDE or SCSI chain.)

When you're done and you've closed up your PC, start Windows. Go to Start→Run, and type diskmgmt.msc to open the Disk Management utility (Figure 6-6). In the lower pane, right-click the box labeled "Unallocated" (which represents your new drive), and select New Partition. (If you don't see an unallocated drive, your new disk may already be partitioned and formatted, which means you can skip this step. If the drive doesn't show up, see "Windows Won't Start.")

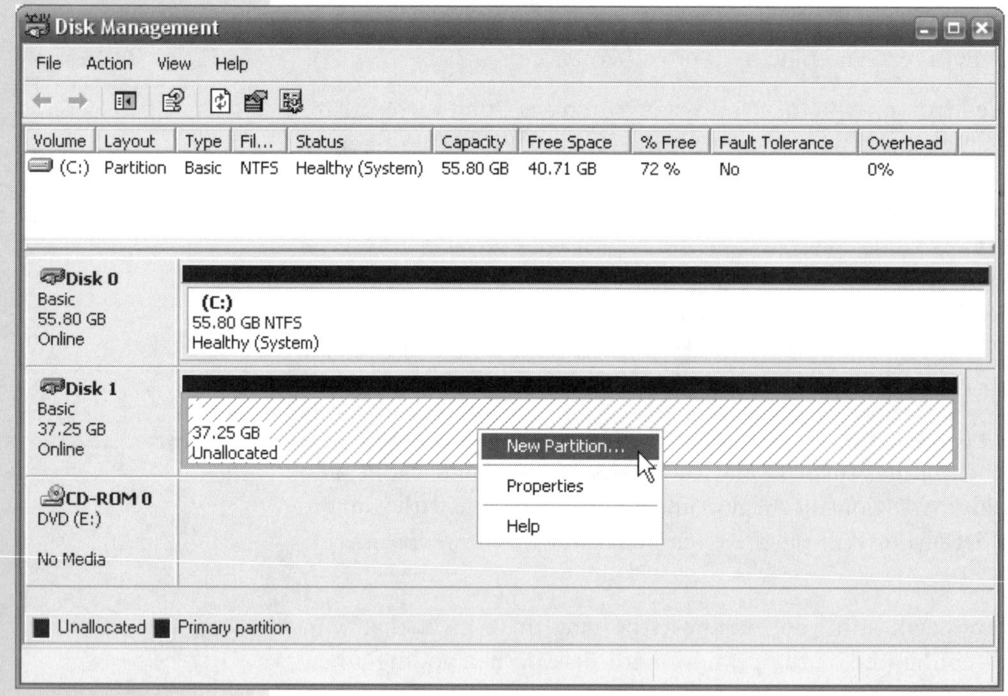

Figure 6-6. Use the Disk Management utility to configure newly installed hard disks.

In the New Partition Wizard, select "Primary partition" and then specify the maximum capacity for the partition size. (Chances are the system has already calculated this number for you.) Next, select "Assign the following drive letter" and choose a drive letter that you'll remember from the list, such as J. On the Format Partition page, select "Format this partition with the following settings," choose NTFS for the filesystem, and leave the other settings on the page unchanged. Click Finish when you're done. Depending on the speed and size of the drive, it may take Disk Management a while to format the drive—anywhere between a minute and half an hour. When formatting is complete, right-click the new drive in Disk Management and select "Mark Partition as Active."

If all you wanted to do was augment your existing storage, you're essentially done. You can begin saving stuff to your new drive, or even move existing files by dragging and dropping them in Windows Explorer (hold the Shift key to move instead of copy).

If, on the other hand, you want to replace your old drive with this new one, you'll need to copy everything from the old drive to the new one. This can be tricky, for several reasons. For one, there's more to a Windows installation than just the files; the boot loader, discussed in "Windows Won't Start," is installed on your disk's boot sector and can't be copied. Also, Windows won't let you copy files that are in use, so you can't simply drag and drop all of the folders on drive *C:* to copy them to your new drive *J:*.

Fortunately, there are a few workarounds that solve these problems:

Norton Ghost

> The easiest solution is to use a disk imaging utility such as Norton Ghost, available at *http://www.symantec.com*; check out the "Enterprise" section on the Downloads page for a free trial. Use Ghost to create an "image" of your old hard disk, and then restore the image to the new drive. When you're done, you'll have an exact copy of your original drive, complete with all the necessary boot information. All that's left to do is to remove the old drive and set the new one as the primary drive (i.e., set your IDE drive to "master" or your SCSI drive to ID 0).

> ---
> **NOTE**
> ---
> *Store the image file on the old drive, not the new one. For Ghost to restore it, the target drive must be empty. If you don't have enough space on the old drive for the image, divide the new drive into two partitions with the Disk Management utility. Save the image file on the second partition, and then use Ghost to restore the image onto the first partition.*

Back up and restore

> If you have a tape backup or other device capable of storing the entire contents of your hard disk, use it to do a full system backup. Then, just restore the backup onto the new drive. When you're done, shut down the PC, unplug the old drive, put the new one in its place, and start your PC. If Windows won't start, you'll need to write the master boot record to the new drive, as described in "Windows Won't Start."

Start from the beginning

Your final option is to install the new drive as the primary master drive, install a fresh copy of Windows XP on the drive, and then install all your applications.

Next, connect your old drive as the "slave," and copy over your data files. Don't forget the stuff in your *My Documents* folder (usually found at *Documents and Settings\{username}\My Documents*), plus the contents of your desktop (*Documents and Settings\{username}\Desktop*) and extras such as your email and web browser bookmarks (typically found in *Documents and Settings\{username}\Application Data*) and your IE Favorites (*Documents and Settings\{username}\Favorites*). Keep your old drive connected for a few weeks (if practical), until you're sure you've gotten everything.

Stop Heavy Hard Disk Usage

THE ANNOYANCE: At seemingly random times, Windows slows down or even stops responding for a few seconds, during which time I can distinctly hear my hard disk thrashing. What's going on, and how do I stop it?

THE FIX: When Windows uses up all your memory, it starts using a portion of your hard disk as "virtual memory." Since hard disks are much slower than memory (RAM), this causes a noticeable drop in performance. Of course, adding RAM will help significantly; the more RAM you have, the less frequently Windows will resort to using virtual memory.

Figure 6-7. Change some settings in the Virtual Memory window to increase performance.

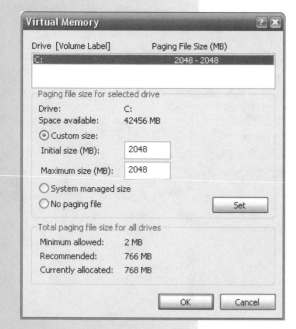

The thrashing problem is caused by the way that Windows handles disk virtual memory by default. The space Windows sets aside for virtual memory is called the *swap file* or *paging file*, which grows and shrinks as needed. As a result, the swap file can become very fragmented, reducing system performance—and increasing the thrashing sound you've been hearing—significantly. You can effectively eliminate the problem by first defragging your hard drive (Start→Programs→Accessories→System Tools→Disk Defragmenter), then setting a fixed swap file size.

Open the System control panel, choose the Advanced tab, and click the Settings button in the Performance section. Choose the Advanced tab here, and click the Change button to show the Virtual Memory window (Figure 6-7).

Highlight your drive in the list and select "Custom size" below. At the bottom of the window, take the "Recommended" paging file size and add 512. Type this number (e.g., 1534 or 2048) into both the "Initial size

(MB)" and "Maximum size (MB)" fields, and then click the Set button. If you typed 2048, it should now say 2048-2048 under "Paging File Size (MB)" at the top of the window. When you're done, press OK in each of the three dialog boxes to confirm your choices. If Windows suggests that you restart your PC, do so now.

Scanner Says It's Not Connected

THE ANNOYANCE: I know my scanner is working and properly connected, but sometimes when I try to scan something, the scanner software complains that the scanner *isn't* connected. I tried unplugging the scanner and plugging it back in, but that didn't help. What gives?

THE FIX: You've encountered a bug in Windows XP that affects USB devices. Although many drivers compensate for the problem, some devices—particularly older scanners—will exhibit the "disconnected" problem as a result. Scanners remain totally dormant, sending no information to your PC until you try to scan something, and Windows misinterprets this inactivity as an opportunity to shut down the USB port to save power.

At the time of this writing, Microsoft hasn't released a patch that effectively fixes this problem. My suggested workaround: the next time you see that error, try scanning again right away. It can take Windows a few seconds to reactivate the USB port, and your scanner software may not have waited long enough for this to happen.

No luck? Restart Windows, and your scanner should be available immediately. But don't dawdle; Windows gives inactive USB devices only a 15–30 minute grace period before cutting power to the port again.

Naturally, you can also try visiting the scanner manufacturer's web site for a driver or software update that may provide a more convenient or reliable workaround.

Troubleshoot Multiple Monitors

THE ANNOYANCE: I connected a larger monitor to an unused monitor port on the back of my PC, but I can't get a picture on it. Am I taking the phrase "plug-and-play" too seriously?

THE FIX: Plug-and-play technology allows Windows to recognize newly attached devices and install drivers for them automatically. Sometimes this is sufficient; other times, you need to help things along. If you plug in a USB microphone, for instance, Windows will change your sound settings immediately so the new microphone works, but monitors do not enjoy the same privileged service. Here's how to get it to work.

If you're using a laptop, there's probably a key on your keyboard (see Figure 6-8) that switches between the built-in LCD screen and any external monitor that might be attached. Press this key (typically while holding the Fn key) repeatedly until the video shows up where you want it.

Figure 6-8. Use this key to switch between your built-in screen and an external monitor, or both simultaneously.

Don't have a monitor key? Want more control? Right-click an empty area of the desktop, select Properties, and choose the Settings tab. If Windows has detected both monitors (as well as both video cards, if applicable), they'll show up here as numbered rectangles (Figure 6-9). If you're not sure which monitor is which, click the Identify button, and an enormous number "1" will appear on the primary monitor.

To use both monitors simultaneously side by side, creating one huge desktop, click the #2 rectangle and place a checkmark by the "Extend my Windows desktop onto this monitor" box.

If you only want to use the second monitor (and turn off the first one), click the #2 rectangle and then place a checkmark next to the "Use this device as the primary monitor" option. When the numbers switch, click the new #2 rectangle, and remove the checkmark next to the "Extend my Windows desktop onto this monitor" option.

If you still have problems, click the Advanced button, choose the Monitor tab, and click the Properties button to verify that the correct drivers are installed for each of your monitors. Then do the same (via the Adapter tab) for your video card(s).

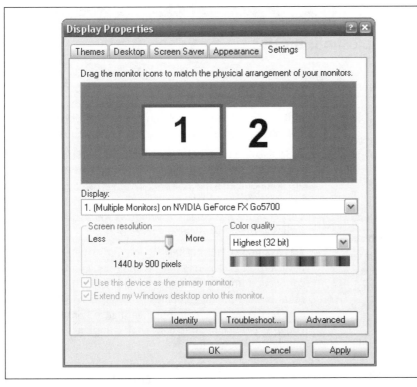

Figure 6-9. Use the Settings tab to enable multiple monitors and choose how the displays are oriented.

Fix Cranky Mice

THE ANNOYANCE: When I move the mouse around, the pointer seems to skip around the screen instead of floating smoothly. Can I whip this rodent into shape?

THE FIX: Both mice and keyboards suffer from the same types of problems, and for the same reasons: despite the fact that they are the primary interface devices for your PC, they're usually the most cheaply built and poorly designed components of your system. Don't hesitate to replace a cranky mouse or a sticky keyboard, rather than spending hours trying to get it to work.

If you're still using a mouse with a little ball on the bottom, you could improve its reliability somewhat by cracking it open and cleaning the rollers and the ball, but you'll be much better off simply replacing it with an "optical" mouse. Optical mice have no moving parts, but rather use a small sensor to more reliably detect the movements of your hand. (If you're in the market for a new one, go down to your local computer store and try out a few models to see which one feels the most comfortable and well made.)

If you're fed up with mice altogether, and sick of the whole "lift and drag" thing—not to mention the wrist pain—consider replacing your mouse with a pen and tablet. Tablets, such as those made by Wacom (http://www.wacom.com), allow you to control your pointer with a cordless, battery-less stylus (pen) with much more precision and comfort than any rodent offers. Features such as pressure and title sensitivity also make working with graphics programs (e.g., Photoshop and Illustrator) far more productive and pleasurable.

Troubleshooting Tips

The most important step—and usually the most difficult—in troubleshooting a computer system is isolating the problem. Some questions to ask yourself:

- **IS THIS AN ISOLATED INCIDENT, OR DOES THIS PROBLEM OCCUR EVERY TIME I PERFORM SOME ACTION?** Crashing is a fact of life on a Windows system. An isolated incident is often just that. On the other hand, if a given error message or crash repeatedly occurs at the same time, in the same place, or as a result of the same mouse click, remember this fact if you hope to solve the problem.

- **DID I INSTALL OR REMOVE ANY SOFTWARE OR HARDWARE JUST BEFORE THIS PROBLEM OCCURRED?** Sudden changes in your computer's behavior are almost never spontaneous; if something suddenly stops working, you can bet that there was a discernible trigger.

- **IS A SPECIFIC APPLICATION, A HARDWARE DEVICE, OR WINDOWS AT FAULT?** You can rule out specific applications if the problem doesn't just occur in one program. You can rule out most hardware by removing or disabling unnecessary devices attached to your system. If applications and hardware aren't to blame, shine the spotlight on Windows.

- **DID I READ THE DIRECTIONS?** I know, I know—a well-designed interface should mean never having to crack open the manual. But the reality is that you've got to read the directions (and release notes) that accompany any product you've bought and installed. While you're at it, go to the vendor's site and make sure you've got the latest updates, drivers, fixes, patches, and so on.

- **HAS SOMEONE ELSE ENCOUNTERED THE SAME PROBLEM?** This is often the most useful question to ask, because odds are someone else has not only suffered the same fate, but discovered a solution and written about it in some online forum... such as the Windows XP discussion forum at *http://www.annoyances.org*!

- **AM I ASKING THE RIGHT PEOPLE?** If you just installed a new version of America Online and now your Internet connection doesn't work, don't call Microsoft. On the other hand, nothing compares to trying to convince a technical support representative that the problem you're experiencing is actually their company's fault and not someone else's.

My last tidbit of hard-earned wisdom? In some cases, it makes more sense to replace a product that's giving you endless hours of grief instead of trying to fix it. Keep that in mind when it's four o'clock in the morning and Windows refuses to recognize your ninety-dollar scanner.

—From *Windows XP Annoyances for Geeks, 2nd Edition*

Of course, even top-of-the-line mice aren't entirely trouble-free. Does your pointer jitter when you move the mouse around? If you're using a cordless mouse, this is almost always a reception problem: either the mouse is too far from the receiver or, more likely, the battery needs to be replaced or recharged.

If you have a corded mouse that plugs into a USB port, plug it into a different port and see if its performance improves. If you're using a USB hub, try bypassing it by plugging the mouse directly into one of your PC's USB ports. Other USB devices can sometimes suck up too much USB power or use too much bandwidth, which can interfere with the mouse as well, so try disconnecting them one by one to see if you notice a difference.

Disappearing CD and DVD Drives

THE ANNOYANCE: Recently, my *D:* drive (a DVD writer) disappeared in Windows Explorer. How do I get it back?

THE FIX: The obvious solution is to open up your PC and make sure the cables are firmly connected, but if that doesn't help, an errant Registry setting may be the cause of the problem.

Open the Registry Editor (go to Start→Run and type regedit), and navigate to *HKEY_LOCAL_MACHINE\SYSTEM\CurrentControlSet\Control\Class\{4D36E965-E325-11CE-BFC1-08002BE10318}*. You'll know if you're in the right place if the (Default) value in the right pane says "DVD/CD-ROM drives."

Highlight the *UpperFilters* value on the right, press the F2 key, rename the value UpperFilters.old, and press Enter. Do the same for the *LowerFilters* value.

Next, navigate to *HKEY_LOCAL_MACHINE\SYSTEM\CurrentControlSet\Services*, and click [+] to expand the Services branch to reveal all the subkeys. Look for the Cdr4_2K key on the tree, and delete it if it's present. Do the same for the following keys: *Cdralw2k*, *Cdudf*, and *UdfReadr*. Close the Registry Editor and restart Windows when you're done.

Send and Receive Faxes

THE ANNOYANCE: Thanks to DSL, I haven't used my old dialup modem in years. But now I have to send a document to someone who apparently thinks it's still 1986 and can only accept it via fax. Isn't that modem supposed to let me send faxes? I'm darned if I can figure out how to do it.

THE FIX: Windows XP's built-in fax service actually works pretty well, but it's not installed by default, and it's not entirely obvious how to use it once you set it up. Here's how you do it.

Open the Add or Remove Programs control panel, and click the Add/Remove Windows Components button on the left. Place a checkmark next to the Fax Services component, click the Next button, and then complete the wizard. (If the Fax Services box is already checked, the required software is installed; click the Cancel button and continue to the next step.)

Once the fax service is installed, you'll need to do a little setup. Open the Printers and Faxes control panel, right-click the Microsoft Shared Fax Driver icon (the name may vary), and select Properties. Choose the Devices tab, find your modem in the list (if it's not there, you'll need to install your modem driver), and click the Properties button. On the Send tab, place a checkmark next to the "Enable device to send" option, and type your phone number in the TSID field.

If It Ain't Broke...

Remember the Golden Rule: if it ain't broke, don't fix it. Many problems are actually caused by people looking for problems to solve. For example, installing a new driver just for the sake of having the "latest and greatest" version on your system may introduce new bugs or uncover some bizarre incompatibility. This doesn't mean that updating your drivers isn't a good idea, but only do this if something isn't working or performing at its best.

—From *Windows XP Annoyances for Geeks, 2nd Edition*

Next, choose the Receive tab. If you want to receive faxes with your PC, place a checkmark next to the "Enable device to receive" option. Give this some thought, though, particularly if you use this phone line for other things (such as placing and receiving phone calls). You may not want your PC picking up the phone every time Mom calls (or then again, maybe you do). There's also a "Manual" setting in the "Answer mode" section, which causes the fax service to listen on your line but only pick up when you tell it to. But beware: this "listening" can wreak havoc with some phones and answering machines and may result in dropped calls.

When you're done with the fax modem properties page, click OK. Back in the Fax Properties window, choose the Tracking tab to configure the fax monitor. The fax monitor is the little progress window that pops up when you send and receive faxes, from which you can manually receive faxes, cancel an outgoing call, and so on. Finally, choose the Archives tab and specify where you want Windows to store your sent and received faxes (the defaults are subfolders of *Documents and Settings\All Users\Application Data\Microsoft\Windows NT\MSFax*\).

Finally, to send a fax, open your document in whatever application created it (e.g., Word or Excel), go to File→Print, and select the fax driver from the list of printers. (A fax machine is nothing more than a remote printer, after all.) Click OK, and the Send Fax Wizard walks you through the rest of the process; type the recipient's fax number, choose a cover sheet, pick a time to send the fax, and you're off!

Find Drivers for Old Hardware

THE ANNOYANCE: I have an old USB webcam that I'd like to use. When I plug it in, Windows recognizes it and prompts me for drivers, but then it tells me that the CD that came with the webcam doesn't have "drivers that match my hardware." What do I do?

THE FIX: It sounds like your webcam was made before Windows XP came out, and as a result, the CD that accompanies it doesn't include XP-compatible drivers. This is a really common problem, particularly among the glut of USB devices that hit the market during the Windows 98 era.

Since few companies will support every product from the original date of sale until the Morlocks roam the Earth, it's possible that—gasp—XP-compatible drivers may simply not exist for your device. But it can't hurt to visit the webcam manufacturer's web site and scour the Support and Downloads sections for any drivers or information for Windows XP.

Of course, the manufacturer may no longer offer *any* drivers for your device. The company may have gone out of business or had its assets bought up by another company. In this case, you'll have to turn to others to find a driver. Start by visiting a driver repository (the web equivalent of an auto salvage

---

> **NOTE**
>
> *Rather than using your PC to receive faxes, set up a free account with an online fax service such as eFax (http://www.efax.com). You get your own dedicated phone number, albeit in a distant area code (local phone numbers are available for a fee), and any faxes you receive are emailed to you as attachments. You use the service's special advertiser-sponsored viewer to read and print your received faxes, all without tying up your phone line.*

yard), such as DriverGuide (*http://www.driverguide.com*) or DriverFiles (*http://www.driverfiles.net*). No luck? Search Google for the word "driver" followed by the name or model number of your device.

If you don't find anything, it may be wiser to simply cut your losses. Instead of spending half a day trying to get a seven-year-old webcam to work with XP, just spend the $15 on a new webcam, and use the old one as a nifty toy for your cat.

What's a Digitally Signed Driver?

THE ANNOYANCE: I'm trying to install the drivers for this new device, and all of a sudden, Windows warns me that the drivers are not digitally signed. Is this something to worry about?

THE FIX: Not even a little. A driver with a digital signature is one that has earned Microsoft's esteemed seal of approval, indicating that it has passed a series of rigorous compatibility tests administered by the Windows Hardware Quality Labs (WHQL). In theory, this warning is supposed to scare customers into rejecting any driver that does not come with Microsoft's digital signature, thereby coercing hardware manufacturers into submitting their drivers to the aforementioned WHQL tests.

In practice, however, digitally signed drivers are rarely any more stable, reliable, or safe than drivers lacking the signature. In other words, if you see this warning, just click the Install Anyway button and forget about it.

If the decision makers at Microsoft had thought about it, they might've applied this sort of warning to all software installations, not just hardware drivers. If Windows users were warned before installing software components that weren't digitally signed, we could probably say goodbye to spyware, viruses, Trojan horses, worms, and all the other forms of malware that can make their way onto your PC without so much as a peep from Windows!

Windows Won't Detect New Device

THE ANNOYANCE: My PC has four USB ports, and they're all full. Rather than using a USB hub, which I've heard can be problematic, I bought a PCI card that gave me another six USB ports and a pair of FireWire ports to boot. When I installed it, however, Windows appeared to detect it but couldn't properly identify it or accept the installation of the included drivers.

THE FIX: There are essentially two reasons why Windows doesn't detect a device, or detects that a device has been added but can't identify it properly: either the device isn't compatible with Windows XP, or some other device is causing a conflict.

You can test the first hypothesis pretty easily by consulting the documentation or checking the manufacturer's web site for XP compatibility (see "Find Drivers for Old Hardware" if these turn out to be dead ends).

The second possibility is a little harder to troubleshoot. You'll encounter this problem mostly in desktop PCs—as opposed to laptops—that have a bunch of internal expansion slots. (Laptops have fewer expansion options, and thus fewer opportunities for conflict.) The system BIOS and chipset are responsible for parceling out IRQs to all the devices in your system, but when you add a handful of cards to the dozen or so devices already built onto your PC's motherboard, devices must share IRQs, and that's when the conflicts start making life difficult.

You can confirm that this is the problem by simply moving the card to a different PCI slot. This fools Windows into thinking the card is an entirely new device, which gives you another shot at installing the right drivers (see "Replace an Incorrect Driver"); the new location may also eliminate a conflict with a device on your motherboard. Despite Windows's plug-and-play capabilities, you may have to shuffle PCI cards in a full system until you find a setup that works.

If you still aren't having any luck, enter your PC's BIOS setup screen (see "Boot with the Windows CD"), find the "Reset Config Data" option (sometimes called "Reset NVRAM"), and set it to Yes. When you're done, save your settings and reboot. This setting makes the BIOS reset and reconfigure all your plug-and-play devices every time your system starts, which forces Windows to do the same. The change may increase boot time, but you can turn it off later, and it may be just the thing to get all your devices to work in harmony.

Replace an Incorrect Driver

THE ANNOYANCE: I installed the wrong driver for a new piece of hardware, and now Windows can't install the correct one. Isn't there any way to uninstall drivers?

THE FIX: Yes—most of the time—but it's not always obvious how to do it. You could open the Device Manager (go to Start→Run and type devmgmt. msc), right-click the device, and select Uninstall, but oddly enough, this usually doesn't remove all traces of the driver. Unfortunately, Windows saves details about uninstalled hardware both in the Registry and in *.inf* files located in the *Windows**inf* folder, which means the next time your device is detected, Windows is likely to detect it incorrectly again. (See "Windows Won't Detect New Device" if this happens right off the bat.)

If it's listed in the Add or Remove Programs control panel, or if there's an uninstaller hiding in your Start menu or in the driver's folder, you may be able to remove the driver completely. However, odds are you'll have to turn to the manufacturer's support web site for help. Search the site for "uninstall," and you might find a procedure or even a downloadable utility to cleanse your system of the driver. If not, search Google for the word "uninstall" and the name of your device. (Don't be surprised if the instructions you find have you deleting obscure Registry keys and renaming DLLs in your \Windows\System32\drivers folder.)

The good news is that uninstalling the driver isn't always necessary. Windows ties each detected device to the port or slot to which it's connected. If you pull a sound card out of PCI slot 2 and insert it into PCI slot 3, Windows will detect the card as a brand new device and offer you a chance to install the device correctly. The same goes for hard disks and CD/DVD drives (all IDE/ATA devices, really), all SCSI devices, cards inserted into your laptop's PCMCIA/PC Card slots, and even USB devices; just plug them into different ports to force Windows to re-detect them, and your plug-and-play woes may simply melt away.

Undo an Unwanted Driver Update

THE ANNOYANCE: During a recent visit to the Windows Update web site, I was tempted by a driver update listed in the "Hardware, Optional" category. I installed the driver and restarted Windows, and now the device no longer works. Did I do something wrong, or did I just fall for a trap?

THE FIX: While Microsoft has the right intentions, it doesn't always have the right drivers. In theory, Windows Update should only suggest a driver upgrade if your device is already using a Microsoft driver, but sometimes it oversteps its bounds. Fortunately, Windows is prepared for this!

Open the Device Manager (go to Start→Run and type devmgmt.msc), find your device in the tree, right-click it, and select Properties. Choose the Driver tab and click the Roll Back Driver button. If all goes well, Windows should remove the new driver and reinstate the old functional driver automatically.

Sometimes this doesn't work, though. If Windows complains that it can't roll back the driver, or if the device still doesn't work after the old driver was supposedly restored, your best bet is to dig through your disks and install the original driver that came with your gadget. Better yet, visit the manufacturer's web site, download the latest driver for your model, and install it over the one already on your system.

Find Out More About Your Hardware

THE ANNOYANCE: I've read of a bug that affects a certain type of motherboard chipset, but this information isn't exactly laser-etched on the front of my PC. How can I find out what's inside my PC without having to pop the hood?

THE FIX: Your PC is made up of dozens of separate components, most of which aren't made by your PC vendor. Although you can certainly open up your computer and look at the label on your hard disk or CPU, most of the "devices" are nothing more than chips soldered to your PC's motherboard. Rather than trying to read the microscopic text on each chip, you can use software to scan your system and produce reports in excruciating detail.

First, open up Windows's own Device Manager by going to Start→Run and typing devmgmt.msc. Here, you'll see a manifest of every device for which a driver is loaded. Unfortunately, the information can be spotty at best. For instance, your FireWire controller is probably called simply "1394 Net Adapter." If you're trying to find out whether or not it's a VIA VT6306, for instance, you'll have to look elsewhere.

One of the best tools for this, and a free one at that, is Everest Home Edition, available at *http://www.lavalys.com*. (Lavalys also offers commercial versions with more features.) Among other things, Everest displays copious details about your hardware (Figure 6-10), digs into your CPU (indicating, for example, whether or not it can be overclocked), and even performs system diagnostics and memory benchmark tests.

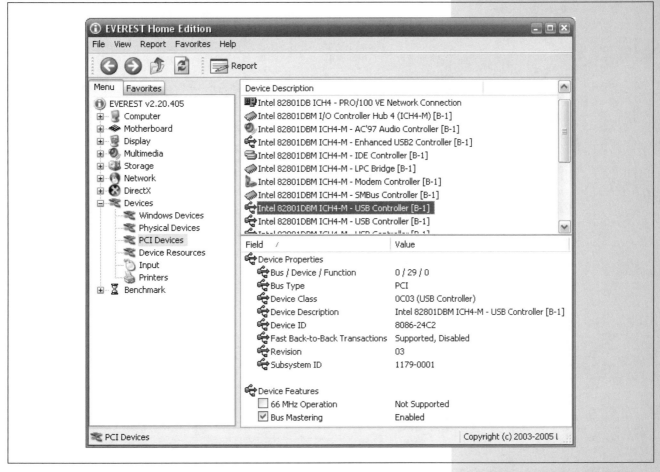

Another worthy tool is WCPUID/XCPUID, available for free at *http://www.h-oda.com*, which provides exhaustive details about your processor (CPU). This tool's output is useful for overclocking, as well as for finding a compatible CPU if you're interested in upgrading.

Figure 6-10. Use Everest Home Edition to display details about the components inside your system.

Index

R

S

T

W

WAV format, 78
WCPUID/XCPUID, 211
Web (see Internet)
web pages
  animations, 119–121
  blank forms, 118
  missing images, 113
  odd characters, 112
web site passwords, 109–110
Welcome screen
  bypassing, 25
  changing picture, 12
  replacing with a logon box, 27
WEP key, 167
WEP security key, 140
WiFi hotspots, 170
WiFi sniffing, 169, 171
WinAmp, 76
WindowBlinds, 8
windows, sprucing up old windows,
    25
Windows 95/98/Me
  connecting to, 152
Windows Explorer, 29–58
  address bar, shrinking, 32
  Advanced Search, 53
  animated character, removing, 53
  changing default of running as sepa-
      rate instances, 41
  cleaning up context menus, 42
  copying files to hidden destinations,
      49
  copy folder path to the clipboard, 33
  default programs, choosing, 46
  deleting an undeletable folder, 41
  Details view, making default, 30
  file dialog boxes, customizing, 50
  file extensions, showing, 45
  file types, protecting, 47
  file types, restoring if overwritten,
      48
  folder icons, customizing, 44
  folder tree, changing views, 39
  folder tree lines, showing, 30
  hiding the tasks pane, 37
  keyboard shortcuts, 49
  moving and copying rules, 48
  navigating folders with keyboard, 36

opening in a custom folder, 40
printing a folder listing, 33
printing file from, 34
recent files, finding, 56
remembering folder settings, 31
searches, saving, 56
searching in a new window, 52
Search Results, expanding visibility
    of, 54
search results, missing paths in, 55
search results, saving, 56
selecting multiple files, 48
showing size of folders and
    subfolders, 35
simple folder view, 30
speeding up opening folders, 45
subfolders, jumping to, 31
Windows Firewall, 113, 162
Windows logo key, 10
Windows Media Audio, 77
Windows Media Center Edition
    (MCE), 90–95
  alternatives, 94–95
  broken TV listings, 91
  DVDs, burning, 95
  HDTV, 92
    capturing programming, 93
    timeshifting problems, 93
  home-theater PC (HTPC), 95
  remote control, 94
  TV hookup, 90
  Windows XP, mimic MCE, 91
Windows Media Encoder, 61, 62
Windows Media Player
  Alt-Tab, 70
  blank videos, 62–63
  buffering, 67
  color, 71
  crossfading, 76
  error codes, 61
  license issues, 81–82
  not playing video clip, 60
  not recognizing MP3 player, 81
  playing incomplete downloads, 61
  quits before burning CD, 101
  simplifying version 10, 70
  skipping ads, 64
Windows Media Stream Editor, 77
Windows Movie Maker, 68
  montages, 69

Windows Picture and Fax Viewer, 46
Windows Recovery Console (WRC),
    184
  settings, 186
Windows Update, 193–197
  getting past validity check, 196
  Internet Explorer, updating safely,
      196
  removing an update, 195
  safe updates, 193
  User Profile Hive Cleanup Service,
      189
Windows Vista, 183
Windows Volume Control, 73
Windows XP, mimic MCE, 91
Windows XP Shut Down box, 27
WinTidy, 10
WinZip, 56
wireless networks, 164–174
  connecting in public places, 170
  connecting to, 168–170
  encryption, 167
  Not Connected messages, 172
  PPPoE, 165
  private, 166
  range and reception, 171–172
  setting up, 164–168
  WEP key, 167
  WiFi sniffer, 169
  Wireless SSID Broadcast option,
      166
  without routers, 173
Wireless Strength widget, 172
.wma files, 77, 78
WMRecorder, 66
.wmv files, 61
WPA security key, 140
wwwroot$, 151

Y

YouSendIt, 132

Z

ZIP files, 55

Better than e-books

Buy *Fixing Windows XP Annoyances* and access the digital edition FREE on Safari for 45 days.

Go to www.oreilly.com/go/safarienabled
and type in coupon code F1RC-VIFQ-1GHV-XTQL-LMHR

Search
thousands of
top tech books

Download
whole chapters

Cut and Paste
code examples

Find
answers fast

Search Safari! The premier electronic reference library for programmers and IT professionals.

Addison Wesley

Sun microsystems

ALPHA

Java

Microsoft Press

Peachpit Press

O'REILLY

AdobePress

SAMS

New Riders

Cisco Press

QUE

macromedia PRESS

PRENTICE HALL PTR